RETHINKING STANDARDS THROUGH TEACHER PREPARATION PARTNERSHIPS

Gary A. Griffin & Associates

STATE UNIVERSITY OF NEW Y

This work was made possible in part by generous funding from The Pew Charitable Trusts, The AT&T Foundation, and the Joyce Foundation. The opinions expressed in this book are those of the authors and do not necessarily reflect the views of these foundations.

Published by
State University of New York Press, Albany

For information, address State University of New York Press,
90 State Street, Suite 700, Albany, NY 12207

Production by Michael Haggett
Marketing by Patrick Durocher

Library of Congress Cataloging-in-Publication Data

Griffin, Gary A.
    Rethinking standards through teacher preparation partnerships /
Gary A. Griffin & associates.
        p. cm.—(SUNY series, teacher preparation and development)
    Includes bibliographical references and index.
    ISBN 0-7914-5439-8 (alk. paper)—
    ISBN 0-7914-5440-1 (pbk. : alk. paper)
    1. Teachers—Training of—United States.   2. Education—
  ndards—United States.   I. Title.   II. SUNY series in teacher
  ration and development.

  G75 2002
    dc21   2002019098

    5 4 3 2 1

RETHINKING STANDARDS THROUGH TEACHER PREPARATION PARTNERSHIPS

SUNY series, Teacher Preparation
and Development

Alan R. Tom, editor

CONTENTS

ACKNOWLEDGMENTS

This book was created with the support of the National Center for Restructuring Education, Schools, and Teaching (NCREST) which was founded nearly a dozen years ago by Ann Lieberman and Linda Darling-Hammond at Teachers College, Columbia University in New York City. In establishing NCREST, Darling-Hammond and Lieberman were visionary and practical, routinely bringing together researchers, practitioners, and policy workers in a variety of forums to debate and shape education reform together. One of the strategies they favored was creating networks of networks, loose affiliations of representatives of reform-oriented partnerships, groups, and projects that met over time to learn from and build upon each others work and perspectives.

This book is the culminating project of one such group, the Leading Edge Professional Development Schools Network, representing six, diverse teacher education programs using a professional development schools (PDS) approach. The idea for this network originated in discussions in a much larger group of PDS partnerships convened by NCREST in the early 1990s. That larger network brought together school-based and university-based representatives of many of the earliest PDS partnerships as well as some newly formed ones to share what was working and what was not as they collaborated day-to-day to reinvent teacher education and improve schooling. For many of us working daily to nurture these new relationships and programs, these NCREST meetings, held over two days several times a year with funding from the Danforth Foundation, were manna from heaven. Most of us were working at the edge of institutional norms, often violating long-established role expectations with little or no support. At the NCREST meetings, we did not have to explain for the hundredth time why we thought school–university collaboration was worth it; we all believed it was. We did not have to convince anyone that private, isolated teaching practice behind a closed classroom door is dysfunctional; we thrived on sharing our ideas and getting suggestions for improving them.

At the NCREST PDS network meetings, we found we could often finish each other's sentences in both our tales of woe and tales of accomplishment. We came to understand that we were not the only ones taking three steps forward and four back, and sometimes even a quantum leap forward, that would take the work to new levels of understanding. We became friends as well as

professional colleagues and developed personal associations that have long out-
lasted the actual meetings.

Somewhere along the way in the unfolding of that network, several of the
PDS partnerships realized that, as helpful as those meetings were, they became
too large and too diverse to really dig in on some thorny issues. For that, we
needed a smaller group. To create this smaller network, NCREST again raised
the funds, and we began meeting in 1996. This book is about what we did together and what we learned about policy, standards, inquiry, inclusion, assessment, and technology. As Griffin and Litman point out in Chapter 1, it is "an
inside-out perspective . . . about the prospects, possibilities, and problems of
making PDSs work."

The Pew Charitable Trusts, The AT&T Foundation, and the Joyce Foundation generously funded this work. We are grateful for the support of: Debo-
rah J. Gore, Kent McGuire, Lallie Lloyd O'Brien, and Russell Edgerton of
The Pew Charitable Trusts; Peter T. Mich and Warren K. Chapman of the
Joyce Foundation; and Marilyn G. Reznick of The AT&T Foundation.

Those of us who had the advantage of attending the network meetings
and activities were only a few of many involved in significant work in each of
the PDSs and partnerships. The authors of the chapters are those who directly
participated in the writing. It is important for readers to understand that many
more were key to the work described. The hundreds of faculty, teachers, staff,
administrators, student teachers, doctoral candidates, and students of the involved schools and higher education institutions should be named but obviously cannot be. We acknowledge their many contributions to the work
discussed in this book and trust that readers will keep in mind that we have not
solved the problem of representing everyone. The views here are those of the
authors and do not necessarily represent others involved in the work.

Typically one or two highly motivated individuals create networks which
are sustained only when others take on leadership roles. The Leading Edge
network was fortunate to have many leaders. Without Linda Darling-Hammond and Ann Lieberman, the Leading Edge network would not have hap-
pened at all. Without Maritza Macdonald, the network would not have
coalesced around the issue of standards and the dyadic themes of inquiry, equity, assessment, and technology. If Gary A. Griffin had not agreed to codirect
NCREST and participate enthusiastically in the network, our energy for dig-
ging more deeply and critically into our work would likely have dissipated. Jon
Snyder, Ric Hovda, Amy Otis-Wilborn, Walter Kimball, Marleen Pugach, and
I all helped out at various points. Margaret Early, editor for the National Society for the Study of Education Yearbooks, and her colleague Carolyn Lyons,
agreed to assist in the editing process which helped us bring clarity to the dynamic and varied nature of writing about PDS work. Patrice R. Litman routinely kept the network humming. Without her graceful, quiet, relentless

prodding, this book would not have come together as designed. Throughout, there was no task too small or too daunting for Patrice. From her cheery e-mail reminders of deadlines to her flawless logistical planning and support for meetings, to working with editors and remaining astoundingly patient and supportive with at least two of us who have been beyond the pale with missed deadlines, she has been the cheerleader and keeper of the faith, contributing substantively and always with kindness and encouragement. To all involved, but especially to Patrice, we thank you.

Betty Lou Whitford, Director
NCREST
January, 2001

CHAPTER 1

Teacher Education on the Leading Edge: Learning With and From One Another

Gary A. Griffin and Patrice R. Litman

INTRODUCTION

The Leading Edge project sponsored by the National Center for Restructuring Education, Schools, and Teaching (NCREST) and generously supported by The Pew Charitable Trust with matching funds from the Joyce Foundation and The AT&T Foundation has demonstrated the power of institutional collaboration to influence how we think about and enact teacher education. We believe that the work reported in this volume is especially timely as a number of concerns about the quality of the nation's teaching force and the preparation of women and men to become teachers come together in powerful and unprecedented ways (Griffin, 1999).

The purposes of the Leading Edge project that have guided our efforts are deceptively simple and easy to understand. We intended to support the enhancement of already exemplary teacher education programs in their work with professional development schools around issues of standards for teacher education. We did this toward the end of providing models of outstanding practice that could contribute ideas for other institutions to study and adapt to their own contexts. To do this, we hoped to provide sufficient evidence of these successful practices so that policymakers, teacher educators, and school-based partners would be persuaded to experiment and to change longstanding but sometimes questionable practices of teacher preparation and school collaboration. Finally, we sought to document the work of the project in sufficient detail and with ample attention to the complexities, dilemmas, and possibilities of achieving excellence in teacher education such that we could join others in shattering the image of learning to teach as a simple, easy-to-accomplish mastery of a set of techniques and proven practices (Oakes & Lipton, 1998).

This book is our collective response to the purposes we set out to achieve. We provide an overview of our work, describe our several institutional settings, present pictures of our individual programs, illustrate how our work together is more powerful than our work alone, and demonstrate many of the policy and practice dilemmas that must be faced by those of us who are serious about ensuring that our nation's children are not shortchanged in their encounters with educational professionals over the course of their years in elementary, middle, and high schools.

We believe that the work presented here is especially timely for a number of reasons associated with teaching and schooling and because of a number of conditions currently confronting our society. Among the issues that spark our intellect and engage our practice are (a) guaranteeing that all students, independent of personal and cultural characteristics, receive education that is rooted in serious conceptions of equity (Cochran-Smith, 1999); (b) responsibly formulating and enacting educational standards as guides for teaching and learning rather than using them as sorting mechanisms to determine success and failure (Interstate New Teacher Assessment and Support Consortium [INTASC], 1992); (c) testing rigorously the degree to which school–university relationships, historically claimed to be important linchpins for effectiveness in teacher preparation, can realize that claim (Whitford & Metcalf-Turner, 1999); (d) understanding and ameliorating the tensions that exist naturally and expectedly between policymakers and practitioners (National Commission on Teaching and America's Future, 1996); (e) making wise decisions about which of the newly advanced practices related to teacher preparation are most worthy of experimentation and implementation; (f) linking technology more directly to the work of preparing teachers; and (g) coming to understand the possibilities and limitations of change in teacher education during times characterized by criticism, disillusionment, and disappointment with the consequences of schooling for large numbers of citizens (Howey & Zimpher, 1999). It is increasingly clear that the intellectual, social, and life-enhancement prospects of children and youth are affected directly by the character and quality of the teachers they encounter and the schools in which they are provided opportunities to learn. Consequently, our work has aimed at making individual and collective sense of the interactive and often confusing dilemmas about how best to ensure that teaching and schooling, influenced as they are by how teachers are prepared, can and should be positive forces for the students who encounter them.

What we discovered in the course of the Leading Edge work will not come as a surprise to those who have come to understand learning to teach and teaching as intellectually complex and institutionally difficult work. An analogy that may be apt is that of opening a long-held and well-remembered trunk in an attic. We have known the trunk was there, we have some memory of its contents, it has been in view each time we needed something near it. But when we finally open it and examine its contents with concentrated attention, we come to new understandings about the layers of objects, the historical antecedents that accompany those objects, and the relationships between what we find and our new perspectives on what we thought was familiar. In teacher education, as with the objects from the trunk in the attic, there are the familiars—methods, content, understandings about the nature of students in educational situations, placements for practica, the longstanding traditions of student teaching, the nature of knowledge and curriculum making, and the like. But again, as with the contents of the attic trunk, the times we live in and the understandings and perspectives we now hold cause us to see the familiar in new and often surprisingly different ways.

The Leading Edge institutions all have strong reputations for their preparation of teachers, have histories of excellence, and are known as leaders in constructing theory, engaging in research, and demonstrating outstanding practice. Yet, as we worked together and reexamined, in community, our work and our thinking about that work, we came to realize that we were facing challenges that pushed us to reconsider our individual and collective past and our current engagement with teacher preparation. We recognized that our understandings needed both reexamination and reconstruction. We acknowledged that the societal contexts, particularly in terms of state and regional policy arenas, were often in conflict with how we conceived of our work. We became conscious of new demands and new realities that must be given attention. And we realized that these new engagements with how we participated in the preparation of teachers could be enhanced considerably by sharing our ideas, critiquing our practices, and engaging one another as critical friends. This book is the story of that journey, of the reseeing and remaking of what many of us once acted out as well-honed and carefully constructed ways of helping women and men realize their ambitions to become exemplary teachers.

WHO ARE WE? THE LEADING EDGE INSTITUTIONS

Six teacher preparation schools, departments, and colleges of education participated in the Leading Edge effort from 1996 to 1999. Each of the programs is described in detail in the chapters that follow. As introduction, though, a brief picture of the settings is provided here.

The Preservice Program in Childhood Education at Teachers College, Columbia University is a graduate level teacher preparation program. The Preservice Program works in collaboration with three elementary schools in New

York City. All of these schools serve students characterized by cultural, linguistic, developmental, and economic diversity. The Teachers College initiatives involve prospective teachers in developing interdisciplinary learning experiences, conducting research, and working as student teachers and interns in restructured urban school settings.

The elementary teacher preparation program at the University of California, Santa Barbara (UCSB) is a minimum 13-month program culminating in a master's degree and state certification after a year-long internship. The program works in collaboration with seven elementary schools in Goleta and Santa Barbara, all of which have substantial immigrant (primarily Spanish-speaking) populations and one of which is a California charter school. UCSB's program emphasizes preparation and practice in support of linguistic and cultural diversity (in particular, a bilingual and cross-cultural emphasis), family and community involvement, professional collaboration, and thematic instruction using authentic assessment.

The University of Louisville's Professional Development School (PDS) Partnership involves seven elementary, two middle, and six high schools in three school districts serving urban, rural, and suburban schools. The Partnership works to a lesser degree with an additional twelve schools that are members of the Greater Louisville PDS Network. The unifying theme of the Partnership work related to teacher education and professional development is "teachers as learners and leaders." This network is a member of The Holmes Partnership[1] and is engaged in a wide array of reforms mandated by the groundbreaking Kentucky Education Reform Act of 1990. The University of Louisville (UL) has been at the forefront in launching models of professional development schools explicitly aimed at school restructuring for greater student success.

The University of Southern Maine (USM) works in partnership with approximately thirty K–12 schools representing a diverse cross-section of Maine schools collaborating in supporting the initial preparation and professional development of teachers. The professional development schools are organized into five sites centered in Portland, western Maine, Gorham, Yarmouth, and southern Maine (Sanford, Wells–Ogunquit, York) as part of the Extended Teacher Education Program (ETEP). ETEP includes (a) an undergraduate degree in arts and sciences and an education minor; (b) a graduate level, full-time, year-long, school-based internship for initial certification; and (c) course work emphasizing assessment in the beginning years of teaching culminating in a master's degree. All sites share a common focus on implementing the recently approved Maine Learning Results, K–12, developing local formative assessments to both inform instruction and document and report students' progress toward and attainment of the standards, and piloting performance-based intern assessment and initial certification.

The University of Wisconsin–Milwaukee (UWM) partnership includes four elementary and two high schools. All of these are urban schools in the Milwaukee Public School system serving students characterized by cultural, linguistic, developmental, and economic diversity. Teacher preparation programs are being restructured under the umbrella of teacher education for urban communities using INTASC standards as a framework. UWM is part of the Four Cities Network funded by the Joyce Foundation, which includes school–university partnerships among five universities and ten schools in Chicago, Cleveland, Detroit, and Milwaukee.

Wheelock College in Boston has established partnerships with eleven public elementary and K–8 schools in Boston, Brookline, and Cambridge. Of these partnerships, six are in Boston, which is a designated Empowerment Zone. Each partnership provides an opportunity for candidates to immerse themselves in exemplary practices that expand the notion of child-centered pedagogy in new directions that are particularly relevant to students in urban communities. In addition, the programs are engaged in transforming preparation and practice to build on knowledge that will enable greater inclusion of special needs children in mainstreamed settings and that will enhance curriculum and teaching practices which are responsive to diversity across all dimensions. Part of the Massachusetts Learning/Teaching Collaborative, Wheelock's work is at the cutting edge of early childhood teacher preparation.

WHAT DID WE SET OUT TO DO AND WHY?

The sponsoring organization, NCREST, has an intense interest in and firm commitment to understanding how educational organizations can be structured to provide both outstanding educational opportunity for students and meaningful and stimulating work environments for educational professionals. NCREST has been a leader in bringing together institutions and individuals concerned with new ways of working toward educational excellence. Whether through research activity, technical assistance, national conferences, demonstration projects, or other collaborative work, NCREST has focused on restructuring and redefining schools. Part of that work has necessarily attended to the nature of teaching as important social and intellectual activity and to conceptualizing, adapting, and inventing school places that support such a view of teaching (National Center for Restructuring Education, Schools, and Teaching, 1993).

Increasingly, it became clear to NCREST that the preparation of teachers for these newly conceived school organizations must be given solid attention. Clearly, too, professional development schools, which are new organizational vehicles for teacher preparation, would provide opportunities for fruitful research and development work. Consequently, NCREST set out to understand better than was the case at that time how teacher preparation programs worked with elementary, middle, and secondary schools in productive ways and to support that work through providing opportunities for collaborative activity across institutions. The goal initially, then, was twofold: to learn about professional development school cooperative work and to document that work in ways that would help others better cope with the often shrill and harshly critical calls for better teachers and better schools.

At the same time, it was clear that the so-called standards movement was in full swing. New standards for students were claimed to be a powerful way to promote deeper and more serious learning. Similarly, professional organizations, states, and regional alliances were promulgating standards for teacher licensure and assessment to be enforced over entire teaching careers. The Leading Edge work, then, originally proposed to focus on standards and how they were implemented, achieved, adapted, or otherwise dealt with by the participating institutions, with particular reference to this implementation in relation to professional development school partnerships.

We were, and continue to be, particularly interested in how new models of teacher preparation programs work, how they are influential upon and are influenced by teaching and teacher education policies, and how they impact all parties involved—prospective teachers, teacher educators, teachers in schools, and, most important, children and youth. We believe that this greater understanding can be used as leverage toward realizing systemic change in teacher education and in widespread improvement of educational opportunity. In short, we believe that work like that presented in this volume, when aggregated with similar efforts, can provide intellectual and practical bases for altering both professional practice and the preparation of those who engage in it.

However, we also believe that individual instances of exemplary practice are often just that—single cases that can be ignored because of a variety of "we can't do that here" perspectives held by observers. Therefore, we set out to provide evidence of individual as well as collective practice and the power that results from a community of interest. In our case, the community is made up of the six institutions described earlier.

The six institutions with, of course, their professional development school partners made up the larger community. Representative university- and school-based teacher educators met regularly over the course of the project to share ideas, puzzle out dilemmas, provide intellectual and psychic support, formulate plans for the future, reflect upon current and past experiences, participate in national and regional professional meetings (e.g., The Holmes Partnership and the annual meetings of the American Educational Research Association), and, importantly, develop personal and professional relationships that were both supportive and critical. We came to understand the substantive and practical conditions that helped us to connect our work, as well as acknowledge and accept the individual context features that often showed how different we were. Our times together were important features of the Leading Edge work.

In addition to the larger community, each of the six settings paired with another around issues of common interest. Remembering that we were all focusing on professional development school partnerships and standards, the dyads chose additional aspects of teacher preparation that we believed were important to explore within this framework of PDSs and standards. Teachers College and the University of California, Santa Barbara focused on standards and assessments with particular attention to the inquiry process. Wheelock College and UWM emphasized diversity and equity while attending to the issue of inclusion. USM and UL cooperated around the issues of evidence-based assessments through standards and using technology for program improvement. The dyad chapters later in this volume provide much greater detail about how this work moved forward, what was discovered, and what issues emerged from the cooperative work in the three pairs of programs.

How Can Our Work Inform the Field of Teacher Preparation?

It is obvious to even the most naïve observer that teacher preparation as it has been practiced historically is in need of serious revision (Holmes Group, 1986). A number of assumptions and beliefs about learning to teach—and teaching— well simply do not hold, if they ever were valid, as we move into a new millennium. These assumptions and beliefs, along with their associated practices and program features, are being challenged in a number of settings and from a variety of perspectives. The Leading Edge work offers a set of related issues for examination, critique, and review. The chapters that follow illustrate in detail how these issues influenced and were influenced by participation in the effort. Several are briefly noted here.

First, our work challenges the one-size-fits-all brand of teacher preparation. It is still assumed by many that teaching is a kind of follow-the-rules activity; that if one knows a set of teaching behaviors, students will respond and learning will take place. Although additional information to challenge this assumption is not needed for the expert teacher educator, there are still educational professionals and policymakers who persist in holding such a view. The work reported here both acknowledges and advances the understanding that teaching is a multifaceted decision-making process, that persons preparing to teach need opportunities to learn how to examine contexts for important features in order to decide how to move ahead with effective teaching, and that the growing diversity of student populations demands that teachers bring to their important work a well-developed repertoire of ways of thinking and acting. Although a number of models of teaching continue to be useful, holding one as absolute rather than knowing how to use a number of them simply does not match the reality of today's classrooms (National Commission on Teaching and America's Future, 1997).

Second, our work reveals the dilemmas associated with the presumed fit (some say fidelity) between institutional priorities and policy decisions. For example, states have become increasingly active in instituting accountability measures for both students and teachers. Leading Edge has begun to examine how these measures influence professional development and teacher education. The Leading Edge institutions, as noted earlier, were selected for this project because of their exemplary status. That is, the programs are acknowledged by peers in the field to be outstanding in the ways they work with prospective teachers, in the manner with which they organize and implement their professional development school partnerships, and in the excellence of their graduates. One might assume, then, that there would be few tensions between these programs and their participants and the policy arenas, state and regional, where they are located. We demonstrate and report in this book that this simply is not the case. Points of view about teaching and what is fundamental to learning to teach, from the perspectives of university- and school-based teacher educators in the Leading Edge settings, are often in conflict with policy directives that are formulated by state agencies, for example. It is striking to discover that excellence, substantiated by both peer review and the demonstrated quality of graduates, continues to be insufficient to guide policy decisions. Several such examples of this conflict appear in the chapters that follow.

Third, our work moves inside the professional development school in intellectual rather than simply structural ways. Although the notion of the professional development school has been part of our thinking about teacher education for more than a decade, there are still only a few serious reports about what they are and how they work from the inside (Whitford & Metcalf-Turner, 1999). Instead, we have observers' reports that most often focus on the structural characteristics and features (e.g., public intentions, hours spent by teacher candidates, role descriptions). The Leading Edge work, by definition, is in large part an inside-out perspective on the professional development school and provides substantial evidence and multiple stories about the prospects, possibilities, and problems of making PDSs work.

Fourth, our work reveals the important impact of long-term relationships among critical friends at the institutional as well as the personal level. It has long been known that, as individuals, we are sustained and supported by our relationships with persons who know us and care about us. The presence of confidants whose judgment we trust and whose critical eye reveals what we sometimes cannot see for ourselves is helpful and sustaining, particularly when that presence persists over time. What the Leading Edge work reveals is that critical friendships can have professional and institutional bases. In the dyad-oriented chapters that follow, a variety of ways of maintaining this broader based set of relationships are described and their impact is presented. Teaching, of course, has been called the lonely profession. Likewise, the work of preparing teachers, even in the company of one's program-based colleagues, can be isolated activity, absent what we believe are important external and supportive sources of inspiration, ideas, criticism, and review. In effect, we came to common cause across institutional boundaries and our work benefitted from it.

Fifth, our work illustrates how recommendations from national organizations and movements can be transformed and translated when considered seriously by leaders in local contexts (Yinger, 1999). In large part because the Leading Edge project focused directly on standards for teaching and teacher education, we were sensitive to and thoughtful about the recommendations for achieving excellence in both of these areas. What we came to understand with greater clarity was the need to be sensitive to the struggles that are inherent in presenting sensible but distanced recommendations for change in our own workplaces. There were no cases in our settings where we simply adopted and implemented recommendations for altering our practices. Instead, we illustrate in this book the difficult work of transforming conceptualizations of teacher preparation so that they made sense where we do our work, whether those places are colleges, universities, or elementary and secondary schools. Similar to the transformations that must occur when we make school subjects out of the traditional disciplines, the construction of local meaning from national recommendations is difficult, time-consuming, and complex intellectual and practical activity.

Sixth, our work adds to the understandings about the power of context to influence ideas and ideas to influence context (Hargreaves, 1994). Directly related to the transformations noted above is our observation that ideas from outside our own contexts are changed as they are shaped to make sense in our ongoing work and that our contexts are changed as a consequence of the introduction of the externally formulated ways of thinking and acting. We came to understand clearly the concept of mutual adaptation, the importance of ideas shaping contexts and contexts shaping ideas.

Seventh, our work helps to focus directly on the political aspects of learning to teach. As can be seen from the chapters that follow, the work of preparing teachers is political activity in larger measure than is typically understood. Although some see teacher education generally as a relatively neutral effort, in political terms, we are aware more sharply than ever before of the ideological struggles around issues of how teachers should be taught, what they should know and be able to do, and especially how they should conceive of their work in terms of influence upon children and the larger society. Whether we are experiencing the tensions associated with competing claims about preparing teachers for multiple language settings or to work with students around the construction of meaning rather than simply passing along what has been called "funded knowledge" or some other similar example, we realize that the assumptions and dispositions that support conflicting perspectives must be understood and, in some cases, opposed in direct as well as subtle ways. Here, particularly, our network of critical friends has been an ongoing source of intellectual and personal, as well as political, support.

Eighth, our work suggests how we can conceptualize the relationship between professional development schools as new organizations and the ongoing professional development of experienced teachers and teacher educators. The history of school–university relationships can probably best be characterized by the statement, "The university teaches prospective teachers *about* teaching and the schools teach them *how* to teach." That is, the theory and propositions related to what teaching is all about are the province of higher education but the "real" learning to teach takes place in elementary, middle, and high schools. Often, however, learning about and learning how have been in conflict. This is perhaps best represented in the oft-repeated claim by new teachers, "I didn't really learn to teach until student teaching. All that theory at the university was a waste of time." Notwithstanding that this claim may have some basis in reality in certain instances, we believe that the closer relationships between higher education and the schools as represented by professional development schools diminish enormously the possibility that such a representation can continue with any vitality. In large part, this is because of the close proximity of university-based and school-based teacher educators. The professional development school provides a meeting ground and an intellectual and practical space for members of both groups to come together to face important questions like these: "What is exemplary teaching?" "Where and when is the best time and place to learn to teach this way?" "Who are the strongest candidates for teaching and why?" "Where is the required knowledge and skill to assist the prospective teacher?" The Leading Edge work pushed us to understand more directly and to appreciate more deeply the power of school–university interactions in this new context of the professional development school.

Ninth, our work adds to the growing inventory of what is needed to be a teacher educator in times of social and cultural conflict and tension (Cochran-Smith, 1999). Throughout this volume, but particularly in those sections dealing directly with issues of equity in teaching and schooling, we provide examples of the ways that teacher educators must directly face the differences that characterize our society and our schools. Difference manifests itself in many ways, but the most common and, in many cases, the most volatile ways are in relation to ethnicity, race, and social class. In some ways, the fact that teachers are increasingly middle class and white while their students are increasingly neither middle class nor white is exacerbated by the overwhelmingly middle class and white teacher educators who prepare teachers. Our experiences demonstrate the tensions that teacher educators must encounter to come to terms with preparing teachers for the so-called new populations of students in schools. Similarly, as teacher educators, we face the political issues noted above and must develop serious agency to do so with greater power than has generally been the case. Also, now that teacher education once again assumes a central fiscal role in higher education as enrollments burgeon, we must learn how to balance our beliefs about quality preparation with the extraordinary national demand for new teachers. Much of the subtext of this volume is focused on redefining the role of teacher educator, whether that role is played out in a higher education setting, a conventional public school, or a professional development school.

Last, our work provides a framework for thinking of learning to teach as a community preoccupation rather than an individual vocational path. This can be conceptualized in several ways. Because of our focus on professional development schools, we are able to speak about communities of interest that include university- and school-based teacher educators working together to bring greater power and authority to the experience of learning to teach. This is in sharp contrast to the historical (and, in all too many cases, current) practice of separating sharply and irrevocably the teacher education practices in higher education from those in cooperating teachers' classrooms, as noted earlier. In addition, however, we can testify to the benefits that are derived from participating in the overlapping multiple communities that characterize the Leading Edge project. We believe that the prospective teachers we work with have received stronger opportunities to learn to teach because of our interactions with one another, because of the multiple realities we have faced together, because of the program initiatives that we have learned with and from one another, and because of the focus the Leading Edge opportunity has given to our work. In effect, this book is largely about how these communities intersect to provide these benefits for our students and for ourselves.

ORGANIZATION OF THE VOLUME

This chapter has introduced the Leading Edge participants, described what we intended to do together, and suggested some of the reasons that we believe the experience was worthy of our time and effort and of others' attention. These advance organizers provide only the briefest of glimpses into the complexity of our experience and the benefits we derived. The remainder of this book describes in detail how our work proceeded and what we learned from that work.

The authors of Chapter 2, Standardization or Standards for Professional Practice? Public and Private Theories of Teaching in Professional Development Schools, argue that standards are most useful when coconstructed in partnership with other local stakeholders. The tension between proscriptive standards and contextualized standards is exposed both by reflective processes and by PDS work. To frame their discussion, the authors define teaching by examining public theories of teaching and those held by university faculty and interns. How do public theories manifest themselves? How do teacher education faculty and teacher candidates negotiate public and private theories of teaching? How does public discourse inform teaching practice? The mission of teacher education to assist students to develop their own theories of teaching is challenged by public theories of teaching embodied in state and national standards, which may not be adapted to local conditions or carefully analyzed by those implementing them. In the context of Kentucky's policies, the authors report that the standards and accountability movements have limited curriculum and student learning opportunities by focusing exclusively on strategies that raise test scores, rather than framing efforts around students' learning needs. Thus, policy levers limit rather than enhance the scope of improvement efforts.

Chapter 3, Assessment and Standards for Professional Improvement, describes the evolution of the collaboratively developed and implemented Extended Teachers Education Program at USM. Collaboration between school- and university-based educators has significantly shaped assessment and standards, the framework in which the program approaches issues of teaching competence and ongoing program development. The authors use three themes to illuminate intern assessment—authenticity (accurate and useful), continuity (developmental, continuous, and explicit), and fairness (genuine circumstances and multiple opportunities to demonstrate). Attention to standards and outcomes encourages a tighter alignment of program expectations, with intern assessment informing teaching practice and providing a unified conception of what interns and teacher educators are working toward. Embedded in this assessment system is the opportunity to use evidence defined by good teaching for continuous program improvement. The authors conclude with a discussion of assessment strategies used to review evidence of teaching quality, showing how technology is used to support interns' interaction and access to information.

In Chapter 4, Getting Beyond the Talking and Into the Doing, the first dyad chapter, a team of authors from USM and UL trace the evolution of a significant and influential "critical-friend" relationship. State policy had consequences for program structures and behaviors. UL found that the implementation of high stakes accountability legislation challenged not only the ethos of experimentation that had marked the teacher education program but also the nature of the PDS as a teacher education model. While USM also experienced recently implemented state standards, school districts develop their assessment systems locally and interns are able to develop lesson plans broadly in response to state standards. USM experienced internal challenges as the program sought to establish consensus across faculty in multiple sites about assessments aligned with candidate performance indicators and corresponding course work. As a dyad, the two sites work to develop their intern assessment systems by sharing program documents and acting as critical friends. Technology is being used at both sites for communication and to share student teacher products.

Researchers at Teachers College describe in Chapter 5, A Professional Development School (PDS) Partnership for Preparing Teachers for Urban Schools, the program structures that actualize the program philosophy in the context of the schools and state policies. The program engages PDS interns in field-related experiences that closely resemble the real life of teaching. Candidates are encouraged to engage in a reflective process about their instruction and learn about multiple instructional strategies to address individual student needs so that they become deliberative practitioners. Domains of knowledge or program-specific standards are reflected in both the program structures and course assignments, and emphasize what the program believes is good teacher education. The authors describe how standards are articulated and enacted through structures and processes.

The author of Chapter 6, Elementary Teacher Education Program at University of California, Santa Barbara, uses three lenses to describe work in teacher education at the UCSB: values, state policy context, and programmatic structures. In the early '90s, the program engaged in a process to make their existing program values more explicit. These explicit values statements served to provide a direction for the redesign of the program, their research agenda, and the nature of the relationship with their school-based partner. Resulting program structures and processes seek to help teacher candidates grow and develop in six interrelated themes that weave through course work, field experiences, and all interactions candidates have with the program. Over the course of the Leading Edge work from 1996 to 1999, externally developed state-mandated policies challenged the existing internally developed values, structures, and processes. This chapter describes how state policies confronted and influenced the program structures and policies.

In Chapter 7, What We Learned From Site Visits, the dyad team from Teachers College and the University of California, Santa Barbara describe how the state policy contexts of each of their institutions affect the teacher candidate experience. To illustrate how "who decides and how?" influences learning opportunities for teacher candidates, the authors present vignettes of practice and three policy contexts that serve as a backdrop to discuss how these policies play out in teacher education programs and in schools. While examining each other's programs, and the role of standards and assessments within those programs, the authors discuss the issues of centralized and decentralized decision making and the role of professional trust in the standards-setting movement. The chapter concludes with a discussion of policy values matching or mismatching, the role of negotiating space in constructive communication, and the need for permeable and open systems of policy making.

The authors of Chapter 8, Beyond Standards: Creating Depth in Teacher Education Reform, professors at the University of Wisconsin-Milwaukee, draw attention to the "distance between standards and reform" to stress that it is the actions taken beyond the adoption of standards that will improve teacher preparation and create long-lasting reform. The UWM process toward action is reported through a description of "dialogue spaces" and a belief that talk reflects knowledge and beliefs that become "fuel for our actions." The chapter describes "a recursive cycle of dialogue and action" including the structures and processes used to develop public and shared commitments to action that are informed by national standards as well as locally defined core values that define what it means to prepare teachers for urban schools.

As reported in Chapter 9, Visions and Outcomes: Developing Standards and Assessments in Wheelock College Teacher Preparation Programs, Wheelock College in Boston, with its funding from Leading Edge, set out to develop standards and assessments appropriate to a small private college whose graduate and undergraduate programs are specifically devoted to preparing professionals for the fields of education, social work, and child-centered work in medical settings. The Wheelock group took as its framework standards developed by INTASC, and adapted them to fit the unique requirements of early childhood and elementary teachers committed to teaching all of the nation's children effectively. Wheelock's experience suggests that standards and assessments are an important but not singular aspect of transforming teacher education. As the nation's school population becomes increasingly diverse, the pool of teachers is likely to remain largely white, female, and middle-class. Therefore, standards must be part of a system that includes a multicultural approach to curriculum and pedagogy, a carefully crafted sequence of field experiences for students, and a campus culture that supports continuing dialogue about equity and diversity. The authors recount the "messy" process of working toward faculty consensus on relevant standards and they explain the specific differences between Wheelock's and INTASC's formulations.

The authors of Chapter 10, Equity in Teacher Education Standards and in Our Practice, describe institutional and state policy contexts of their teacher education programs at University of Wisconsin-Milwaukee and Wheelock College. Similarities between these dissimilar institutions include a commitment to equity, teacher preparation in urban settings, and PDS partnerships. These commonalties form the basis of their discussions about equity as cross-institutional research partners. The authors argue that the national standards movement does not adequately address issues of equity but instead substitutes a multicultural diversity perspective, and thus falls short of supporting the preparation of teachers able to address the persistent achievement gaps among students. They identify program structures and activities that address teacher education in urban settings.

NOTES

1. The Holmes Partnership, founded in 1986 as the Holmes Group, is a consortium of research universities, public school districts, and professional organizations which is committed to high quality teacher preparation, continued faculty development, and the renewal of public schools through identifying best practices, research, and professional development school partnerships. [*http://www.holmespartnership.org/*]

REFERENCES

Cochran-Smith, M. (1999). Learning to teach for social justice. In G. A. Griffin (Ed.), *The Education of teachers: The ninety-eighth yearbook of the National Society for the Study of Education, Part 1* (pp. 114-144). Chicago: University of Chicago Press.

Griffin, G. A. (Ed.). (1999). *The Education of teachers: The ninety-eighth yearbook of the National Society for the Study of Education, Part 1*. Chicago: University of Chicago Press.

Hargreaves, A. (1994). *Changing teachers, Changing times: Teachers' work and culture in the postmodern age.* New York: Teachers College Press.

Holmes Group. (1986). *Tomorrow's teachers.* East Lansing, MI: Author.

Howey, K., & Zimpher, N. (1999). Pervasive problems and issues in teacher education. In G. A. Griffin (Ed.), *The Education of Teachers: The ninety-eighth yearbook of the National Society for the Study of Education, Part I* (pp. 279–306). Chicago: University of Chicago Press.

Interstate New Teacher Assessment and Support Consortium. (1992). *Model standards for beginning teacher licensure and development: A resource for state dialogue.* Washington, DC: Council of Chief State School Officers.

National Center for Restructuring Education, Schools, and Teaching. (1993). *Vision statement: Professional development schools network: Purposes, commitments, and enabling conditions for professional development schools.* New York: Author.

National Commission on Teaching and America's Future. (1996). *What matters most: Teaching for America's future.* New York: Author.

National Commission on Teaching and America's Future. (1997). *Doing what matters most: Investing in quality teaching.* New York: Author.

Oakes, J., & Lipton, M. (1998). *Teaching to change the world*. Boston: McGraw-Hill.

Whitford, B. L., & Metcalf-Turner, P. (1999). Of promises and unresolved puzzles: Reforming teacher education with professional development schools. In G. A. Griffin (Ed.), *The Education of Teachers: The ninety-eighth yearbook of the National Society for the Study of Education* (pp. 257–278). Chicago: University of Chicago Press.

Yinger, R. (1999). The role of standards in teaching and teacher education. In G. A. Griffin (Ed.), *The Education of Teachers: The ninety-eighth yearbook of the National Society for the Study of Education, Part I* (pp. 85–113). Chicago: University of Chicago Press.

CHAPTER 2

Standardization or Standards for Professional Practice? Public and Private Theories of Teaching in Professional Development Schools

Steve Ryan, Phyllis Metcalf-Turner, and Ann Larson

Perhaps the central threat of the so-called standards movement in education is that the development, promulgation, and implementation of standards will lead to standardization (Kohn, 1999; Newmann, Secada, & Wehlage, 1995). That is, public theories—as represented by the variety of standards documents currently pervading educational policy and practice discourse—may dominate private theories. Because standards specify what individuals should know and be able to do, they are akin to curriculum in that they attempt to bring order to the conduct of schooling. Teacher standards, for example, attempt to define what effective teachers should know and do, and as such represent a theory of teaching. As a piece of public policy, standards for teachers offer a public theory of teaching that like other policies are presented through a "rhetoric of conclusions" or as "official knowledge" (Apple, 1993; Schwab, 1962). Rarely are the deliberations that led to the developed standards included in their dissemination—two exceptions are the standards developed by the National Board for Professional Teacher Standards (NBPTS, 1999) and the Standards for Effective Teaching developed by the Center for Research on Education, Diversity, and Excellence (Tharp, 1999)—and so the theory of teaching that emerges is absent the underlying epistemological assumptions.

In this chapter, we argue that our essential task as teacher educators is to assist our students in developing their own private theories about teaching. Our teacher preparation programs are structured to provide students individual and collective experiences and promote inquiry so that they can negotiate their own way into and through the teaching profession. Our concern is that our students' private theories can be silenced when standards not only set forth a broad vision of effective practice but also prescribe individual action. This chapter describes how this tension between public and private theories of teaching creates dilemmas for our professional development school (PDS) work and argues that teaching standards, like other pieces of curricula, must be explored by those implementing them and must be adapted to local contexts (Bullough & Gitlin, 1995). We begin by briefly discussing the historical context for our PDS work and by describing our elementary and secondary teacher preparation programs.

A BRIEF HISTORY OF OUR
SCHOOL–UNIVERSITY COLLABORATION

The School of Education at the University of Louisville (UL) has been working closely with local school professionals for more than ten years to reconceptualize teacher education and professional development. Compatible school district and university goals supported the development of PDSs. In 1984, the Jefferson County Public Schools created the Gheens Professional Development Academy to support the professional development of the district's teachers and administrators. The academy emphasized collegial interaction and district leadership for fundamentally restructuring schools (Schlecty, Ingwerson & Brooks, 1988). In 1986, the UL School of Education became a charter member in the Holmes Group (now The Holmes Partnership), which supported the reform of teacher education programs. That same year the Center for the Collaborative Advancement of the Teaching Profession was funded by Kentucky's higher education governing board. The center adopted as its primary function the enhancement and support of school–university collaborative activities aimed at improving preservice preparation and professional development of teachers, modeling exemplary practice, and conducting research.

Early on, local leaders emphasized innovation and experimentation rather than compliant implementation. After the district had initiated a process for planning site selection, 24 district schools worked on two major PDS goals: (1) becoming exemplars of best practice and (2) becoming centers for the induction and continuing professional development of teachers and administrators. During the planning phase, the district conducted seven all-day seminars for representative school teams on the problems confronting local educators and some of the potential means to solve them. These seminars explored the social and organizational characteristics of schools and the teaching profession, the conditions of teaching and learning in schools, and some of the obstacles to reform. A vision statement—six beliefs and six sets of standards about exemplary practice—was drafted by academy leadership, approved by seminar participants, and guided the establishment of PDSs. Fairdale High School was chosen as the first PDS pilot site (Whitford, 1994).

More recently, as a partnership school for over a decade, Fairdale High School was selected from a field of 95 applicants to serve as one of twenty university–school partnerships in a pilot project to test the draft of the National Council for Accreditation of Teacher Education (NCATE) on Professional Development School Standards. As a pilot site for NCATE's Standards Field-Test Project, Fairdale has collaborated with the university to examine, critique, and apply the draft standards to programs and practices through a self-study process and through research into the learning of adolescents and teacher candidates in the partnership. The pilot PDS standards define four functions of a partnership school that we explicated as: (1) improving the lives, learning, and opportunities of all students; (2) enhancing the curriculum, structures, school culture, and community ties for the high school and the university staff and faculty; (3) preparing new educators in a professional, collegial environment within the context of experiences that they will likely face in their early years as teachers; and (4) researching, assessing, reflecting upon and/or disseminating the partnership work. The Fairdale High School and UL partnership has continued to explore the interconnections of these four functions with the attributes of a Professional Development School as defined by NCATE: learning community; collaboration; accountability and quality assurance; organization, roles, and structure; and equity. A long-standing commitment to Fairdale, as well as to other partnerships with local schools, helped to earn the School of Education two citations in 1997 from NCATE—the Citation for Exemplary Practice in Design and Delivery of Curriculum and the Citation for Exemplary Practice in Collaboration.

Although local efforts were consistent with nationally recognized reform recommendations (e.g., Holmes Group, 1990), local leaders emphasized a selective adoption of national reform recommendations. One of them explained:

> Where recommendations from national groups have been found to be relevant in our local context, they have been pursued. Where national reports can be used to help local audiences better understand local initiatives, they are used. And where the recommendations of national groups are judged to be inappropriate in the local context, those recommendations are disregarded.

Such selectivity was possible early on because the national PDS agenda had yet to be established. There was no public theory of school-based professional development, so private theories—those that grew out of local contexts and were informed by local actors' beliefs and commitments—were ascendant. By the time the Department of Early and Middle Childhood Education adopted the PDS model for its teacher preparation program in 1993, however, there was much greater consensus, informed both by the efforts of colleagues in the department of secondary education and national leaders in professional development schools, about what constituted "good" practice in PDS's.[1] Thus, the elementary and secondary teacher preparation programs emerged from different historical contexts, which led to different program structures.

About Our Secondary Teacher Education Program

Our secondary teacher preparation program is a 33-credit, fifth-year, graduate-only program leading to a Master of Arts in Teaching (MAT) degree. In the fall semester, teacher candidates enroll in education courses for nine credits—Pre-student Teaching and Special Methods. Pre-student Teaching (6 credits) is offered at one of three local high school PDS sites and includes a classroom internship and participation in a school-based change project. Candidates enroll in Special Methods (3 credits) by content area. Methods faculty, in consultation with district representatives, make student teaching placements for the spring semester. In the spring semester, candidates student teach for 15 weeks (earning 8 credits) and participate in a weekly Student Teaching Seminar (3 credits) and the Capstone Seminar (1 credit) that culminates our program. In addition to education courses, students enroll in 12 credits of graduate academic courses, usually in their content area. Nearly all of our students earn an MAT within one year of admission to the program, although many students have already spent one year taking academic support courses or completing their teaching majors prior to admission.

Students in our teacher preparation program—about 90% European American, 5% African American, and 5% other—come from a variety of backgrounds, including recent college graduates, mid-career professionals, and former military personnel. We admit between 75 to 90 students per year, of whom approximately 70% are women. The department recommends students for a variety of teaching certificates: Biological or Physical Science, English, Mathematics, and Social Studies (7–12); Business Education (5–12); and Art Education and Foreign Language (P–12). Art and Foreign Language candidates have split student teaching placements (usually, seven weeks in an elementary or middle school classroom and seven weeks in a high school classroom). Nearly all of our graduates teach in public or private schools in Jefferson County or the immediate surrounding counties.

About Our Elementary Teacher Education Program

The 36-credit, fifth-year elementary program includes heavy involvement in and commitment to teaching in public schools. Interns in the elementary program are admitted to a cohort and for the entire academic year are immersed in a classroom in one of six elementary PDS sites, where they are assigned to work with one or more teachers. They spend one semester each at the primary and intermediate levels. Generally, one of these placements is in an urban school and the other is in a rural or suburban school. Methods courses (12 credits) are offered throughout the year on campus. Throughout the elementary program, student performance and progress are measured against discipline-based standards such as those of the National Council of Teachers of Mathematics and the state's Experienced Teacher Standards.

THE CONTEXT OF THE KENTUCKY REFORM

As an early model of PDS work nationally, the School of Education earned recognition for its efforts. The new form of teacher preparation at the center of early efforts fits well with the state's widely heralded passage of the Kentucky Education Reform Act (KERA) in 1990. KERA sought to equalize educational opportunities for all students through new school funding principles and through a heightened focus on school, district, and university accountability. Published test scores, rewards for schools that reach improvement targets, and sanctions for those that fail to improve contribute to a schooling environment where "teaching to the test" is a sensible response to the uncertainty of an increasingly prescriptive state context (Jones & Whitford, 1997). Selective adoption of reforms is hardly an option when local educators are expected to show how any school improvement or professional development is expected to raise student achievement (as measured nearly exclusively by state test scores). As a result, the scope of school improvement and professional development activities has focused only on those areas that might have a direct and immediate impact on student achievement.

Of course, the process of defining those areas is itself informed by theories about how students learn, whether all students can learn at high levels, and the purposes of schools. While others have suggested that PDSs themselves are not concerned enough about issues of equity and social justice (Abdal-Haqq, 1997; Murrell, 1998), we believe that the current dominant public theory of school reform in Kentucky and elsewhere contributes to this shortcoming. The idea that raising standards for students and teachers and holding schools more accountable for student achievement will create better schools has ironically created a deprofessionalizing reform context that limits the ability of PDSs, or any school reform effort, to adequately address equity and social justice issues. The announced intention that the move to raise standards and hold schools accountable would in fact induce local educators to develop new competencies and create new curricula has not yet materialized. Instead, educators seem to be frantically hunting for the right curriculum, the right program, or the right strategies for raising student test scores without considering how students learn or what the purposes of schools may be.

As with many other systemic reform efforts, Kentucky is seeking to align student learning goals with state assessments, teaching standards, and teacher preparation, certification, and induction practices. Following the development of learner goals and academic expectations, the Education Professional Standards Board (EPSB)—an autonomous body appointed by the governor—created a committee to assist the Board in the development of a performance-based system of teacher preparation and certification by

- developing and recommending standards and performance criteria for the certification of experienced teachers in Kentucky;
- recommending steps for developing the assessment tasks;
- recommending a process to support certification using the recommended standards. (Kentucky Department of Education, 1994)

The EPSB explained that the standards were to be used by colleges and universities in the state to restructure teacher education programs for teacher candidates and experienced teachers as part of Kentucky's "results-oriented, primarily performance-based system of teacher preparation and certification" (p. 2). Although this statement from the preamble to the standards expresses the EPSB's intended use of the standards, teacher educators and others who use the standards to assess and evaluate teachers do so in ways that are informed by their own theories of teacher performance and evaluation. The preamble cautions that the standards should not be used as a checklist for teacher behaviors, but many teacher educators and others familiar with the use of behavioral objectives in evaluating teaching have used them in just that way.

DEFINING TEACHING IN PROFESSIONAL DEVELOPMENT SCHOOLS

Working in PDSs—institutions created, in part, to redefine the ways we think about teaching and teacher education—inevitably exposes tensions between public theories of teaching and private theories held by individuals and groups. Darling-Hammond (1994) argues that "PDS's aim to provide new models of teacher education and development by serving as exemplars of practice, builders of knowledge, and vehicles for communicating professional understandings among teacher educators, novices, and veteran teachers" (p. 1). As university and school faculty create these new models, they do so within existing structures and cultures (including that of standards-based reform) that can constrain or enable innovation, development, and professional dialogue.

Few individuals in our society would be hard-pressed to define "teaching." Images of teachers from the classrooms of our individual and collective histories evoke memories of recitations, requirements, reprimands, and relationships. One often repeated observation is that anyone can teach. Teaching takes place naturally in any culture, and perhaps it should not surprise us that so many claim to know so much about what teaching *is*. As researchers (including practitioner-researchers) study teaching more closely, however, it becomes clearer that the special relationship between teacher and student is not easily defined and that good teaching varies across contexts, institutions, and classrooms (Ball & Wilson, 1996; Cochran-Smith, 1991; Davis & Sumara, 1997; McDonald, 1992).

In the remainder of this chapter, we define teaching in three ways. First, we describe the Kentucky Experienced Teacher Standards as a public theory of contemporary teaching. Although these standards were developed with only Kentucky's educational reform in mind, they share many characteristics with other public theories of teaching, as manifested in other standards documents. Next, we look briefly at how faculty in the elementary and secondary programs mediate this public theory of teaching by looking at how we and our colleagues use these standards. Of course, how we do so is influenced by our work with P–12 educators and our students. Finally, we examine the private theories of one group of university interns working in a PDS to determine how they are negotiating their way into the teaching profession.

The Kentucky Teacher Standards: A Public Theory of Teaching

Because our graduates receive a master's degree (and advanced rank in Kentucky), we use the Kentucky Experienced Teacher Standards rather than the New Teacher Standards as an important measure of our students' development. The standards, developed by a committee of university faculty, district-level and school administrators, teachers, and business community representatives, "describe what experienced teachers do in authentic teaching situations and those teaching behaviors and processes that are most critical to student learning" (Kentucky Department of Education, 1994). Thus, these standards put forth a public theory of teaching that concentrates on teaching behaviors that are closely associated with student learning. This was especially important since new K–12 student assessments, initiated in the wake of KERA, placed a heavy burden on teachers and schools to be held accountable for student performance. Similarly, the emphasis on performance implied in the standards sent out a clear message that teacher preparation programs should seek to provide students with experiences that would enable them to demonstrate their ability to meet these standards. The committee that developed the standards was also given responsibility for monitoring their implementation by teacher education programs.

Nine standards for an experienced teacher were established in 1994:

1. Demonstrates professional leadership;
2. Demonstrates knowledge of content;
3. Designs/plans instruction;
4. Creates/maintains learning climate;
5. Implements/manages instruction;
6. Assesses and communicates learning results;
7. Reflects/evaluates teaching/learning;
8. Collaborates with colleagues/parents/others; and
9. Engages in professional development.[2]

The majority of the standards involve classroom practice. Standards 3 to 6 establish a linear pattern of lesson planning, instruction, and assessment. These teacher behaviors are linked to student development through a common phrase added to each standard. For example, standard 5 reads, "The teacher introduces/implements/manages instruction that develops student abilities to use communication skills, apply core concepts, become self-sufficient individuals, become responsible team members, think and solve problems, and integrate knowledge." Interestingly, standard 7, which might also be conceived of as a standard for classroom practice, omits this connection to student development. It reads simply, "The teacher reflects on and evaluates teaching/learning." In this way, the standards focus on reflection *on* practice rather than reflection *in* practice, in which reflection can be seen as an integral part of teaching rather than a tool to be used "after" instruction and assessment (Schön, 1991).

The remaining standards involve professional knowledge and the professional community. Standards 2 and 9 focus on teachers' content knowledge and professional development respectively and do not make a connection to student learning. For example, standard 2 reads, "The teacher demonstrates content knowledge within own discipline(s) and in application(s) to other disciplines." This standard describes teachers in relation to the content that they teach, but not in relation to the students they teach. As such, the standards do not directly link teachers' content knowledge or learning to that of their students. In contrast, standard 1 focuses on "professional leadership within the school, community, and education profession to improve student learning and well-being." Standard 8 asks teachers to collaborate with "colleagues, parents, and other agencies to design, implement, and support learning programs that develop student abilities to use communication skills, apply core concepts, become self-sufficient individuals, become responsible team members, think and solve problems, and integrate knowledge." The mixed message given here is that what teachers do individually and collectively is more important to student learning than what they know.

An emphasis on effective practice. The absence of a connection between teacher thinking, knowing, and learning and student development (in standards 2, 7, and 9) highlights the public theory of teaching represented by the standards. That is, the standards set forth a technology of teaching that emphasizes what teachers do rather than what they know or think. Despite the contention in the standards that they "identify what effective experienced teachers know and do" and that "they imply more than the mere demonstration of teaching competencies," the standards clearly see teaching behaviors as linked to student development, while teacher thinking, knowing, and learning are not. Thus, what is known by those who developed the standards (the public theory of teaching) is privileged over what teachers know based on their content knowledge, experience, and professional development (a private theory of teaching).

The standards portray a technical–rational theory of teaching. Their aim is to enlist teachers in the implementation of effective teaching behaviors that will lead to student development (Clandinin & Connelly, 1995; Snyder, Bolin, & Zumwalt, 1992). For example, teachers are to "design and plan instruction that develops student abilities to use communication skills, apply core concepts, become self-sufficient individuals, become responsible team members, think and solve problems, and integrate knowledge." Certainly, just writing lesson plans cannot accomplish all of these things. To take one example, teachers have to know *which* communication skills can be taught within a lesson or series of lessons without making the learning of the communication skills more important than the content. They must decide whether or not the content being taught provides a context in which to develop communication skills. This is not simply a performance task; it involves at least the following factors: teachers' deep understanding of students' developmental level, teachers' knowledge of how students learn, teachers' capacity to create contexts that support such learning, and the delicate balance between teaching content and process. Teachers and other observers of classroom instruction are well aware that it can be just as easy for teachers to overemphasize learning processes at the expense of important content as to overemphasize content.

Designing instruction that develops communication skills requires teachers to know something about their students' communication styles (which may be affected by cultural differences) and how to draw on students' strengths and address areas of weakness. This means that the same lesson will not achieve the same results for different students, so teachers must be able and willing to modify their lessons accordingly. The will to modify is significant here. As a large body of research makes clear, teachers' beliefs are just as important as teachers' skills (Gay, 1995; Hunsaker & Johnson, 1992; McLaughlin, 1987). Teaching to high standards is much more complicated than writing a lesson plan, which can provide necessary structure and a clear set of goals but cannot ensure the "success" of the plan.

An underlying assumption of the EPSB appears to be that lesson planning is necessary but not sufficient, and a separate implementation standard also exists. Again, the standard emphasizes what teachers do—introduce, implement, and manage "instruction that develops students' abilities to use communication skills" (p. 3). Absent are the beliefs that guide teachers' actions and missing, too, is any consideration of schooling contexts.

Using Standards: Fidelity or Mutual Adaptation?

The Kentucky Experienced Teacher Standards are to be "used by colleges and universities in Kentucky as a guide for restructuring teacher education programs" (p. 2). The expectation is that the standards will shape the actions of teacher educators throughout the state. Just how the standards are to be used and which actions are to be shaped is not specified, but the EPSB approves all certification programs through its review of program folios. Moreover, the EPSB specifies the contents of the folios, which must include a description of program experiences showing how they relate to the standards. Clearly, then, one central policy assumption underlying the standards is that teacher educators and teachers will faithfully promote and emulate the vision of teaching suggested therein.

This assumption is not verified by our experience. First, the task of defining teaching is not a routine one for us as teacher educators, particularly teacher educators who work collaboratively with local P–12 educators. The public theory of teaching suggested by the standards was introduced into an ongoing conversation about teaching among university faculty and school-based educators. In a way this conversation created a set of institutional standards or another kind of public theory of teaching (which we hope is a more democratic public theory) that not only relies on "expert" knowledge but also is responsive to individual and contextual differences. Before returning to this theory below, we look first at how standards are used in our teacher preparation programs.

As part of our Leading Edge work, we conducted an interview study regarding how standards were being used in our teacher preparation programs.[3] Results of the study suggest that faculty are pleased that the standards provide a "common framework for expressing expectations for MAT student learning and for assessing student progress toward those expectations" (p. 3). Many faculty members explained that the standards help make our programs more coherent by providing a "common language" (p. 17). For example, both programs use the standards as organizers for intern portfolios, although the secondary program has recently begun to require interns to develop evidence-based portfolios demonstrating their development toward each standard. In this way, the secondary program is attempting to show the connections between various standards and reduce the emphasis on discrete teacher behaviors or performances.

In describing the benefits of the standards for program development, faculty members' responses show the narrow boundary between standards and standardization. Some faculty described the standards as setting targets, serving as benchmarks, expressing clear expectations, and helpful reminders. Other faculty reported that the standards "require you to look at students within specified parameters" (p. 16), and that teacher educators "have to be operating in a certain frame of mind when we observe and evaluate" (p. 16). These latter responses reveal the tendency to apply standards in a rigid or prescriptive way, demonstrating that private theories influence how individuals implement standards. Given this condition, teacher educators must publicly deliberate about what standards are and how they ought to be used. Without such deliberation, standards hold little promise for influencing teaching practice, because they are likely to be used in idiosyncratic and unpredictable ways.

Many faculty members interviewed also expressed a concern that the standards' emphasis on teacher performance could lead to their use as a pro forma checklist of best practice. There was hardly unanimity of opinion on this matter, however. One faculty member suggested that "until the standards are used as a set of teacher expectations of practice there will be little change [in schools]" (p. 21). Faculty members complained that, although the standards had helped bring coherence to teacher preparation programs, they had been adopted as "program goals" without adequate deliberation. One faculty member worried that the standards neglected contextual influences and therefore skirted diversity issues. Others were concerned that the standards failed to adequately address teachers' attitudes or such ethical dimensions of teaching as care and inclusion.

To address this latter concern, the secondary program added an overarching program theme, "Understanding the complex lives of children and adults in schools and society," which attempts to make public the privately held theory of many secondary education faculty that issues of equity and social justice are essential elements of teaching. This theme leads some faculty members to develop course projects that challenge interns to view themselves as change agents and develop their capacity to act as such. Thus, the phrase "teacher as learner and leader" that summarizes our programs' conceptual framework is not viewed as an empty platitude but rather as a moral challenge to question the current order and to conceptualize change as an ongoing process aimed at developing caring and inclusive classroom and school communities. While we adapt our programs to address state standards, we also maintain our autonomy to pro-mote teachers' development not only in terms of their teaching performance but also in their ability to think, inquire, and work collaboratively for school betterment.

Defining teaching in collaboration with school colleagues. Maintaining our auton-omy to use standards flexibly is even more important for us as teacher educators working in PDSs. Because we now work together with school-based educators in preparing new teachers, we no longer hold a privileged position from which to define teaching. Instead, we work in a single professional community com-posed of experienced teachers and interns. The definition of teaching that emerges is shaped by multiple sources of input and is the result of negotiation. Of course, PDSs were originally designed, at least in part, to increase the rele-vance of teacher education experiences.

The powerful influence of the existing school culture and new teachers' own schooling experiences are two of the primary reasons why PDSs hold such appeal for university teacher educators. A PDS provides a real context in which to ex-plore various theories of teaching and learning. Teacher educators, experienced teachers, and teacher candidates can analyze and elaborate these theories, assess their implications for practice—and acknowledge their limitations.[4] Working with candidates in PDSs, university teacher educators can ask them to reflect on their experiences as interns and on how these experiences relate to their own school histories, which may differ significantly from those of their students.

Working collaboratively with school-based educators is not easy. We try to help them understand teacher development issues, but they have many other priorities competing for their time. Although we are in schools more than ever before, we are still not in daily contact with our interns and mentor teachers. Some PDS staff members still view us as ivory tower university types who do not really understand what's going on in the real world. But these expected ten-sions lead us into an inevitable negotiation with our school-based colleagues to define teaching (as well as teacher education), as we work toward creating a single professional community.

This is a constructivist view of teacher education, one that situates teach-ers and teacher educators in real-world settings, sharing teaching responsibili-ties. This is particularly true in the elementary program where interns are immersed in PDS sites for the entire professional year. For example, the re-sponsibility of guidance and supervision of the elementary student interns is entrusted to the collaboration of a mentor teacher and a university liaison (usu-ally a teacher education faculty member). Together, university- and school-based educators have redefined their role as that of a facilitator. The term *mentor teacher* was selected to connote the new and more complex role these teachers assume—coach, guide, supporter, and advocate—in contrast to the mostly supervisory role they previously filled. The university liaison is released from teaching one course in order to spend at least one day per week collaborating with mentors and other school staff in determining how university resources can benefit the PDS and how best to induct new interns.

This collaboration has led to other significant changes in the elementary program. One such change was organizing course work in the elementary program around five interrelated areas: Human Development and Learning, Sociocultural Awareness, Curriculum Perspectives and Development, Instruction and Management, and Professional Leadership Skills. Thus, we were able to develop courses that helped interns become an active part of the PDS community. Another example is related to the elementary program's admission process. School and university faculty work together in the recruitment, selection, and admission of interns. Prior to admission, prospective teacher candidates are assessed by a variety of cross-role teams who assess course work, examine applicants' portfolios, and conduct interviews. School-based educators play a key role in identifying the personal and professional qualities necessary for candidates to work successfully in their PDS sites. These qualities include reflectiveness, understanding of diversity issues, understanding the roles of schools in contemporary society, effective communication skills, enthusiasm and energy, and a commitment to the teaching profession.

The major goal of our program is to develop reflective educators who view learning as a constructive, lifelong process. They reflect on the rationale for, and origins of, their behavior, as well as on the materials they will use and the ideological and sociological constraints operating in the classroom, school and societal contexts in which they work (Duckworth, 1987; Ross, Bondy, & Kyle, 1993). It is during the reflective process of observation, analysis, interpretation, and decision making that teachers function as learners.

As reflective educators, we strive to prepare our graduates to nurture human development in all children. This includes learning appropriate strategies for including children with disabilities as well as those who are gifted; to understand and respond constructively to sociocultural and linguistic differences among students (Banks & Banks, 1993); to develop and implement school curriculum and technology; to assess student progress and outcomes; to be skilled in pedagogy and building classroom community; and to possess the knowledge, values, and capacity necessary to function as change agents in an era of education reform.

Providing opportunities for interns to define teaching. Our teacher education curriculum is an instantiation of our faculty's theories of teaching. We believe that our interns must develop their own private theories as they negotiate their way into and through the profession. We view our role and the role of our school-based colleagues as providing interns with a variety of opportunities to consider the complexity of teaching. We employ many conventional activities such as reflective writing, personal history writing, case studies, and practice teaching, but we also ask our students to participate in a variety of inquiry projects, including action research projects. For example in the professional year, university interns at the secondary level participate in a school-based change project that helps students investigate the culture of schools and the difficulty in making changes in them (Sarason, 1982). We cannot give students a recipe for how to become a change agent; instead these projects require them to grapple with issues of reform, commitment, and resistance and send a clear message that teaching involves more than classroom competence. It also means, among other things, taking on a role within a professional community and contributing to its development.

Taking on such a role is not always easy for the interns. During an afternoon class discussion one intern expressed the frustration of many of his colleagues. "They [the teachers] expect us to do all of the thinking for them. We're not change agents. You're not teaching us to be change agents." Indeed, we are asking interns to act as change agents and to learn how by completing these projects. As a class, we read selections from the school change literature, but we view participation in the change projects as the primary lessons of what it means and what it takes to become an effective school agent. We rely on this experiential strategy for at least two reasons. First, we believe that school change must be understood in relation to school context and, second, we believe that school change requires grassroots commitment that may best be accomplished through on-site inquiry and communication.

After completing the change projects, the subjects of which are decided by school faculty and are consistent with the objectives of the PDS site's school improvement plan, we ask our students to assess their group's accomplishments as well as their group process. We also lead a debriefing session that asks interns to discuss what they learned about the process of school change, about the relationship between school context and school change, and about themselves as change agents. Finally, we ask students to reflect on the question, "What is a professional teacher?" Interns' answers to this question reveal their private theories of teaching, theories often concealed by the more widely discussed public theory embodied in the teaching standards. Because writing this essay takes place near the midpoint of the professional year, it is influenced by the entire range of activities in which interns engage, not just those related to the school-based change project.

Interns' Private Theories of Teaching

Five themes emerged from interns' responses. These themes constitute a theory of teaching quite different from that of the teaching standards or that of our university faculty, one more grounded in teacher and student development. A majority of interns identified *continuing teacher learning* through professional development, self-exploration, and collegial interaction, as an important characteristic of a professional teacher. As one intern explained:

> I think being a professional teacher means that you model education not only by engaging in professional development—learning about your profession, getting ideas, and then implementing them in your classroom—but learning as well. A professional teacher recognizes *learning is change.*

Another intern expressed her belief that teacher and student learning went hand in hand, "She [a professional teacher] is a woman of the world, who still has a lot to learn, but is elated about discovering it together with her students." All of the interns who discussed learning as a key component of teaching echoed this sense that it is invigorating and exciting. By contrast, the standards do not acknowledge the emotions of teaching (Hargreaves, 1998).

The interns held a vision of teacher learning that was necessarily connected with commitment to developing a professional community. About half of the interns also noted that *responsibility to students* and *knowing students* are important traits of a professional teacher. The same number explained that being a professional teacher meant becoming part of a professional community. These interns described the many hats teachers must wear, but insisted that teachers should think of students' welfare above all else. Some of these interns acknowledged that working with students means working with colleagues, parents, and the community. One intern explained, "A professional teacher knows her students individually, knows her fellow teachers, knows the parents, and knows the community. . . . A professional teacher is a listener. She hears and values the needs and perspectives of others." One of her peers agreed: "You have to be able to engage your students in active learning, but you must also be an engaging member of your department and school community." One can clearly see how these interns strongly valued the connection between their learning and that of their students, a concept not found in the standards.

As a whole, the interns expressed a view of teaching as a construction of individual and collective learning and interaction. Many interns described *teachers' values*—integrity, care, a concern for equity, and a sense of fairness—as important characteristics leading to a *commitment to student achievement.* The interns, many of whom were frustrated by the resistance they encountered in working on school-based change projects such as writing across the curriculum or implementing block scheduling, mentioned the importance of participating in school projects and taking a leadership role in helping colleagues grow. The interns saw commitment to student achievement as a professional obligation that must be shared with and encouraged in colleagues; they viewed collaboration as a good in itself and not just a means to the end of improved student achievement.

One might ask if interns' theories of teaching are valid and if their development as teachers is sufficient to create visions of teaching that satisfy our current preoccupation with standards. To examine these private theories, let us look at how portfolios (a favored tool within the standards movement) might exemplify the interns' theories of teaching: continuous teacher learning linked to student learning; engagement in a professional community; responsibility to students; teacher values including caring and inclusiveness; and a commitment to student achievement.

First, the portfolios would highlight teacher learning rather than teacher performance. Rather than simply showcasing their best work, interns might use portfolios to examine their own learning, reflect on how far they have come, and what direction they anticipate for future learning. Second, the portfolios would link intern learning with that of their students. As such, a lesson plan would not suffice as evidence of lesson planning, but would have to include a classroom videotape, a sample of student work, and a reflection on what the intern learned about teaching, curriculum, and students by teaching the lesson. Third, the portfolios would demonstrate the influence of the professional community on interns' development. This might include work with mentor teachers, work associated with school change initiatives, and work that extends beyond the school into the community. Finally, the portfolio would provide a way for interns to reflect on their values related to teaching and learning and to analyze particular artifacts with an eye toward the extent to which such pieces are congruent with those values. We believe these would be exciting portfolios to create and read and would more than adequately demonstrate important talents and dispositions associated with effective teaching.

CONNECTING PUBLIC AND PRIVATE THEORIES OF TEACHING

We do not reject the public theory of teaching suggested by the Kentucky Experienced Teacher Standards. Indeed, with our colleagues we rely on those standards as a way of focusing our students on some important aspects of teaching. We do reject, however, the idea that the standards constitute the *only* way to think about the qualities of effective teaching. Moreover, the technical–rational vision of teaching implied by the standards fails to adequately link teachers' beliefs and learning with student learning, and as such, fails to see teaching fundamentally as a relationship between teacher-as-learner and leader and student-as-learner and future leader. Standards provide a good starting point in considering the complexity of teaching, but they cannot be allowed to standardize teaching, to reduce it to a set of behaviors to be performed instead of an active process of discovery and negotiation.

We have great faith in the ability of university- and school-based educators to assist interns as they develop their own private theories of teaching. Inevitably, teacher standards will play a role in that process. Our experiences working within PDSs, listening to our school-based colleagues and our interns, have helped us develop our own theories of teaching as teacher educators. We believe our students, other teacher candidates, and the experienced teachers who mentor them deserve the same learning opportunities that we enjoy. Professionalizing teaching requires it.

When we engaged ourselves in the work of school reform by creating PDSs, we sought to leave behind the world of defining teaching outside of real school contexts. In arguing for a more limited role for standards, we do not seek to avoid accountability. Rather, working with fellow teacher educators and teaching scholars, school-based educators, and our teacher candidates, we seek to construct theories of teaching that promote high-level learning for all students. We believe that this goal is fundamental not only if we are to treat teachers as true professionals and improve our educational system, but also if we are to strengthen our democracy by educating all of our citizens for active participation in that democracy. Coconstructing theories of teaching within local contexts—that is, with community members and local educators—is the only way to make those theories truly public.

NOTES

1. More recently, NCATE has developed a set of draft standards that describe the institutional commitments and defining characteristics of PDSs. A set of 20 representative PDSs is currently engaged in piloting the standards.

2. A tenth standard, "Demonstrates Competence in Educational Technology," was approved by the EPSB in May 1999.

3. This study was conducted by Letitia Fickel and Donna Gaus, both former doctoral students at the University of Louisville, in 1997.

4. Marilyn Cochran-Smith (1991) describes this working together as collaborative resonance and contrasts it with the critical dissonance that typifies much traditional teacher education which separates university theory from school practice and generally has little influence on teachers' development.

REFERENCES

Abdal-Haqq, I. (1997). *Professional development schools: Weighing the evidence.* Thousand Oaks, CA: Corwin Press.

Apple, M. W. (1993). *Official knowledge : Democratic education in a conservative age.* New York: Routledge.

Ball, D. L., & Wilson, S. M. (1996). Integrity in teaching: Recognizing the fusion of the moral and intellectual. *American Educational Research Journal, 33*(1), 155–192.

Banks, J., & Banks, C. (1993). *Multicultural education: Issues and perspectives* (2nd ed.). New York: Allyn & Bacon.

Bullough, R. V., Jr., & Gitlin, A. (1995). *Becoming a student of teaching: Methodologies for exploring self and school context.* New York: Garland.

Clandinin, D. J., & Connelly, F. M. (1995). *Teachers' professional knowledge landscapes.* New York: Teachers College Press.

Cochran-Smith, M. (1991). Learning to teach against the grain. *Harvard Educational Review, 61*(3), 279–310.

Darling-Hammond, L. (1994). Developing professional development schools: Early lessons, challenge, and promise. In L. Darling-Hammond (Ed.), *Professional development schools: Schools for developing a profession* (pp. 1–27). New York: Teachers College Press.

Davis, B., & Sumara, D. J. (1997). Cognition, complexity, and teacher education. *Harvard Educational Review, 67*(1), 105–125.

Duckworth, E. (1987). *The having of wonderful ideas.* New York: Teachers College Press.

Fickel, L., & Gaus, D. (1997). *Leading edge: Report to the faculty of the Department of Early Childhood & Elementary Education, and Secondary Education, School of Education, University of Lousiville.* Unpublished report. University of Louisville.

Gay, G. (1995). Modeling and mentoring in urban teacher preparation. *Education and Urban Society, 28*(1), 103–118.

Hargreaves, A. (1998). The emotional practice of teaching. *Teaching and Teacher Education, 14*(8), 835–854.

Holmes Group. (1990). *Tomorrow's schools: A report of the Holmes Group.* East Lansing, MI: Author.

Hunsaker, L., & Johnston, M. (1992). Teacher under construction: A collaborative case study of teacher change. *American Educational Research Journal, 29*(2), 350–372.

Jones, K., & Whitford, B. L. (1997). Kentucky's conflicting reform principles: High-stakes school accountability and student performance assessment. *Phi Delta Kappan, 79*(4), 276–281.

Kentucky Department of Education. (1994). *Experienced teacher standards for preparation and certification.* Frankfort, KY: Author.

Kohn, A. (1999). *The schools our children deserve: Moving beyond traditional classrooms and "Tougher Standards."* Boston: Houghton Mifflin.

McDonald, J. P. (1992). *Teaching: Making sense of an uncertain craft.* New York: Teachers College Press.

McLaughlin, M. W. (1987). Learning from experience: Lessons from policy implementation. *Educational Evaluation and Policy Analysis, 9*(2), 171–178.

Murrell, P. (1998). *Like stone soup: The role of the professional development school in the renewal of urban schools.* Washington, DC: American Association of Colleges of Teacher Education.

National Board for Professional Teacher Standards. (1999). How the standards are developed. Retrieved 11/15/99 from http://www.nbpts.org/nbpts standards/how-standards.htm

Newmann, F. M., Secada, W. G., & Wehlage, G. G. (1995). *A guide to authentic instruction and assessment: Vision, standards and scoring.* Madison, WI: Wisconsin Center for Education Research.

Ross, D. D., Bondy, E., & Kyle, D. W. (1993). *Reflective teaching for student empowerment: Elementary curriculum and methods.* New York: Macmillan.

Sarason, S. B. (1982). *The culture of the school and the problem of change.* Boston: Allyn & Bacon.

Schlecty, P. C., Ingwerson, D., & Brooks, T. (1988 November). Inventing professional development shools. *Educational Leadership, 46*(3), 28–31.

Schön, D. A. (1991). *The reflective turn: Case studies in reflective practice.* New York: Teachers College Press.

Schwab, J. J. (1962). The teaching of science as enquiry. In J. J. Schwab & P. F. Brandwein (Eds.), The teaching of science (pp. 1–103). Cambridge, MA: Harvard University.

Snyder, J., Bolin, F., & Zumwalt, K. (1992). Curriculum implementation. In P. W. Jackson (Ed.), Handbook of research on curriculum: A project of the American Educational Research Association (pp. 402–435) New York: Macmillan.

Tharp, R. G. (1999). Effective teaching: How the standards came to be. Retrieved 11/15/99 from http://www.crede.ucsc.edu/HomePage/Standards/Development/development.html.

Whitford, B. L. (1994). Permission, persistence, and resistance: Linking high school restructuring with teacher education reform. In L. Darling-Hammond (Ed.), Professional development schools: Schools for developing a profession (pp. 74–97). New York: Teachers College Press.

CHAPTER 3

Assessment and Standards for Professional Improvement

Walter H. Kimball, Nancy Harriman, and Susie Hanley

The University of Southern Maine (USM) is a comprehensive university that serves approximately 10,000 students, the majority of whom are commuters. The Extended Teacher Education Program (ETEP) is a master's degree program. Two thirds of the program is a full-time internship year, which meets the state professional education certification requirements. The remaining third consists of courses completed during the beginning years of teaching which emphasize classroom assessment, research techniques, and historical, philosophical, and social issues in education. These courses are designed to support the new teachers as they refine their teaching and assessment practices.

The average age of students in the university is 28, and it is not unusual for a cohort of interns in the ETEP to range in age from 23 to 55 years. Many of the candidates have traveled abroad and have had experience in other professions.

USM has a rich heritage in teacher education, having provided teachers for the state since the 1800s. The College of Education and Human Development asserted a commitment to graduate teacher education for people with a degree in the arts and sciences by eliminating the undergraduate degree in elementary education in 1989. The move in 1989 from a program serving three hundred undergraduate majors to one serving ninety preservice teachers in a full-time, year-long internship required strong leadership and a faculty ready to defend the decision with evidence of higher quality graduates. ETEP has done this. In 1998, in an area of the state with at least one hundred applicants for every elementary teaching position and an abundance of secondary social studies and English teachers, 78% of those completing the internship year obtained full-time teaching positions. An undergraduate elementary education certification strand for students in Arts and Sciences began in 1998 to provide an option for undergraduate students and to strengthen the connections between professional education experiences and a liberal arts education.

The ETEP program was collaboratively developed and is collaboratively delivered by faculty from the university and professional development schools in five districts. Site coordinators (a university-based teacher educator and a school-based teacher educator) facilitate linkages between teachers and school development initiatives in the PDSs and the preservice program. Each school year, cohorts of 15 to 20 interns are admitted to each site by a panel of site coordinators, university faculty, and school faculty for an integrated program of course work and internship. Establishing a site-based PDS model for preservice teacher education has had significant ramifications in the teacher education department and in the schools consistent with the findings of national research. Lyons, Stroble, and Fischetti (1998) have documented some of the cultural changes in schools, departments, and colleges of education and professional development schools resulting from this collaboration, including the appointment of school-based teacher educators to university departments, inquiry connecting theory and practice, constructing new knowledge, and making knowledge public. The last three are particularly pertinent to the system of intern assessment designed to support the interns' development as teachers.

Preservice teachers in ETEP strive to become learner-centered teachers who design learning experiences that balance presenting necessary knowledge to their students with asking, modeling, and making suggestions, based on student work. Discourse with mentor teachers, faculty, and peers about the purposes and outcomes of teaching interactions complement interns' classroom experiences and provide models for becoming learning-centered professionals. Formal and informal conferences in which students present their work and receive feedback are conducted at several points during the internship year. What guides the discourse? Assessment and standards for professional improvement provide the framework. However, our understanding of the respective roles and purposes have shifted over time. Faculty have strived to attain a satisfactory balance between encouraging individual creativity and defining clear expectations for performance. How have the uses of standards and assessment processes changed as the ETEP program has evolved? What kinds of evidence provide the answers school and university faculty seek to assure them that teacher candidates have met the quality standards of the program? In what ways has the kind of evidence sought changed as the program has evolved? How is the evidence used to support the interns' ongoing development? How is the evidence used in evaluation decisions?

Questions such as these have played a central role in the continuous refinement of the ETEP program. University and school faculty have worked closely together with preservice interns to clarify expectations, practices, and forms of evidence that exemplify professional standards for teaching. A prevalent concern from the outset was that clearer articulation of the standards should not dictate a prescribed and narrowly defined set of teaching behaviors. Faculty were also concerned that assessments be fair and consistent, yet flexible enough to allow for adaptations to fit the unique culture of each PDS site and the various students and teaching situations that teachers address. In this chapter we will first briefly describe the organization of the ETEP program and the context in which it is delivered, then focus on the significant role standards and assessments have played in its evolution. The significance of three themes (authenticity, continuity, and fairness) will be explored, and the outcomes of strategies for implementing assessment practices addressing these themes will be described.

TEACHER ASSESSMENT FOR IMPROVEMENT AND EVALUATION

Teacher assessment has two generally acknowledged functions: improving teaching and evaluating teaching. Teacher assessment is a process of gathering and analyzing data on aspects of an individual's teaching that demonstrate (a) effective instruction and assessment to support student learning; (b) participation in program development, mentoring colleagues, and service on teaching teams and school and district work groups; and (c) reflection upon the place of education in the community and society at large. Our standards and assessment system, to be addressed later, deal not only with curriculum, instruction, and assessment but also with such areas as citizenship, diversity, and professional collaboration.

Improving Teaching

Assessment for improving teaching involves ongoing self-appraisal, reflection, and explanation of one's own teaching as well as review by others, including feedback on performance and suggestions on next steps and new directions. Assessment is a process of gathering a body of evidence on the current status of one's teaching through observations, teaching plans, and student work. It includes also the articulation of how one's teaching beliefs and practices are aligned and reflection on purposeful decision making throughout planning and teaching processes. Assessment starts at an intern's current level of performance and documents progress incrementally. It is based on immersion in the work of teachers and students with repeated practice, reflection, and feedback.

Evaluating Teaching

The most crucial function of evaluating teaching in preservice teacher education is the decision to recommend a candidate for initial teacher certification.

Evaluating teaching is making a decision about the quality of teaching performance: Has the candidate demonstrated teaching of high enough quality to be recommended for initial certification?

In the past, the criteria used in judging performance were individual and, for the most part, implicit. They were revealed after the fact by the instructor, supervisor, or mentor teacher, by feedback after a teaching observation or by a grade after an assignment had been completed. Too often, students who quickly figured out the criteria were rewarded with the highest ratings on performance.

Assessment for evaluating teaching should involve clear criteria and guidelines, real tasks and exercises, feedback on the quality of one's performance according to the criteria, and opportunities for the individual to use feedback to make changes. The process for evaluating teaching cannot be a floating measure idiosyncratic to the individual. Judging always involves standards or criteria against which performance is judged. The standard may have loose or tight specifications. In ice skating or the visual arts, the standards or criteria are a combination of technical requirements with unwritten elements that are generally accepted by the skating or arts community, giving judges a moderate degree of latitude. In drafting and engineering, the specifications are exact; designs and products are compared to a model or criteria with little room for variation (Eisner, 1992). In any evaluation, standards exist, either in the mind of the judge or in the public record. In teacher evaluation, the standard needs to be known as a consistent measure that is consistently applied, although ranges of acceptable performance certainly will exist and, in fact, are necessary as teachers strive to help each of their students learn to use varied teaching practices as required.

THREE ATTRIBUTES OF ASSESSMENT SYSTEMS

Given that the primary purpose of teacher assessment is to improve teaching, can we embed a system of evaluating teaching within an overall system for assessment? What roles do standards play? What evidence provides an accurate, meaningful, and useful picture of learning and teaching performance? How can this evidence be reviewed, and how can it inform judgments about certification? Can the dual purposes of improving teaching and evaluating performance be served through preparing and judging a multifaceted body of evidence? We have used these questions in devising a year-long intern assessment system, which is designed to support the intern in professional improvement and to evaluate performance on program outcomes leading to the recommendation for certification. The system is built on developing and reviewing a multifaceted body of evidence, including observations of teaching, a major interdisciplinary unit, professional judgment of cooperating teachers and site coordinators, interns' presentations of teaching and analysis of student work, and their vision of teaching. Significant events in the year-long assessment system are:

Internship Orientation. The program outcomes and the Intern Assessment System are introduced, and the intern's vision of teaching (a written piece) is required.

First Placement Outcomes Review and Goal Setting at Midpoint. In October, cooperating teachers use the ETEP Outcomes Review and Feedback Form to complete a midplacement appraisal of the intern's work. The purpose of the midplacement review is to assess the intern's progress in each of the eleven outcomes thus far. Interns use the form for self-assessment leading to setting goals.

First Placement Exit Conference. The exit conference consists of a 45-minute exchange among the intern, cooperating teacher, and site coordinator (supervisor). The objective of the meeting is for the interns to present evidence of their learning and teaching and the work of their students. They address the outcomes in this presentation.

Midprogram Outcomes Review. The site coordinators use the outcomes review form after the exit conference, incorporating the midplacement review, observations, the intern's projects, the exit conference, and the cooperating teacher's final narrative for evidence. The form is given to the intern to review and is discussed at a meeting between the intern and site coordinators.

Spring Midplacement Outcomes Review. In March, cooperating teachers use the ETEP Outcomes Performance Review and Feedback Form to complete a midplacement appraisal of the intern's work, and the interns use it also for self-assessment.

Second Placement Exit Conference. This conference repeats goals and procedures of first exit conference. See above.

Intern Exhibition. Presented in May, the intern's exhibition aims to celebrate and share accomplishments, ideas, and future directions, and address the ETEP Outcomes. The intern presents to a panel of the internship supervisors and cooperating teachers with whom she or he has worked during the year, focusing on the progress made. A question-and-answer exchange between the intern and the panel follows. The intern then departs and the panel caucuses about the presentation, work, and outcomes reviews accumulated during the year. An agreement is reached regarding the recommendation for certification. The intern returns for the findings and feedback.

As the foregoing summary shows, the system includes a series of events where both interns and faculty use the program standards as the basis for reviewing intern progress and ultimately making the decision for certification. Three attributes essential to the design of the assessment system are discussed below.

Authenticity

Authenticity is the extent to which learning experiences are relevant to the individual, school, district, or community. In assessment for P–12 students, Grant Wiggins (1989) has recommended two criteria for authentic assessment: (1) mirroring the challenges, work, and standards that engage practicing professionals; and (2) involving the individual interactively through opportunities for explanation, dialogue, and inquiry. Features of authentic instruction have been proposed by Newmann and Wehlage (1993): (a) Students construct meaning and produce knowledge; (b) students use disciplined inquiry to construct meaning; (c) students aim their work toward production of discourse, products, and performances that have value or meaning beyond success in school (p. 8). It is not coincidental that these features of assessment and instruction deemed authentic are so similar; assessment and instruction are closely linked.

The Coalition of Essential Schools, Central Park East School in particular, has been developing an alternative to the accumulation of Carnegie units for graduation whereby students prepare portfolios in fourteen areas of study, seven of which are presented to teachers. Portfolio development and presentation is a two-year process embedded in the curriculum at Central Park East, a New York City school that has adopted many reform practices (Meier & Schwartz, 1995). There is strong interest among teachers and researchers in developing classroom assessment systems which are fair and valid and provide important information for both teachers and students about the current status of students' authentic learning, which in turn can be used to prepare future learning experiences likely to maintain progress.

Consideration of authenticity is appearing in teacher assessment. How can preservice teacher assessment ground its judgments on an evolving picture of the complexity of teaching and learning which builds over time, treats students as individuals with a mix of backgrounds and ways of learning, and is useful beyond the immediate classroom (Shulman, 1987, 1988)? The farther removed assessment is from the real work of teachers, the weaker the inference about interns' learning and performance. Interns in ETEP complete six major projects during the internship year: an interdisciplinary unit, an individual student case, an internship journal, a vision or philosophy of teaching, a videotape of teaching-with-reflection, and a teaching portfolio and presentation. Criteria for the intern projects reflect what teachers do and think about. For example, the intern case study involves the review of student records in the cumulative folder and the special education folder, if applicable; an interview with the parents, observations of the intern, review of her or his work in the classroom, and connection of the intern's learning, behavior, and social interactions to developmental theory.

These projects were developed in part to address evaluation data during the early years of ETEP in which interns rated at 3.58 on a scale of 1 to 5 the degree to which internship courses complemented each other and were integrated (Kopp, 1998). Although a satisfactory rating, it was clear from interns' comments that there were both redundancy and fragmentation among the courses (e.g., all courses requiring separate journals and several courses teaching lesson planning in different ways). Establishing major projects in the internship helped the faculty establish quality assessments directly connected with the outcomes rather than falling into the quagmire of trying to align individual objectives and assignments across multiple courses. It was enlightening to see the agreement across courses when we asked how we assess the interns' learning (journals, designing and teaching lessons, conducting informal assessments) instead of asking what in our specialty areas we expect interns to know. It is important to note that the improvement of intern assessment was occurring simultaneously with the development of new assessment strategies in the schools. For example, the Literacy Committee in one of the partner school districts has been developing a literacy guide for teachers outlining the developmental stages of reading and writing, together with appropriate assessments such as Informal Reading Inventories and individual book conferences. The emphasis is on assessment which gauges the progress of interns and their students and provides teacher educators and classroom teachers with data which inform instruction.

What difference does it make to have the intern assessment process grounded in developing and explaining a multifaceted body of evidence about performance and thinking in experiences that are closely linked to the complexity of teaching? It makes a great deal of difference. Through preparing and presenting evidence of performance, the intern provides a valuable source of assessment data; the intern's explanations not only clarify the documented evidence but become part of the assessment. When the evidence and explanations are focused on lessons and units that have been taught, student work, communicating and conferencing with parents, and reflections on issues faced in teaching (e.g., differentiating instruction), the assessment process is more closely connected with its primary purpose—improving teaching for improved learning by all students.

Connecting authenticity and evidence is important for judging and documentation. What exhibits provide the most relevant picture of a teacher's performance and understanding? What exhibits provide the most meaningful data for review and assessment? How is the evidence reviewed in a way that contributes to improving teaching? To what extent is student work included in the intern's exhibits and assessment? The evidence reviewed in the assessment process should be closely connected to the intern's performance in reaching the primary goal of helping students learn. In this way, the preparation, presentation, and judging of a body of evidence require the intern to think about important issues, and the feedback is more useful in improving teaching.

Continuity

Continuity refers to how understanding deepens and teaching performance improves over time and across professional experiences. Continuity in the assessing process allows for constructive goal setting and designing one's own professional development plan for exploring topics of interest, attending to specific certification requirements, and improving in areas needing attention. When assessment is explicit, supportive, collegial, and ongoing, it is embedded in the curriculum and structure of the program. Intern assessment is designed to support learning and progress through a year-long relationship of coaching and mentoring.

A commitment to basing judgments on multiple sources of evidence over the course of an extended learning experience yields a higher degree of confidence that the evidence is truly indicative of what the intern is capable of doing in the classroom than was engendered by course grades and isolated ratings by cooperating teachers. For example, the intern's performance on the outcomes is reviewed in mid-October, January, and mid-April by cooperating teachers and site coordinators. The intern receives direct feedback on progress in the outcome areas throughout the year. The October review is guided by the question, "If progress continues in the same way, will the intern be ready to successfully complete a week of lead teaching in December?" The expectations are raised in the spring. The March review is guided by the question, "If progress continues in the same way, will the intern be ready for responsibility for his/her own classroom next fall?" Using evidence to support judgments has a direct influence also on mentoring of the intern by program faculty. In situations of questionable or possibly inadequate performance by the intern, the first step is to look for evidence rather than leaping to judgments. The intern contributes to the collecting of evidence on which judgments are based. Engaging in this process on an ongoing basis, the intern not only builds a body of evidence, but refines and sharpens skills and knowledge.

Fairness

If interns are being judged on their readiness to enter the teaching profession, it makes sense that they should be given maximum opportunity to teach and work with students. Inferences from course work and untaught lesson plans are too far removed from whole-class, full-time teaching and the accompanying reflection. Moreover, the interns should be given maximum opportunity to work, learn, and perform under genuine circumstances. They should be evaluated, receive feedback, and set goals for themselves. This is not relegating theory to a background role in favor of the world of practice; rather it places theory squarely in the world of practice with a primary role open to examination by interns, cooperating teachers, students, supervisors, and others. The validity of the assessment process is directly related to its fairness. Messick (as cited in Moss, 1992) characterizes validity as "the degree to which empirical evidence and theoretical rationales support the adequacy and appropriateness of inferences and actions based on test scores or other forms of assessment" (p. 241). Messick (1994) argues that the issues of consequences, evidence, and fairness at the heart of validity need to be applied fully to performance assessment. What are the consequences of performance assessment for those involved and for the quality of education? What difference does assessment make? Applying the criteria of consequences reveals several possible effects. First, it forces the intern and the program faculty to make students' learning the paramount concern. The question "What is the impact of the program on the students?" makes clear that the interns' learning should not take precedence over their students' learning.

Stiggins (1987) proposed that validity relates to assurances that "performance ratings reflect the examinee's true capabilities and are not a function of the perceptions and biases of the persons evaluating the performance" (p. 33). Does the evidence assure that accurate judgments are being made, that the individual does indeed possess the skills, knowledge, and disposition inferred from the performance? Moss (1992) argues for integrative interpretations in which multiple sources of data are reviewed and aggregated to develop coherent judgments supported by evidence. ETEP program development and the intern assessment have both been influenced by shared dialogue about sources of evidence. The internship projects described earlier resulted from faculty seminars during which we shared the assessments and assignments being used in courses and classroom placements in the internship. Common assessments emerged (e.g., a dialogue journal between intern and faculty, an individual student case study, and an extended teaching unit). Study of examples of such assessments and the relevant professional literature resulted in the establishment of criteria for the assessment projects.

The year-long internship assessment system culminates in presenting a portfolio or exhibition to a panel of mentor teachers, site coordinators, and university and school faculty with whom the intern has worked during the year. There are also invited guests, such as principals and the dean of the College of Education and Human Development. Following the presentation and questions and answers, the panel discusses the evidence, both from the presentation and the intern's work during the year, and makes the recommendation for certification. At least three, and many times four, professionals have come to know that intern's work well and can make the decision about his or her readiness to take responsibility for a classroom.

The field of special education informs this discussion of fairness. Special education emphasizes due process for validating decision making and planning and guaranteeing constitutional rights and equity under the law for students with special needs and their parents. Principles of individual protection influencing the intern assessment include: (a) notice of criteria and standing by which interns examine the eleven program outcomes from the beginning to the end of the program and participate in the midyear review evaluating their level of performance with regard to each; (b) multiple performances with feedback opportunity for practice and learning as interns teach for the entire internship year and complete projects directly related to what teachers do and think about; (c) multiple sources of evidence considered together to provide a more comprehensive picture; (d) multiple perspectives with school and university faculty judging the body of evidence both independently and jointly; (e) mediated action planning for interns to design and follow through, with program faculty, on goals and action steps in areas needing improvement. These provisions are embedded in the program, not as legal protection, but as part of the individualized and self-directed learning process. There are no surprises in the system. Interns are apprised of their status and provided support in continuous improvement throughout the internship year.

STANDARDS FOR TEACHING

Although clearly identifying the attributes of a good teacher was considered early on in developing the ETEP program, we realized a few years into it that a vision for the program and a list of the qualities expected of our graduates did not suffice. We needed a public statement of the principles of teaching and learning on which the program was based and more specific articulation of the knowledge and performances expected of graduates represented by the program outcomes. Shortly after the outcomes were produced, several small grants were secured through the Maine State Board of Education to develop results-based outcomes for our teacher preparation program. The State Board was interested in the introduction of outcomes-based and results-based certification systems in other states and wished to investigate the feasibility of such an approach in our state. Ultimately, the work of our ETEP faculty at USM and faculty from other participating campuses became the foundation for a proposed statewide results-based initial certification and performance assessment process.

It is not coincidence that the standards for teaching currently being used at state and program levels have so much in common. The standards of the Interstate New Teachers Assessment and Support Consortium (INTASC) and the guiding principles of the National Board of Professional Teaching Standards (NBPTS) were being developed and refined concurrently with the standards for our own teacher education program and subsequently the proposed state of Maine standards. Our own program outcomes developed in 1992–93 are certainly consistent in viewing planning, knowledge of content, teaching, assessing student learning, and classroom management as closely connected. They are consistent, too, in viewing knowledge of students and developmental theory as important and collaboration with educators and community members as vital to improving education. Likewise, they recognize the significance of teachers' professional behavior and knowledge of, and participation in, broader educational issues. Although definitions of quality teaching vary, the standards and outcomes represent functions of good teaching.

Our major challenge was how to use the standards to improve teaching and our program. Have standards strangled or strengthened our program? We have seen considerable evidence that they have provided strength and consistency. Our coaching/supervising/mentoring process has supported continuous improvement. The outcomes statement has provided common targets for all participants in the program, targets grounded in good teaching which serve as guides for continuing intern progress in teaching from the beginning of the internship to the end.

However, we discovered from initial program evaluation data that interns perceived the outcomes as more crucial to the development and presentation of their final portfolios than to their actual teaching performance (Harriman, 1998; Walters & Harriman, 1995). This prompted us to explore strategies for formally introducing the outcomes earlier in the program and integrating them more functionally into the supervision and evaluation process throughout the year. Site coordinators implemented strategies that included (a) introducing the outcomes at orientation in August, (b) having interns observe and confer with mentor teachers about their modeling of the outcomes during the first few weeks of school, and (c) developing protocols for periodic evaluations requiring interns to document throughout the year evidence of their own growth related to the outcomes. During the next 3 years, evaluation data collected at each site indicated improvement in interns' satisfaction with the clarity of expectations related to the outcomes, integration of the outcomes and program, and feedback on progress (Harriman, 1998).

Strengthening a preparation program in a professional development school requires finding effective ways to include the many constituent groups involved in delivering the program. In our case, those groups include university- and school-based site coordinators, other university- and school-based faculty who teach courses in the program, and mentor-teachers in each of our 29 partner schools. Through projects such as the Leading Edge Professional Development School Network and the Teacher Education Initiative of the

National Education Association, we have been able to support curriculum retreats and workshops on performance assessment. These opportunities have significantly "raised the conversation" and helped us strengthen the coherence of the standards and assessment components of our program across sites.

Results of focus groups and surveys of mentor–teachers and program faculty in 1996–97 provide evidence of this improvement. "ETEP and the schools are talking the same language around teaching and learning" (Ridlon & Major, 1997, p. 18). Interns can make self-evaluations and teachers and site coordinators can make evaluations and talk about them. When the outcomes call for using student assessment data to adapt teaching, and this target is shared from the beginning, people in the program know where they are headed. The teacher education curriculum has a framework.

STRATEGIES FOR BUILDING AND REVIEWING EVIDENCE

The portfolio has been a central assessment tool for both improving and evaluating teaching since the beginning of the program (Lyons, Stroble, & Fischetti, 1998). Until the National Board for Professional Teaching Standards (NBPTS), the Teacher Assessment Project (TAP) at Stanford University, directed by Lee Shulman, was the most comprehensive look at teacher assessment, focusing its attention on currently certified teachers pursuing professional advancement or recertification. This project explored the use of specially defined assessment exercises and the preparation of portfolios under careful guidelines for certification and recertification. TAP found that procedures through which teachers present and reflect on existing situations in their own classrooms show how teaching involves complex interactions of contextual variables of teachers and students working together over time for deeper learning, and does this better than do assessment center exercises where the teacher responds to simulated circumstances under specified conditions and scenarios (Wolf, 1991, 1994). This finding directly influenced our effort to connect as directly as possible the intern projects and other evidence in the assessment system to the work of teachers and students.

In the early years of the program, the portfolio as the centerpiece of assessment was the collecting point for excerpts from the case study, units taught, student work, and so forth. However, as faculty worked to further embed the standards in the curriculum and build criteria for the other projects, it became apparent that they were becoming stand-alone, portfolio-like exhibits. Each of the six projects in the internship—interdisciplinary unit, case study, vision or philosophy of teaching, videotape and reflection, intern journal, and portfolio and presentation—now has its own criteria and contributes to the multifaceted body of evidence.

Each project is completed in a drafting and feedback process. Each one is directly connected to the program outcomes. These projects join teaching observations, other lessons and student work, a record of collaborative parent conferences, and team planning, as multiple sources of evidence in the assessment system. The body of evidence includes exhibits that are both required by the program (the six projects and teaching observations) and selected by the interns from their work in classrooms and academic courses.

As important as targets and shared language is the impact of standards and criteria on the feedback system. First, feedback has become more focused. When interns are responding to relevant criteria or guidelines, getting feedback related to those criteria, and making improvements based on that feedback, their work is improving and their thinking deepening. They are engaged in the same process they are being taught to use in their teaching. For example, the process for each intern's case study was adapted from the work of a graduate of the program who had taught in middle school. Steps in the process for developing the case study are:

1. The interns examine exemplars of outstanding case studies.
2. Class time is devoted to introducing each section and the interns work together in gathering and sharing information profiles of the community and each intern's school.
3. They gather data about the subject of their case study and draft each section. Each section is based on functions in which they, as teachers, will engage: reviewing records, knowing the community and available services, talking to parents, using classroom observations and assessment, using knowledge of lifespan development to think about their students, etcetera.
4. The tuning protocol developed by the Coalition for Essential Schools (Cushman, 1995) is used by the interns to share their data and drafts with each other and provide feedback through questions and comments.
5. The interns submit drafts of the section and receive feedback from faculty, which leads to seeking further information or considering other questions or issues to deepen thinking and analysis.

This same process is also used for another of the intern's major internship projects, the interdisciplinary unit.

Internet Technology

Technology is proving to be a valuable tool in both providing universal access to information and convenient opportunities for interactions between interns. A Web site contains the program calendar, an explanation of the assessment system, intern project guidelines, and helpful resources, such as Internet links. The Internet provides opportunities for discussions at a distance. Web conferencing systems allow people to post messages and responses which are clustered together—a message and its response following each other. Using the chat function allows a text-based real-time conversation which can then be printed out for future use. This conferencing system has been used to support the interns' development of their vision or philosophy of teaching. During the fall, a Web discussion is held around three questions: How do people learn? What is quality teaching? and What is the purpose of education? Not only are they interesting discussions, they provide the brainstorming and initial ideas for the vision statement. We have conducted an eight-week discussion around these questions. The interns then print particularly helpful entries and bring them to the seminar session where we discuss the vision statement. Their thinking is already underway as they begin to share outlines of the vision statement; thus, we save class time that might otherwise have been spent brainstorming and recording on chart paper. Web conferencing has been used to exchange ideas with interns in programs from different parts of the country. Currently, a discussion is being conducted between interns at the University of Southern Maine and the University of Louisville about the book *Possible Lives* by Mike Rose. The internship Web site is located at http://www.usm.maine.edu/ ~wkimball/gorwebpg/Homepage.htm.

CONCLUSION

Close attention to assessment and standards for improving and evaluating teaching has yielded an assessment system that is the same for all interns. Interns who are approaching competence and interns who are approaching excellence all work to improve their teaching. They all receive feedback and revise lessons and projects. The three or four professionals working together with the intern throughout the year use the program outcomes and their own experience for feedback (improving teaching) and to come to agreement on the recommendation for certification (evaluating teaching). This assessment should be distinguished from others (e.g., INTASC) in which the interns are not known to the assessors and have no opportunity to explain their exhibits or respond to questions. The opportunities for interns to elaborate and explain have been invaluable and are the heart of the assessment process.

Elementary (K–8) and secondary (7–12) interns progress through the system together. Both elementary and secondary perspectives are shared as interns exchange and discuss their intern projects. Thus, interns are gaining a view of the full spectrum of schooling. In addition, we have found that the interns are able to extend their own time frame in planning and teaching. In the past, interns were thinking in terms of individual lessons or possibly a unit of several weeks. Now interns are learning to conceive and teach extended units and are devising curriculum maps for their literacy program or social studies program over the course of a year.

Perhaps most important, the range in quality of projects has diminished as overall quality across projects has increased. The process of displaying models, posting public guidelines or criteria, feedback, and drafting and revising allows many opportunities for success. Assessing for evaluation of program outcomes is embedded as a series of checkpoints in a year-long system of assessing for improving teaching. Data are used by the program faculty to make adaptations in the program and by the interns to improve their teaching for their students. In short, the system itself is based on good teaching.

REFERENCES

Cushman, K. (1995). The tuning protocol: A process for reflection on teacher and student work. *Horace, 11*(4), 2.

Eisner, E. W. (1992). Do American schools need standards? Macie K. Southall Distinguished Lecture, Peabody College, Vanderbilt University, November, 1992.

Harriman, N. (1998). Program evaluation results, 1995–1998. Unpublished data. University of Southern Maine.

Kopp, H. (1998). *Extended teacher education program evaluation results.* Gorham, ME: University of Southern Maine, Center for Educational Policy, Applied Research, and Evaluation.

Lyons, N., Stroble, E., & Fischetti, J. (1998). The idea of the university in an age of school reform: The shaping force of professional development schools. In M. Levine & R. Trachtman (Eds.) *Making professional development schools work: Politics, practice, and policy* (pp. 88–111). New York: Teachers College Press.

Meier, D., & Schwartz, P. (1995). Central Park East: The hard part is making it happen. In M. W. Apple & J. A. Beane (Eds.), *Democratic schools* (pp. 26–40). Alexandria, VA: Association for Supervision and Curriculum Development.

Messick, S. (1994). The interplay of evidence and consequences in the validation of performance assessments. *Educational Researcher, 23*(2), 13–23.

Moss, P. A. (1992). Shifting conceptions of validity in educational measurement: Implications for performance assessment. *Review of Educational Research, 62*(3), 229–258.

Newmann, F. M., & Wehlage, G. G. (1993). Five standards of authentic instruction. *Educational Leadership, 50*(7), 8–12.

Ridlon, A., & Major, C. (1997). *NEA-TEI Report, 1996–1997.* Gorham, ME: University of Southern Maine.

Shulman, L. S. (1987). Assessment for teaching: An initiative for the profession. *Phi Delta Kappan, 69*(1), 38–44.

Shulman. L. S. (1988). A union of insufficiencies: Strategies for teacher assessment in a period of educational reform. *Educational Leadership, 46*(3), 36–41.

Stiggins, R. J. (1987). Design and development of performance assessments. *Educational Measurement, 6*(3), 33–42.

Walters, S., & Harriman, N. (1995). *Initial teacher certification project: Final report to the Maine State Board of Education.* Gorham, ME: University of Southern Maine.

Wiggins, G. (1989). A true test: Toward more authentic and equitable assessment. *Phi Delta Kappan, 70*(9), 703–713.

Wolf, K. (1991). The schoolteacher's portfolio: Issues in design, implementation, and evaluation. *Phi Delta Kappan, 73*(2), 129–136.

Wolf, K. (1994). Teaching portfolios: Capturing the complexity of teaching. In L. Ingvarson & R. Chadbourne (Eds.) *Valuing teacher's work: New directions in teacher appraisal.* (pp. 112–136). Victoria, Australia: Australian Council for Educational Research.

CHAPTER 4

Getting Beyond the Talking and Into the Doing

Ann Larson, Steve Ryan, Phyllis Metcalf-Turner, Walter H. Kimball, Nancy Harriman, and Susie Hanley

Between 1995 and 1999, there have been at least ten opportunities for different faculty members and partner school personnel from the University of Southern Maine (USM) and the University of Louisville (UL) to visit each other's sites. Reasons for the visits have included research projects, invited consultations, professional conferences, and documentation visits for the Leading Edge work. Each type of activity has contributed to an increased understanding of the context of the universities' teacher preparation programs. For those school and university faculty who have often engaged in collaborative activities over the years, relationships have deepened with time. The importance of those personal, professional relationships cannot be understated. Personal, professional relationships among network partners provide a centrix for commitment and growth just as they do within a professional development school (PDS) (Miller & Silvernail, 1994).

In 1995, the Extended Teacher Education Program (ETEP) at USM was one of seven teacher preparation programs with a reputation for preparing learning-centered teachers selected for an in-depth study (Silvernail, 1997, p. 1). Two faculty members from UL, Betty Lou Whitford and Gordon Ruscoe, along with research assistant Letitia Fickel, served as documenters and authors of a case

---

The dyad participants responsible for this chapter are Nancy Harriman, Susie Hanley, and Walter H. Kimball of the University of Southern Maine and Phyllis Metcalf-Turner, Steve Ryan, and Ann Larson of the University of Louisville.

study on ETEP for that project. During their initial visits, the study team conducted extensive interviews with teachers, administrators, faculty, and students and observed program activities in site schools (Whitford, Ruscoe, & Fickel, 2000). As the case developed, participants and researchers engaged in discussions of mutual interest, such as year-long internships and intern assessment, and they decided to follow up with other faculty.

CROSS-SITE EXCHANGES BETWEEN USM AND UL

Betty Lou Whitford suggested that the director of the Center for Professional Development at UL, Ric Hovda, attend a session at the American Association of Colleges of Teacher Education (AACTE) given by the ETEP site coordinator team from Gorham, Maine in February, 1996. The site coordinator team composed of a university-based and a school-based teacher educator is responsible for a graduate level year-long internship for a group of 15 to 20 preservice interns in the Gorham PDS. They had been invited to present the workshop by David Imig, president of AACTE, who had recently visited USM with Dick Clark from the National Network for Educational Renewal, of which USM had been a part since its inception in the late 1980s. Of particular interest to the AACTE audience were samples of interns' work and the completed observation and evaluation forms used to illustrate and analyze their strategies.

Several follow-up activities ensued from that first encounter at AACTE. The exchanges took different forms over time. The two Gorham site coordinators attended Louisville's Professional Development School Conference in March, 1996 and continued the AACTE conversations in conjunction with school visits. Then they were invited to return in June, 1996, to consult with all university- and school-based teacher education faculty.

This first collaborative visit at Louisville focused on examining the processes and tools used in the year-long intern assessment system developed at the Gorham ETEP site. The two site coordinators used as workshop materials the same forms and guidelines used with interns (i.e., working documents rather than materials created only for the workshop). Samples of intern work were displayed, rationales explained, and the site coordinators' reflections were shared. The idea was not to replicate the Maine system in Louisville, but to present and discuss it in enough detail so that Louisville faculty could identify implications for their own programs. Consulting with the Louisville faculty helped USM's teacher educators to clarify the explanations and materials they used with interns and provided welcome ideas for revisions and improvements. The relationship started to acquire a Critical Friends Group approach (Costa & Kallick, 1993).

Faculty from both sites soon realized that simply reviewing and discussing the use of tools and work samples from each other's sites often stimulated new ideas and practices. One such review was of the draft of a new handbook for

UL's Master of Arts in Teaching Program, which included guidelines, activities, requirements, and policies for teacher education in their professional develop-ment schools. The handbook showed what the PDSs did, how they did it, and how it was portrayed to the public. This review of the handbook by represen-tatives of both UL and USM resulted in changes at both institutions.

For example, one of USM's observation forms was adopted and adapted by Louisville to incorporate the program outcomes at the bottom of the form, so that the observer might note those that were particularly emphasized during the observation. This led the Maine site coordinators in turn to incorporate the listing of outcomes on the bottom of their observation forms (Figure 1). Of even more importance was the related discussion of the purpose for the change and how the revised forms might be used to enhance the feedback and reflec-tion process for interns and mentors in their application and documentation of the standards. True to the site's goals of developing collaborative workers and community contributors (Gorham School Department, 1994), program docu-ments, teaching techniques, and assessment processes continued to be revised.

When the Leading Edge project was launched, USM and UL asked to form a dyad because of their similar programs, interests, and desire to grow the fledgling relationship that was evolving. In the fall of 1996, a team from Louisville (Betty Lou Whitford and Phyllis Metcalf-Turner from UL and Linda Brown from Fairdale High School) came to Southern Maine for the first Leading Edge cross-site visit. The cross-site documentation approach was in-tended to assist sites in documenting their work through the review, feedback, and suggestions of an informed visiting team. The focus of the first visit was to assess faculty's perceptions of where USM should start in addressing the Lead-ing Edge areas of inquiry: (a) standards for teachers, (b) standards for students, and (c) helping teachers use standards.

The documenters asked university- and school-based faculty questions in-cluding: How do you view standards and assessments? What have been the im-portant changes in the program to support this focus on standards? What is the nature of documentation of progress toward standards? Data from this visit confirmed a common interest in assessment issues as well as differences in the state contexts within which each university operated.

Other occasions for cross-site meetings were national conferences. For three successive years a team of USM faculty and mentor teachers attended the Professional Development School Conference hosted by UL. The conference includes a day of site school visits and two days of presentations and profes-sional development sessions. Joint sessions on site at Louisville provided a forum for school and university faculty to engage in an ongoing discussion of issues and practices. These discussions, however brief, were important to main-tain progress. The sharing of practices and ideas led to the development of a common language. Terms such as *assessment system, ongoing feedback, projects and*

Susie Hanley, Gorham School Department
Gorham, ME 04038

Lesson Observation

Date: Intern:

Observer: Topic:

What I Saw and What I Heard

Affirmations, Suggestions, Comments

ETEP Outcomes
1. Student Development   5. Assessment   9. Professionalism
2. Subject Matter   6. Diversity   10. Improving Teaching
3. Planning   7. Teaching Belief 11. Classroom Management
4. Instructional Strategies 8. Citizenship

Figure 1. Lesson observation.

project guides, continuous improvement, and *body of evidence* were jointly understood. During an early discussion, it was observed that, although the primary emphasis in Leading Edge was standards, our work was as much about assessment as about standards. Later, we surmised that while standards are useful in focusing on assessment, the standards alone are not sufficient for making important judgments about teaching and teacher condidates' performance.

THE FOCUS AND EPICENTER OF CHANGE FOR UL

The Departments of Early and Middle Childhood Education and Secondary Education at UL have been working closely with local school professionals for more than ten years to reconceptualize teacher education and professional development for school-based educators. Early on, local leaders emphasized a selective adoption of national reform recommendations that led to innovation and experimentation rather than compliant implementation. A vision statement of six beliefs and six sets of standards about exemplary practice was drafted by a leadership team, approved by participants in seminars to plan partnerships, and used to guide the establishment of PDSs. Fairdale High School was chosen as the first PDS pilot site. Currently, UL has approximately twelve variations of PDSs in local and regional schools.

As an early model of PDS work, the departments earned national recognition for their efforts, but several shifting currents have created turbulence for this work in recent years. The widely heralded passage of the Kentucky Education Reform Act (KERA) in 1990 led to a variety of changes in the political climate in the state, including a heightened focus on school, district, and university accountability. The high-stakes nature of the accountability system (Jones & Whitford, 1994) worked against the experimental ethic that drove early collaborative efforts between the university and local schools, as "teaching to the test" became a sensible response to the uncertainty of a shifting state context. In the last several years, a growing teacher shortage, particularly in mathematics and science, has fueled concerns that teacher preparation within a PDS model may not be an efficient way of educating teacher candidates for the state's classrooms when teachers are in short supply. Exacerbating this latter tension is a university effort to attain Research I status, including greater emphasis on faculty grant writing and research productivity. Maintaining strong relationships with local schools, keeping teacher education enrollments high or expanding them, and increasing research and dissemination activities without additional resources or personnel are difficult demands to balance and present a real challenge for UL programs and others like them that may emerge in the next several years in response to teacher shortages. The faculty take such change as a natural condition of educational institutions. They are interested in inquiry approaches—not only about learning and development, but about leadership, change, and resiliency in the face of change. A metaphor that faculty frequently use to describe the nature of inquiry approaches is "riding the rapids."

The teacher education programs at UL are grounded in sets of beliefs that reflect a commitment to preparing teachers to adopt a problem-solving perspective with respect to their practice. Faculty attempt to model effective practices and encourage teacher candidates to experiment with similar approaches in their early field experiences in classrooms, in their curriculum planning, assessment practices, and student teaching placements. Additionally, there is an emphasis that these practices are context-sensitive and not inherently effective or best practices. Particularly in urban settings, faculty believe that teacher candidates must understand the contexts that shape their work and understand how to negotiate these contexts to provide challenging and engaging learning opportunities for their students. With the influence of high-stakes assessment in a local policy context, UL faculty are constantly reminded of the great importance of guiding teacher candidates to collect data about their students' learning and about their own teaching practices, to form critical friendships with colleagues, and to reflect on their own practice through journal writing, constructing metaphors about teaching, collaborating with other teachers, and seeking continued professional development. All of these efforts, it is hoped, will help teacher candidates focus on their students' learning rather than on primarily skills-based, potentially dehumanizing pedagogy (Ryan, Dittmer, Stroble, and Larson, 1999).

RELEVANT INITIATIVES AT THE
UNIVERSITY OF LOUISVILLE

Inquiry is a central pedagogical theme throughout the teacher education programs at UL. Curriculum is organized around a series of individual and group projects that challenge novice teachers to contemplate central questions facing educators in urban schools: What is the relationship between schools and their communities? How do schools change and what are the impediments to change? What does it mean to teach all students? How does one's personal history shape one's perspective of schools and teaching and learning? Occasionally, these questions are discussed directly, but more often they are used as important organizers—a way of maintaining a focus on big ideas as teacher candidates work on authentic projects in schools and communities. In this way, faculty attempt to strike a balance between helping teacher candidates develop practical skills that will help them survive in their early careers and a problem-posing and problem-solving orientation to their practice.

The Secondary MAT program is guided by the theme, "Understanding the Complex Lives of Children and Adults in Schools and Society." While this phrase seems fairly simple, thinking about how to support teacher candidates' learning as it relates to this theme is complex. First, what does it mean to understand as opposed to think, believe, or know? How do structures of the teacher education program support teacher candidates' developing understandings of race, ethnicity, culture, gender, class, and language ability, rather than simply reinforcing their opinions, which may be biased by a limited set of previous experiences? Second, how can faculty avoid using the theme as a convenient catchall for explaining away much of the complexity that the phrase attempts to communicate (Ryan, Dittmer, Stroble, and Larson, 1999)?

Curricula in the Secondary MAT courses prior to student teaching focus on problem-based or contextual learning projects that require teacher candidates to work with faculty and staff members at schools sites and with course instructors. The major inquiry project is called "Enabling School-based Change." Project themes are defined from initiatives that are taken directly from the school's consolidated plan (a state-mandated document that lays out a two-year agenda for school improvement). Over a period of six to eight weeks, student groups collect data about the history and context of the problem, meet with faculty and staff members to gain a broader understanding of the issue, find out how other local schools have addressed similar concerns, read journal articles, interview students and parents, and propose a series of possible solutions or perspectives for future consideration by the school's staff. The projects focus on real issues: enhancing decision-making strategies and enabling appropriate choices for 9th graders, writing across the curriculum, the effects of teaming on 9th-grade students, the impact of block scheduling on student achievement and school climate, and literacy strategies for cross-content curriculum, for example. These projects result in authentic tasks that challenge teacher candidates to see themselves as active members of a school community who are collaborative leaders.

Teacher candidates present their findings on the problem-based project to their classmates and instructors. More important, they also present their findings to school faculty and staff, students, site-based decision-making councils, and school district officials. Following the presentations, a debriefing session concludes the project, during which students meet to reflect on what they have learned, assess their learning and performance both individually and as a group, report to the instructors on this learning, and present a portfolio-worthy project that includes products created and a written reflection that summarizes what was learned about school change, the importance of the school context in shaping products, and suggested innovations for school administrators, faculty, staff, and students.

Since 1998, secondary and early and middle childhood faculty have joined with school district partners and School of Education administrators to determine future PDS initiatives and to explore alternative possibilities for program delivery. Areas of inquiry that have been collaboratively identified are PDS site selection, definitions of PDSs and partnerships, continuous assessment, the role of PDS liaisons, professional development, the relationship between PDS models and student achievement in these schools, and issues of teacher education program design.

Faculty at UL are committed to establishing conditions that reflect a learning community, among their teacher candidates, who, they hope, will likewise foster such a community in their future classrooms. Several assumptions underlie the faculty's understanding of such a community. A learning community cares about its members and the quality of its work, fosters cooperation and connections among individuals in the community, respects individuals and provides diverse opportunities for leadership, adopts standards for performance and makes them known, seeks improvement through ongoing assessment and feedback, and governs itself through participatory means. Only through shared inquiry can such a community be established, and UL faculty look forward to further opportunities to collectively shape their work as teacher educators.

Linking in recent years with USM colleagues as "critical friends" has been an important element in understanding a learning community and has enabled faculty to reflect and deliberate about the work they engage in. Rich and multiple opportunities across contexts—the UL and USM campuses, elementary and high schools, professional meetings and national conference presentations—have made it possible to engage in dialogue, share work, interview each other, consider alternative methods for continuous assessment, and review student portfolios around sets of standards and problem-based learning projects. Additionally, working with USM colleagues has allowed us to further develop and refine the use of such teaching and learning protocols as "tunings" and "consultancies" that originated in the work of Theodore Sizer and colleagues in a Critical Friends model (See Coalition for Essential Schools in References). The collaboration has also motivated UL and USM faculty to incorporate in course syllabi virtual links between teacher candidates to examine, discuss and reflect on differing perspectives and experiences they have in urban and rural classrooms in Kentucky and Maine. And because teacher candidates in both institutions are in multiage placements K–12, in their virtual dialogues about course texts and educational issues, they are challenged to expand their thinking in light of particular settings and differing sets of experiences. The traditional dimensions of teacher candidates' classrooms are expanded as they are asked to consider, and discuss with each other, what lifelong learning is and how the complex lives of the students in their classrooms affect teaching, assessment, social justice, and learning communities. Finally, there is common interest across UL and USM faculty to further develop, pilot, and summarize findings of a USM draft of a professionalism rubric which assesses teacher candidates' knowledge, skills, and dispositions in this area, something not being addressed in sets of content area standards and teacher standards yet a part of continuous assessment NCATE recommends.

THE FOCUS AND EPICENTER OF CHANGE FOR USM

At USM, the ETEP faculty have traditionally met in the fall and spring for day-long "advances"[1] to examine practices in employing, supporting, and documenting improvements in the program related to outcomes, assessments, and curriculum. From 1996 to 1999, many of these advances were devoted to work related to Leading Edge. (See Chapter 3 for a description of events leading up to this point.) Other faculty in the Teacher Education Department and in the partner schools serving as mentors or course instructors were invited to participate. During the fall of the first year of the project, faculty contributed to the development of goals and a local plan of action for the project.

At one of the first Leading Edge faculty advances, case studies of interns from previous years were shared and analyzed to better understand what role standards play in the evaluation process. School and university faculty reviewed the documentation for two interns from different PDS sites: one for a typical and one for a marginal candidate. A case was also developed for an intern who was an experienced teacher. This case served as a reference point in more clearly articulating the differing expectations for preservice students and induction-level candidates. Delving into the complicated, ponderous documentation collected on each intern over the course of the program was a somewhat overwhelming experience, but an enlightening one.

Although standards and assessment are inextricably intertwined, we continue to struggle with clearly defining the boundary between acceptable and unacceptable performance. What is the nature of documentation of progress toward the standards? How much is enough? How soon in the internship year should areas of concern be identified and action planning initiated to address them? At what point is it determined that the candidate is not going to be able to meet the standards (Harriman, Kimball, & Hanley, 1997)?

The discussion became somewhat rancorous at points. The nature of how each PDS site went about the process of evaluating candidates was a more sensitive issue than we had anticipated. Although a common set of standards had been used for several years (Walters & Harriman, 1995), different processes for collecting evidence and evaluating candidates had evolved at each site. Moreover, the autonomy the PDS sites had exercised in the past was highly valued. Many faculty were reluctant to relinquish practices that had been collaboratively established as part of the culture of an individual site for the sake of attaining standardization, and possibly more reliability in judgments, across sites. We emerged from the first year of Leading Edge work realizing we needed to slow down and examine in more depth some of the structures and practices established previously (i.e., evaluation of standards, shared assessments, coordination of course work). Also, it became apparent that we could benefit from an outside facilitator and reinforcement of norms for "public testing of ideas" (Argyris & Schön, 1996).

Thus, activities in the second year focused on revisiting the shared assessments agreed to in 1995. (A list of the common set of products and performances used to evaluate interns across courses and sites is given in Chapter 3.) The goal was to study the implementation of each shared assessment, including how the assessment was being implemented in each site, how courses supported students' development relative to the assessment, and what quality work students were demonstrating on the assessment. First, all faculty who teach courses in the program were invited to attend a curriculum advance at which we would lay out our syllabi and examples of assignments across sites. Much of the discussion throughout the day involved distinguishing between the roles of assessments for evaluation and assessments for improvement. Could a system be developed which addresses both improving teaching and evaluating teaching? Faculty concluded that we could (and had) but that documentation of improvement should not be confused with documentation of competent performance. Improving our assessment system began to have increasing impact on the teacher education curriculum. As the shared assessments or intern projects were more clearly defined, with their knowledge and skill requirements specified, the alignment of the projects with the outcomes and with courses became clearer. The roles that different courses would play in supporting and guiding the intern projects were discussed (e.g., Lifespan Development and internship seminar). Thus, the intern projects served both assessment and teaching functions.

Concerns addressed included broader programmatic considerations (i.e., the purpose of the shared assessments and parallels between expectations for interns and learning standards for their students) and specific classroom performance considerations, which are the most critical performance indicators for an assessment. An outside facilitator and a carefully designed agenda with specific tasks of relevance to all participants resulted in consensus on several important broad as well as specific issues. All present agreed that the shared assessments were purposeful and should be continued and that they served several critical functions:

- common experiences for interns across sites,
- common documentation toward outcomes across sites,
- authentic sources of evaluation (representative of tasks teachers do),
- formative assessments throughout internship,
- summative assessments for courses and program,
- designing, teaching, and evaluating an extended unit of study that synthesizes many elements of teaching,
- external validity (representative of assessments in other programs or professions).

Louisville's use of similar projects entered the discussion as did sample materials from INTASC and NBPTS assessments.

The tone of this advance was constructive, and most participants indicated they had learned a lot. Participants left with a better understanding of standards and assessments in the context of the whole program. Instructors of sections of a course offered across PDS sites, in particular, had a rare opportunity to meet. In terms of the Leading Edge goals, we had collected a lot of data, including lists of performance indicators for each assessment. The next step was to incorporate these data into functional tools to increase consistency in implementation of the shared assessments across sites.

Jim Curry facilitated the next "advance," at which a format was developed to incorporate all the collected information into a type of product descriptor that we called an "assessment guide" (Curry & Samara, 1999). These tools were refined and piloted by many instructors across sites throughout the second year.

Several professional development activities with various groups continued this work in the third year, with an emphasis on testing external and internal validity of the guides. In 1998, Rick Stiggins, a visiting scholar invited through USM's Libra Scholar program, facilitated a review of our work within his framework for developing and evaluating a sound assessment system (Stiggins, 1998). He focused on two questions: How do we assess our interns' work? What are we teaching our interns is vital about classroom assessment practices?

Other USM work in the form of ETEP inservice workshops for school-based faculty have been quite successful. We have used our focus on standards for the Shared Assessments to improve mentor teachers' work with interns by increasing their understanding and analysis of the case study. We also introduced the assessments at a session for mentor teachers on how to set goals, provide feedback, and note improvements in interns' abilities.

CONTINUING THE CROSS-SITE RELATIONSHIP: EVALUATING STUDENT WORK

By 1999, based on our research on assessment, faculty from the two campuses were ready to share intern work for direct constructive feedback, rather than simply sharing tools and practices. The Leading Edge meeting at The Holmes Partnership Conference in Boston allowed participants from both universities to gather for a full day together. UL faculty brought with them samples of lesson plans for secondary classrooms, and USM representatives brought samples from K–12 interns' disciplinary/interdisciplinary units.

First, faculty from each campus shared four types of information: (1) the program rationale and criteria for the project, outlining the outcomes or standards it was intended to address and why it was required; (2) the guidelines given to interns for the project; (3) samples of intern work; and (4) the mechanism used for feedback to interns. Then time was allowed for participants (in mixed groups) to review and discuss work samples. Finally, groups reported and discussed:

- the features of the project that represent high quality teaching and assessment,
- how the project documentation can provide evidence of meeting or exceeding program outcomes (standards), and
- what exhibits or sections are most useful.

The presentation, comments, and questions led to at least three common focus areas: (1) reflective thinking by interns about their teaching and their students' learning, (2) levels and layers of feedback to interns, and (3) learning standards. Faculty in both programs emphasize the development of reflective thinking; yet through the review of each other's products it became apparent that anticipatory thinking was equally as important as retrospective analysis. Through a unit plan which emphasizes assessment, an intern could demonstrate his or her ability to think ahead, plan a series of lessons, and assess incremental growth toward long-term student outcomes. However, through the individual lessons the intern could reveal details of thinking related not only to the methodologies chosen, but also to aspects of classroom management and personalization of learning.

This led to a discussion of the difference in richness of details noted in lesson plans developed after the fact as opposed to before the teaching events. Obviously, it is best when interns prepare lesson plans prior to teaching, but we have found that some assignments and structures prompt a richer kind of thinking after the fact as a result of the intern's reflection and peer and mentor feedback. In some respects, this may be more in alignment with the continuous feedback and reflection cycles that practicing teachers experience and depend on for planning. In a later discussion at USM, Sue Walters suggested that pre-observation conferences might be even more important than postobservation conferences.

In both sites, the continuous feedback cycle for the review of intern work is crucial to performance and improvement, which are highly valued in each site's program. Given different intern projects assigned over the course of the year, site coordinators, other interns, mentor teachers, and course instructors can all be a part of the feedback loop for the intern. Focusing many eyes and minds on the work of interns is seen as valuable within the systems and ultimately crucial to interns' development. Formal feedback forms and scoring guides for all intern projects were the most valuable tools shared across sites and visits and were reported by interns in both sites as constructive springboards for the most growth in their work and thinking.

Another issue raised was the difference in state contexts. The degree to which meeting content standards carries high stakes (Kentucky) heavily influences the range of freedom interns are encouraged to exercise in teaching content and methodology. In Maine, the state Learning Results (Maine Department of

Education, 1997) are relatively new. All school districts are aligning their local curricula with the new student standards but have the freedom to develop their own comprehensive assessment systems to complement the statewide assessment that students take at fourth, eighth, and eleventh grades. The expectations for interns reflect these differences. For example, the Louisville lesson plan format directly addresses the student standards being emphasized. In Maine the student standards, in conjunction with teacher-developed assessment, are emphasized at the unit level but not so directly at the lesson level. We do not know to what extent these contextual differences may also result in differences in the content of feedback that interns receive from faculty and mentors.

TECHNOLOGY

Another area of collaboration that emerged from the dyad is the use of technology in the two teacher education programs. USM and UL have approached the use of technology in two different, yet compatible, ways. UL has investigated technology as a way for interns to showcase their work and prepare electronic assignments, lesson plans, and portfolios for sharing with peers, instructors, and others, such as prospective employers. Many times the electronic materials can be posted on the web as well as on a disk or disk drive. UL has been using technology to gather and archive useful intern materials such as lesson plans, making them available to interns and instructors. Faculty have Web pages for individual courses with course syllabi and curriculum resources on the Web as well as intern space on the Web server where interns can save and retrieve teaching materials and assignments. Faculty have recently developed a "Technologies Competencies Self-Assessment" as a rubric to prepare teacher candidates to meet a 1999 standard added to the Kentucky Teacher Standards—"Demonstrates competencies in educational technology." This assessment is both formative and summative, and teacher candidates are asked to provide both written and performance-based evidence of their skills, competencies, and dispositions about the applications and implications of new technologies in educational settings as they proceed through the program.

USM narrowed its focus to Web-based technology supporting the yearlong internship. The cross-platform accessibility works very well for students and faculty using a variety of computers and operating systems. The opportunity to access a website anywhere there is a connection to an Internet browser complements the variety of intern schedules and information needs, allowing many interns with multiple information needs to use the same system. USM has been looking at technology as a clearinghouse for program information and as a vehicle for promoting exchange of ideas across time and distance. The internship Web site has a program description, course syllabi in a consistent format, a Web-based calendar, and various forms and guidelines.

In both programs interns are working full-time in schools and taking concurrent seminars or courses. Thus, the emphasis has been on how to use technology to improve communication and the sharing of materials and ideas in a clinical setting rather than how to use technology to enhance presentations in courses on campus.

Showcasing and sharing work across the two sites is another step. Both sites use a similar lesson plan format that would be simple to make consistent across the two sites. Both sites have the interns teach extended interdisciplinary units. Most interns are comfortable with Internet access. It is reasonable to begin to scan in unit and lesson plans and samples of student work that the interns can use in building collections of artifacts representing their teaching. As at UL, such work can be done at a computerized video editing station, where the interns can excerpt video, organize word processing files, and scan other documents such as student work and pictures and save the work to a hard drive or a disk.

In the future, we will be seeking technology to promote real time interactions across our sites, looking at topics of common experience and assisting each other in areas of need. For example, both our programs have standards or outcomes on which students are assessed for certification.

What are we doing, and planning to do, together? How has the partnership enhanced our innovations? At a simple level, interns and faculty across the two settings have access to the Web materials assembled at each site. Interns respond positively to a collection of Web resources that have been categorized in the course syllabus (e.g., assessment, standards, planning, and classroom management). At another level, the same discussions and intern server mechanisms we have in our individual sites are available across sites. With no extra time, and no extra effort, we can exchange information and materials across students who are engaged in common activities (e.g., designing assessments and learning activities that relate to our state standards). In other words, the resources we are using in our individual sites and the work the interns are showcasing can be made accessible across time and distance with no extra time or effort on the part of the instructor. Graduate assistants or technology support staff can mount the existing materials on the Web. The simple things are often the most powerful. Interns crave useful resources and the web provides a multitude of resources beyond the print materials available only in library collections and limited to library hours.

After realizing how our existing web applications could be shared, we began to clarify our purposes. Our most immediate goal beyond information and resources is providing venues for the exchange of ideas. The most immediate application is a Web-based discussion area allowing for threaded discussions in which entries—whether new topics or responses—are clustered. The system is asynchronous; that is, entries can be posted at any time. An individual has the opportunity to post a new entry or respond to an existing entry. The system has worked best when the Web conference is focused on questions such as "What is quality assessment?" rather than attempting an open-ended repository of ideas and comments. Of course, the Web conferencing system requires minimal preparation and maintenance. The first entry is best done during a class where someone can explain the system and model an entry, and the interns can access the system and post their first entry with someone immediately available to answer questions and troubleshoot. We are currently examining four Web-based applications connecting USM and UL: (1) archiving lesson plans with direct attention to assessment and content standards; (2) Web-based discussions for exchange of ideas on issues such as diversity through a discussion of Mike Rose's *Possible Lives*; (3) compressed video or other conferencing systems for intern presentations, sharing, and feedback on projects; and (4) digital portfolios for organizing and displaying intern exhibits and projects. Using technology to disseminate materials and interact anytime, anywhere has complemented the individual experiences and face-to-face support and conversations that are so important in the internship.

VALUE OF THE DYAD

One of the greatest effects of partnerships built across institutions has been maintaining the ability to stay on target. Our work can be characterized as being a string of "little tries," allowing us to reflect, revise, and improve incrementally over time. The partners in this Leading Edge dyad took a similar and constructive approach to change and improve their work. Two major qualities surfaced—a genuine trust in each other and a validation of quality in the work being done. Our work stayed "on the ground" because we kept it simple, practical, and useful to all the layers of partners involved. We shared curricula, intern work, and difficult issues for critical feedback while maintaining appreciation of accomplishments and embracing opportunities for continued professional growth.

NOTES

1. These sessions were called "retreats" until colleagues at Montclair State University pointed out the self-defeating attitude inherent in the term.

REFERENCES

Argyris, C., & Schön, D. (1996). *Organizational learning II: Theory, method and practice.* Reading, MA: Addison Wesley.

Coalition for Essential Schools. Retrieved 1/01, from http://www.essentialschools.org/fieldbook/strategies/inquiry/examstudwork/consultancy.html

68   LARSON, RYAN, METCALF-TURNER, ET AL.

Costa, A. L., & Kallick, B. (1993). Through the lens of a critical friend. *Educational Leadership, 51*(2), 49–51.

Curry, J. A., & Samara, J. P. (1999). *Differentiating curriculum, instruction, and assessment for students with diverse needs.* Austin, TX: Curriculum Project.

Gorham School Department. (1994). *Gorham learner outcomes* (program document). Gorham, ME: Author.

Jones, K., & Whitford, B. L. (1994). Kentucky's conflicting reform principles: High-stakes school accountability and student performance assessment. *Phi Delta Kappan, 79*(4), 276–281.

Harriman, N., Kimball, W., & Hanley, S., (1997, June). *Final report: Leading Edge Project, 1996–97.* Gorham, ME: University of Southern Maine.

Maine Department of Education. (1997). State of Maine learning results: High standards for all students. (Department of Education document). Augusta, ME: Author.

Miller, L., & Silvernail, D. (1994). Wells Junior High School: Evolution of a professional development school. In L. Darling-Hammond (Ed.), *Professional development schools: Schools for developing a profession* (pp. 28–34). New York: Teachers College Press.

Ryan, S., Dittmer, A., Stroble, B., and Larson, A. (1999, June). Inquiry as a theme for urban teacher education. Paper presented at "In Praise of Education" National Conference, Seattle.

Silvernail, D. (1997). *Results from surveys of graduates of exemplary teacher education programs and the employers of these graduates.* Gorham, ME: University of Southern Maine, Center for Educational Policy, Applied Research, and Evaluation.

Stiggins, R. (1998). *Leadership for excellence in assessment: A school district planning guide.* Portland, OR: Assessment Training Institute.

Walters, S., & Harriman, N. (1995). *Initial teacher certification project: Final report to the Maine State Board of Education.* Gorham, ME: University of Southern Maine.

Whitford, B. L., Ruscoe, G., & Fickel, L. (2000). Knitting it all together: Collaborative teacher education in southern Maine. In L. Darling-Hammond (Ed.), *Studies of excellence in teacher education: Preparation at the graduate level.* New York, Washington, DC: National Commission on Teaching and America's Future and American Association of Colleges for Teacher Education.

CHAPTER 5

A Professional Development School Partnership for Preparing Teachers for Urban Schools

A. Lin Goodwin and Alexandria T. Lawrence

The Preservice Program in Childhood Education (hereafter known as the Pre-service Program) is a graduate level elementary teacher preparation program housed within the Department of Curriculum and Teaching at Teachers College, Columbia University (TC). Steeped in the philosophy of John Dewey and framed by a progressive tradition, the Preservice Program emphasizes child-centered practice and the social construction of knowledge, teacher decision making and reflection, and teaching as a moral and political endeavor. Under-girded by this philosophical mindset, the program acknowledges that there is no single truth in education but many realities given the uniqueness of individual children and the highly contextualized nature of teaching. Consequently, there can be no one superior prescription for educating children and each teacher must thoughtfully develop an educational platform that embraces a spectrum of appropriate alternatives and approaches in order to truly achieve child-centered practice. As teacher educators, we are obliged to introduce our students to multiple instructional strategies and models as well as the important differences among them—so that they may understand the limitations of fixed formulas and will constantly search for the best way to reach each child.

The intention of the Preservice Program is therefore to instill the knowl-edge domains of teaching that transcend the practicalities of teaching skills and tools. These knowledge domains become the professional basis for teaching and serve to educate teachers as deliberative practitioners (Zumwalt, 1988) rather than teachers who merely implement instructional recipes. The program defines deliberative practitioners as teachers who engage in what Dewey (1929) described as intelligent and flexible practice that emphasizes decision making,

69

experimentation, and reflection. Deliberative practice conceptualizes teaching and learning along dimensions of the reflective and ethical. The mark of the professional is not merely knowing what to do and how, but knowing when and whether to do (Mitchell & Kerchner, 1987).

THE STRUCTURE OF THE PROGRAM

The Preservice Program is approved by New York State and leads to elementary education certification. Upon successful completion of the 40-credit program, graduates earn a Master of Arts degree in Elementary Education and are eligible for N–6 certification in New York State and for Common Branches certification (K–5) in New York City. Students can also choose to use their electives, extend the program to earn an Early Childhood certificate for New York City or a New York State Middle School extension for grades 6–8, or both.

Our students enter the program with baccalaureates in noneducation fields and come to us with little or no experience with or preparation in professional education. Most of our students are European American females from middle- to upper-middle-class backgrounds; males usually comprise less than 10% of the group. The program has, however, been quite successful in recruiting minority students resulting in a yearly cohort that is typically 25–30% students of color. Our students are generally quite evenly divided between those who are changing careers and those who come to us directly from undergraduate study. The majority of the career-changers have been out of college about three to five years; only a small number are leaving well-established professions. This translates into a mean student age of mid- to late-twenties. Students come to the program from all over the country although many of them live in or have moved to the tristate metropolitan area encompassing New York, Connecticut, and New Jersey. The average person who applies to the program has a 3.2 grade point average from a reputable university, has devoted significant time to volunteer services, has had experience working with children, and has spent time outside the United States. The program is competitive and rigorous, and demands a strong academic background. Still, about one third of applicants are accepted because the program has the luxury of selecting from a very accomplished and academically strong applicant pool. However, it is important to say that a healthy grade point average alone is not enough to ensure admission; program faculty weigh carefully all components of the application portfolio.

The candidacy period for completion of the master's degree is five years, but most of our students choose to attend the university full-time and typically complete their initial teacher preparation within 16 months. A common schedule begins with one or two summer sessions (two are offered each year), continues during two academic terms and concludes the following summer with another one or two sessions. Like most teacher certification programs, the program requires students to complete course work in several areas (i.e., child development or educational foundations, such as history or philosophy of education), subject specific methods (e.g., reading, science, mathematics), and special education (learning or physical disabilities, for instance). In addition, students complete a minimum of two twelve-week periods of student teaching in two different classrooms and grade levels. Students are placed in a wide variety of mostly public schools in New York City and spend three mornings and one full day, or about 20 hours per week, in their placements.

What distinguishes the experience from a simple progression of courses plus field experience is the preservice core which integrates curriculum and instruction in elementary schools, curriculum design, social studies methods, and models of teaching. Each year, a cohort of approximately 90 students complete the preservice core along with student teaching and reading (which is also an academic year-long course and is designed to support students' field experience). The preservice team, which includes three professors, one full-time lecturer, four instructors who are also doctoral students in the Department of Curriculum and Teaching, and two clinical faculty members, together plan for and teach the weekly, five-hour-long core and collectively make programmatic and instructional decisions. Thus, the preservice core, which accounts for only 16 of the 40 required credits, is actually the most demanding and intensive aspect of the program for faculty and students alike. It brings them together for serious work around teaching and children, work which is conceptually linked to and embedded in the daily classroom lives of student teachers. In essence, the preservice core is the heart and the identity of the program.

THE PRESERVICE CORE

The preservice core is offered only during the academic year and follows a fall–spring sequence. In the fall, core explores the questions: What do children need? How do we know what children need (and by whose authority do we derive that knowledge)? How do we organize instruction to address children's needs in the classroom? In attempting to answer these questions, topics such as child development, lesson planning, management, organization of the learning environment, and understanding classroom and school communities are examined. In the spring semester the same topics and questions continue to be investigated within the context of developing curriculum, focusing particularly on the teaching of social studies and on schools as organizations. Students integrate what they have learned during the year by completing culminating projects and presentations such as a student teaching portfolio and a multigrade curriculum framework.

The Models of Teaching component of core enables students to learn a variety of teaching models so that they develop a repertoire of pedagogical strategies. During the fall semester, students engage in the learning and application of two models of teaching—group process/discussion and cooperative learning. In the spring they are introduced to six models: inductive thinking, concept development, inquiry training, graphic organizers, role play, and simulation. Developing a repertoire of models of teaching is more than mastery of a series of steps. Rather than specific things to do, models represent ways of thinking about what to do. These models of teaching become the building blocks for curriculum development.

As indicated earlier, alongside core, students are spending three half days and one full day a week in classrooms. Learning to teach is a developmental process; we believe that teacher growth cannot be regimented. Our experience tells us that the vast majority of our students will make the journey from student to novice teacher, but the journey will be different for each individual. Our expectation is that over the year, each student teacher will have experiences teaching a wide range of subject areas, utilizing a variety of activities, materials and techniques, working with various instructional groupings (individuals, small and large groups, whole class), handling general classroom management (transitions, snack, materials distribution, small and large groups, etc.) and planning for instruction (spontaneous lessons, lesson sequences, mini-units, etc.). We know that some students will be able to skillfully handle the many demands of teaching by the end of the first student teaching term while others will still be exploring their roles even as they begin the second term in the field. However, we anticipate that all of our students will achieve all basic standards by the end of the year, and most do. The few who do not are usually required to complete a third term of student teaching. The additional time, support, and practice are what most students need to be successful. For the very few for whom additional student teaching experience proves insufficient, faculty provide assistance and counseling so that they are able to make alternate vocational choices. The process is never easy but has, in each case, ultimately been the right thing to do, both for the profession and for the student.

Each semester, students are assigned a supervisor who observes them in their classrooms at least six times per semester and meets with them after each visit. The college supervisor also meets with the cooperating teacher and with preservice faculty, reads and responds to the daily reflective journals kept by student teachers, and facilitates midterm and final evaluation conferences with the student teacher and cooperating teacher. The Preservice Program subscribes loosely to a clinical supervision model (Glickman, 1981); thus the observation cycle generally begins with a preobservation conference for goal-setting purposes and concludes with a postconference where the student and supervisor can discuss and assess the observation conducted. All supervisors gather in biweekly supervisory meetings with preservice faculty to review student teacher progress and discuss issues. It is these meetings that interrupt the isolation of the super-visor–cooperating teacher–student teacher triad and ensure that program per-sonnel keep fully apprised of what is going on in the field.

THE PROFESSIONAL DEVELOPMENT SCHOOL

Each year, the Preservice Program places student teachers in 12 to 15 schools located in Manhattan, the Bronx, and Brooklyn. Most of these schools (and co-operating teachers) have longstanding relationships with the program and are seen as valued collaborators. In 1988, the Preservice Program, along with Com-munity School District Three (one of the school districts adjacent to Teachers College), and the United Federation of Teachers (the New York State teachers union), initiated a professional development school (PDS) partnership which redefined all notions of collaboration. The basic thrust of this partnership is to improve the professional lives of teachers, both those in service and those en-tering the profession. Drawing upon the combined wisdom and knowledge of teachers, administrators and professors of education, the partnership has aimed to create: (a) improved learning experiences for the preservice teacher, (b) new roles and professional development opportunities for the classroom teacher; (c) an integration of academic and clinical work; and (d) a collaborative approach to the continuing education of teachers. Since 1988, the Preservice Program has created and maintained PDS relationships with three elementary schools in District Three, and places at least 25% of its students each term in these schools. The bulk of these are at PS 87, Teachers College's first and best estab-lished PDS.

PS 87 is located in Manhattan's Upper West Side where spacious, luxuri-ously renovated brownstones nestle near dilapidated, packed, and crumbling tenement houses. Small neighborhood sundry shops and a once sizable Latino community have been pushed uptown by fancy ice cream parlors, pricey restau-rants, boutiques, and many upscale women's apparel shops in the area immedi-ately surrounding the school.

Constructed in 1954 in the traditional egg crate style, PS 87 serves ap-proximately 1,000 students in kindergarten through fifth grade. The 59 teach-ers provide a full curriculum that includes art, music, drama, physical education, and special programs for children with learning and physical dis-abilities, as well as the more traditional school subjects. The school also pro-vides an afterschool program to accommodate the needs of parents as well as children. Parents are actively encouraged to participate in the school—they work in classrooms teaching and "room mothering," and run after-school classes in dance, problem solving, puppetry, and sports. Parents designed and built the Wood Park playground behind the school and are on call to help out with everything from providing classroom snacks to major fundraising for the school. Indeed, during the 1998–99 school year the Parent Association raised about $190,000 for the school.

PS 87's distinctly progressive educational vision is captured by the philosophy statement contained in the school's brochure and is closely aligned to the philosophy of the Preservice Program. The PS 87 philosophy emphasizes: (a) heterogeneous grouping, (b) respect for feelings, (c) celebration of diversity, (d) integrated curriculum, (e) active learning, and (f) academic excellence. Overall, the staff agrees with these principles and strives to achieve them in their classrooms. The alignment of PS 87's philosophy with that of the Preservice Program, coupled with its reputation as an excellent school, resulted in PS 87 being deliberately chosen as the first PDS site because the purpose of the project was not to save a school but rather to create a setting where teacher professionalism would be supported, and where educational experiences for students could be improved (Snyder, 1993).

Since the partnership was formed, 12 of the teachers at PS 87 have collaborated with program faculty on action research projects and teacher-driven inquiry around such questions as: What kinds of difficulties do student teachers experience as they make the transition between their fall and spring placements? In addition, each year two classroom teachers serve as clinical faculty in the Preservice Program. These clinical faculty members remain in their full-time classroom teaching positions while they participate in the preservice core as coplanners and teachers. Thus, clinical faculty serve as teacher educators in the program and assume many of the same responsibilities as other program faculty, including advisement, and reading and grading the assignments of a group of preservice students. These rotating positions are filled through an application and interview process with most clinical faculty serving in this role for two or three years.

As part of their PDS commitment, the Preservice Program places large clusters of about 15–20 student teachers at PS 87 both in the fall and spring semesters, a small number of whom are PDS interns. In the TC context, interns are defined as student teachers who have been selected to participate in an intensified student teaching experience at PS 87. This experience, called "the PDS internship," is an opportunity available to all of the Preservice students. Historically, however, fewer than 10% of the roughly 90 student teachers apply to become interns, and generally 5 to 8 students are selected.

The PDS internship begins with an application process followed by an interview with the PS 87 principal, PS 87 teachers, and PDS director. The initial criteria for selection are fairly broad—interest in urban schools, willingness to commit to the internship experience, enthusiasm. Once accepted as PDS interns, the students remain at PS 87 for the year, unlike other student teachers who are placed in a different school each term. Interns work with PS 87 teachers who must meet certain qualifications: five or more years of classroom experience, successful completion of a course in supervision, and a written indication of their desire and ability to work with an intern.

Aside from staying at PS 87 for both semesters, the interns agree to take on additional responsibilities. Each week they attend an on-site seminar at PS 87 taught by various classroom teachers. Seminar topics include classroom setup, teaching reading to lower and upper grades, designing integrated curriculum, and other topics related to practical classroom application. For two weeks in January, during the college's semester break, the interns assume full responsibility for their fall placement classroom. Interns plan for this takeover with their cooperating teacher and take full responsibility for the class. In the spring, another takeover occurs, this time for six weeks from mid-April to the end of May, once the regular student teaching semester is over.

During these takeover periods, the interns are in the classroom all day, five days a week. They generally plan for all daily aspects of the curriculum including scheduling, planning and implementing lessons, informally assessing students (including planning and collecting homework, if appropriate), managing transitions, and maintaining contact with parents, along with the general day-to-day running of the classroom. In January, the cooperating teacher usually remains in the classroom for the first few days to lend support. As the days progress, the cooperating teacher begins to leave the room for short periods of time as deemed appropriate. By the spring takeover, it is expected that the interns will be able to run the classroom alone. Many cooperating teachers leave their classrooms completely and use this time to pursue professional development opportunities (such as visiting other schools, attending conferences, and analyzing data from action research projects).

One supervisor is assigned to all of the interns during the internship takeover periods. This supervisor is on site much of the time and holds regular meetings with the interns. On-site supervision changes the nature of the supervisor–student teacher relationship and changes the dynamic between the supervisor and the cooperating teacher. Thus, while interns continue to schedule observations of particular lessons with the supervisor, the supervisor usually takes on more of an advisory role and drops in on the classroom frequently to offer support and to give advice. While the supervisor still meets formally with the cooperating teacher and the intern, the supervisor's relationship with the cooperating teacher typically becomes more informal, collaborative, and collegial. This informal, collaborative relationship is supported by a dialogue journal where reflections about this intensive teaching period can be shared. A three-ring binder is placed in each intern classroom during the takeover period. In this binder, the intern, cooperating teacher, and supervisor record their thoughts, ask one another critical questions, and reflect upon their practice. This daily dialogue is ongoing and supports continuous conversation among the triad even as opportunities for face-to-face interaction become less available. The journal ensures that even in the midst of each busy classroom day, intellectual space for important teaching talk is carved out.

The internship demands a great deal from students, cooperating teachers, and faculty. But the payoff is handsome—students have a field experience that mirrors the real lives of teachers and, as a consequence, is rich and deeply instructive; cooperating teachers have the opportunity to fully induct and socialize a fledgling teacher into their classroom practice and profession, and they are also given significant school-supported time to attend to their own professional development; faculty gain insight into student teachers' development through an alternate practicum model and are afforded an additional mechanism to strengthen the university's partnership with the school; finally, the district has access to well-prepared teachers who are already knowledgeable about the culture of the school and the district. In fact, at the conclusion of the internship, the Superintendent of Community School District Three takes into consideration the performance of the interns and often gives them priority over other candidates for teaching positions within the district for the following year.

The internship framed by PS 87 as a PDS and the preservice core are the focus of the study on which we embarked with the University of California at Santa Barbara. Together, we sought to understand: (a) what are appropriate standards for the preparation of teachers, and (b) how are these standards articulated and enacted.

STANDARDS FOR THE PREPARATION OF TEACHERS

The philosophy of the Preservice Program is developed through five themes or knowledge domains. These five domains have evolved over time, but each has its roots in our understanding that "personal illumination and liberation" are in reality more practical than "how-to's" (Dewey, 1929, p.15). We avoid prescription from the outset, believing that our students should be exposed to and should critique many perspectives on teaching. We also believe that our students should, in turn, be able to identify and refine their own perspective, and be able to defend the perspective they assume. The five knowledge domains become pedagogical lenses through which our students move beyond teaching as an imitative process to good teaching as the consequence of numerous decisions, development, and reflective practice that grow out of the dialogue surrounding teaching. The domains have enabled the program to develop the reflective and ethical dimensions of work with novice teachers and include:

1. Personal knowledge: autobiography and philosophy of teaching;
2. Contextual knowledge: understanding children and schools;
3. Pedagogical knowledge: models of teaching and curriculum development;

4. Sociological knowledge: plurality and diversity in race, class, gender, and ethnicity; and
5. Organizational knowledge: cooperative, democratic group process.

Each is briefly described in the following sections. (For a more complete discussion of the Preservice Program and the five knowledge domains, see Bolin & Goodwin, 1992; 1995.)

Personal Knowledge

Every person who enters a teacher preparation program has been through a laboratory in teaching. That is, candidates hold impressions about who teachers are and what they do from years of being students. These impressions may involve a loose collection of ideas about what the student teacher does not want to be as a teacher. Or impressions may be positive and articulated in terms of a favorite teacher the student hopes to emulate. Actual teaching practice is often shaped by these positive and negative images that constitute personal knowledge of teaching rather than by a teacher education program (Lortie, 1975). Thus prospective teachers' autobiographies necessarily become the foundation upon which teaching practice is built.

Contextual Knowledge

A perennial dilemma in preparing teachers is the fact that no one teacher education program, no matter how extensive or comprehensive, can possibly prepare each fledgling teacher for every situation that might arise in the classroom or school. Classrooms are complex and dynamic places, and the children who inhabit them defy categorization, despite constant attempts to do so. Schools are equally complex and constitute the larger context for teachers' work. As teacher educators, it would be presumptuous of us to believe that we can identify *a priori* all that our student teachers will need to know in order to be successful with the wide range and variety of human beings with whom they will work. What we can do, however, is provide our students with ways of thinking about teaching and children, with educational problem-solving and fact-finding skills, and with strategies for identifying issues and contextual variables which inform solutions. In essence, we need to provide students with several sets of questions through which to view classroom- and school-based events.

Pedagogical Knowledge

The common dictionary definition of pedagogy is the art or science of teaching or teaching methods. Yet methods defined as "tricks of the trade" provide a false sense of security, particularly to the beginner, because we know there are few tricks of the trade that work universally. Of far more value than a collection of how-to's is the ability to study a situation, notice what students care about, what is important to them, and invent appropriate practices. This ability comes from habits of mind more than from knowing specific methods. Habits of mind are developed as student teachers are challenged to understand and thoroughly integrate program content (knowledge about human growth and development, subject matter content, and pedagogical craft) with prior experience and current student teaching field practice. The goal of the program is to foster deliberative practice. This is clearly in the Deweyan tradition, and may be linked to Dewey's notion of soul action in the classroom, or the activity that occurs as the teacher skillfully uses knowledge of pedagogy, child growth and development, and subject matter content to engage the student.

Sociological Knowledge

American society is marvelously diverse and therefore needs teachers and curricula which respond to and respect that diversity. Indeed, interdependence on a global level is brought home daily as human struggles to live in harmony and achieve equity are paraded internationally on television and in newsprint. The demands of a pluralistic world society have resulted in changes at national and state policy levels in the United States. One change is that teacher certifications regulations in many states have been revised and now, for example, require teacher education programs to prepare teachers "to work effectively with students from minority cultures, students from homes where English is not spoken, students with handicapping conditions, and gifted and talented students" (State University of New York, 1992, p. 1). Changes in practice, however, have been uneven and slow (Grant & Secada, 1990). Although teacher educators support the need to help new teachers work with culturally diverse populations and sociocultural issues, the profession as a whole is struggling to understand and define what pluralistic education is, and what multicultural educators ought to be able to do. No teacher education program is immune to this struggle and subsequent confusion.

Organizational Knowledge

In a rapidly shrinking and increasingly complex universe, where work necessarily involves others outside one's immediate environment, the ability to participate effectively in democratic, cooperative groups is essential to teachers who are going to exert leadership in the field. In the United States, current discussions of teacher empowerment and school governance suggest that teachers have a place in shaping the profession. If teachers are to participate in the determination of school goals and policies and be given the right to exercise professional judgment about curricular content and means of instruction as we believe they should be, they must be equipped for these roles. This requires both professional expertise and professional authority to participate meaningfully in decision making. Teachers need to be skillful in their interactions with individuals and groups, recognizing that different dynamics are at work with each. Teachers who acquire these democratic group process skills, we believe, will naturally create settings in their classrooms where cooperation, mutuality, fairness, participation, and equality are the norms.

These knowledge domains serve as our standards and guide the curriculum we offer, the experiences we provide to our students, the work of supervisors, and the student teaching practicum. They embody the program's beliefs about good teaching and teachers. As such, they represent both standards and values. Further, they exemplify our definition of teaching as praxis, a complex activity undergirded by thoughtful decisions.

HOW THE STANDARDS ARE
ARTICULATED AND ENACTED

The program relies on a number of structures and processes to make our standards explicit. These structures interrelate and help to build coherence across the program. They include: (a) the curriculum of the preservice core, (b) student teaching placements, (c) the role of clinical faculty, (d) biweekly supervisors' meetings, and (e) weekly preservice core planning meetings.

The Curriculum of the Preservice Core

Program standards are made explicit in the syllabus for the preservice core seminar. The curriculum is designed to directly reflect the knowledge domains while assignments enable students to apply and practice the standards. For example, entering students write an autobiography that becomes a lens for consciously examining one's attitudes and expectations about schools, children, and teaching. Such an examination exposes students' preconceptions to self-critique and encourages them to develop new ways of thinking and acting that are related to personal knowledge. Autobiography is further reinforced in the student teaching journal kept in conjunction with field practice. In the journal, students write daily about classroom experiences, reflecting on what they mean. The journal is not a report of events but an account of the way students are thinking about these events. The purpose of the journal is to develop students' skills as deliberative, reflective teachers. It provides a daily link or dialogue between the student teacher and supervisor.

Contextual knowledge is embodied in a child study and a school study. The child study requires students to identify one child whom they follow over the course of ten weeks. Students conduct observations using a variety of data collection strategies, describe in detail the classroom context in which the child operates, and collect and analyze samples of the child's work. They begin to build a holistic, comprehensive portrait of a young learner in order to make informed educational judgments appropriate to the child's needs. The school study directs students to consider the larger institutional context and its relationship to and influence on what occurs in individual classrooms. In examining the school, students begin with a description of the physical environment and gradually move into a deeper examination of school structure and organization, leadership and decision making, and the interaction of school community members, curriculum, and instruction. Both studies are designed to engage students in a critical examination of teaching and learning and the purpose of schooling. Key questions that drive the studies include these: Where is the power? What sociopolitical and sociocultural influences are at play? What is the relationship between the intended and the enacted curriculum? In what ways does the setting support adults and children? We believe that these assignments render concrete the complexity of teaching and schooling and underscore the myriad decisions that teachers must make in order to teach well.

Pedagogical knowledge and organizational knowledge are emphasized through the exploration of various models of teaching and instructional strategies, through an emphasis on the invention of practice where teaching recipes are eschewed in favor of context-specific and child-relevant instruction, and through the engagement of students in much group and cooperative work. For example, students work collaboratively with a team of classmates to design a theme-based social studies curriculum for several consecutive grade levels. In order for the groups to be successful, students must practice positive group behaviors that build consensus, articulate their ideas and educational platforms, learn to resolve conflict, and negotiate numerous pedagogical decisions with their peers. It is not an easy process but it is one that helps students understand that democratic process does not occur by happenstance and that there are numerous strategies for creating and sustaining such a process.

Sociological knowledge runs as a theme throughout the preservice core. Students are exposed to models of multicultural curriculum design, principles of culturally relevant teaching, cultural ways of knowing, learning and developing, and the hegemonic history (and continuing practice) of schools and society. In each assignment and class session, students are guided to consider questions of race, gender, and language, and to always question normative practice.

Student Teaching Placements

The student teaching placement is equally important in ensuring that the standards of the program are realized. The nature of students' experiences and growth can greatly depend on the atmosphere of the school. The Preservice Program reserves the right to select the placements it uses, both the schools and the individual classrooms. Therefore, the school selection process is deliberate and thoughtful and a close working relationship with schools is sought. It follows then that we choose to place our students in settings defined by progressive, child-centered practice, where decision making by teachers is the norm and where diversity is an asset upon which curriculum is built. While the gap between the university and the school is never fully closed, our students witness the actualization of program standards on a daily basis.

The Role of Clinical Faculty

Clinical faculty serve as a crucial link between theory and practice and between the university and the field. Their integration as teaching partners and coplanners has been instrumental in cementing the relationship between the PDS and the program. At the university, they offer the program (and students) insight into the culture and inner workings of the school and help us always to be cognizant of the practical implications of all that we teach. The illustrations that they provide of the theories, models, and ideas presented in the preservice core, serve as evidence to students that what they are learning in the program has meaning in the classroom and that the standards are credible. The program relies on their input and wisdom in ensuring the practicality and fidelity of the standards. Similarly, at the school site, clinical faculty help their colleagues, our students' cooperating teachers, to interpret the relationship between our assignments and learning to teach, and they provide a rationale for the program's standards. As school–university liaisons who understand and live in both worlds, their role in making the standards come alive cannot be minimized.

Biweekly Supervisors Meetings

Every other week, supervisors gather to discuss the student teachers' progress. Supervisors are introduced to the standards at the first supervisory meeting and these standards are reinforced at each subsequent meeting. This reinforcement takes the form of updates on preservice core activities in order to enlist supervisors' assistance in supporting students' understanding of and work towards meeting the standards. Therefore, supervisors are explicitly directed to ask students many of the same questions they are presented with in preservice core, to look for the strategies, models and concepts explored in class, and to provide students technical assistance as they conduct observations or plan for instruction. The program relies on supervisors' support of the curriculum and consequently the standards and sees them as another vital link between the university and the classroom.

Weekly Preservice Core Planning Meetings

Meeting weekly to assess each core class and engage in ongoing, collaborative planning fosters constant reflection about the enactment of standards. A collaborative approach to teacher education demands explicit discussions about what we are doing and why. Decisions about activities, the selection of topics, and criteria for assignments all depend on our commitment to continuous self-assessment and professional dialogue. The struggle to align philosophy with practice is constant, but our discussions are always guided by the knowledge domains we have articulated.

PROGRAM STANDARDS AND THE STATE CONTEXT

All teacher education programs in New York operate under the aegis of the State Department of Education. The Preservice Program is no exception and is registered with and approved by the New York State Education Department (NYSED). The State mandates that all teacher education programs conform to certain guidelines for teacher preparation and reviews requests for program registration with these requirements in mind. The requirements for kindergarten-to-fifth grade certification are quite concrete in some cases—for example, 180 hours of student teaching, six credits in the teaching of reading—and more open-ended in others, such as the requirement mentioned earlier, that new teachers be prepared "to work effectively with students from minority cultures, students from homes where English is not spoken, students with handicapping conditions" (State University of New York, 1992, p. 1). In terms of the former, teacher education programs seeking NYSED approval simply respond directly to the requirements and indicate how they will accommodate what is prescribed. As far as the more flexible requirements are concerned, each teacher education program, in its application for NYSED approval, must first interpret the requirements and then articulate clearly how it plans to meet them. Approval is granted by NYSED if it is felt that the teacher education program in question has responded appropriately to all requirements.

The program approval process aside, NYSED will grant certification only to those candidates who have passed the New York State examinations for teacher certification. Thus, a student could successfully complete a state-approved program and still not receive certification if she or he fails these examinations.

The Preservice Program has consistently responded appropriately to NYSED mandates and requirements, as evidenced by the fact that it has not experienced difficulty acquiring state approval. The relationship between TC and NYSED can be characterized as cordial and professionally respectful. Thus, the interpretation of standards and mandates engages both institutions in dialogue and allows some negotiation to occur. Consequently, while the creation of the knowledge domains (standards) was internal and self-contained rather than administratively imposed or driven by state mandate, they reflect and are informed by state and city certification requirements, principles of good practice supported by national conversations about good teaching, and the cumulative wisdom and research of the education profession.

However, the flexibility that the Preservice Program appears to exercise in terms of standards does not relieve it from state requirements. Where the program enjoys flexibility is in how it conceptualizes good teaching. Notions of good teaching, although implicit in the NYSED requirements, are not explicitly mandated by the state. The Preservice Program's definition of what constitutes adequate teacher preparation or what new teachers ought to know and be able to do is not limited by NYSED requirements which represent minimum competencies. Thus, the program has felt free to go beyond NYSED guidelines and has typically required much more than the minimum of its students. For example, the program had required two semesters of student teaching—one at a lower elementary level and the second in an upper elementary classroom—more than a decade before NYSED required this of all teacher education programs in 1993. Perhaps the fact that the program consistently goes beyond minimum requirements ensures NYSED that it is internally driven towards high standards and rigorous teacher preparation. This enables NYSED to work with the program as a professional partner rather than as an entity that requires constant policing. This process of external standards promoting internal review is further supported by the integral involvement of many faculty in the Department of Curriculum and Teaching, including Preservice Program faculty, in helping to define and create public standards for teacher education. Therefore, preservice faculty often serve as architects of national reform in teacher education even while they effect changes within the program. Many have also served on various state commissions, permitting their beliefs about good teaching to find their way into state policy. Finally, the fact that 95 to 98% of TC's preservice teacher education students pass the NYS teacher exams cannot help but assure the state that, as an institution, TC is doing what is required.

Given this state context, the Preservice Program is able to work from a stance that begins with the articulated values and goals of the program and then moves outward to integrate the larger educational universe. Thus, although the program philosophy is what guides the work of the program, as opposed to external standards handed down from policymakers, the program is far from exclusive or separate from the public world of education. Rather, the program constantly strives to take its own advice, that is, to engage in the same intelligent and flexible practice that emphasizes decision making and experimentation which we encourage our students to adopt (Dewey, 1929). Like our students, we examine and critique many perspectives on teaching before we identify and refine our own perspective, a perspective that we can support and explain. This process of critique and examination of public standards enables preservice faculty to first weigh the appropriateness of such standards before using them to assess the curriculum of the program. External standards help the program to identify gaps, redundancies, and weaknesses and to facilitate changes that ensure current thinking about standards for teaching is incorporated.

CONCLUSION

The Preservice Program structures and requirements and the PDS relationship with PS 87 are all based on the standards, and values held at the core of the Preservice Program. The design of the program, specifically the design of the preservice core, the requirements for awarding a master's degree from the program, and the choice to partner with PS 87 are all decisions that enhance the philosophy of the Preservice Program. Each of these decisions is based on what the Preservice Program believes is good teacher education.

The structures described in this chapter have grown out of the five knowledge domains. The assignments are the practical applications of the domains within the Preservice Program. As intellectual tools, the five knowledge domains recognize that, in the end, teacher preparation is an initiation. We choose to spend our few short months initiating our students into a process that will continue long after they leave us. For us to carry out this mission we must be able to place our students in learning environments where these values can be reinforced and can be played out by our students. Thus the relationship with schools and with the PDS is critical. The Preservice Program relies on the match of the philosophy of the teachers at PS 87 and the Preservice Program standards for the internship to be successful. Similarly, it seeks out schools and classrooms that embrace the basic values of the program. A teacher preparation program depends on the school to provide the atmosphere in which interns and student teachers alike can have a chance to practice the knowledge, standards, and values they are exposed to at the college. Ultimately, it is the context of the school that allows us to actualize our philosophy.

REFERENCES

Bolin, F. S., & Goodwin, A. L. (1995). The knowledge domains of teaching. In C. Richards (Ed.), *Dirktor (The Director) (Russian Journal for School Administrators)*, Moscow.

Bolin, F. S., & Goodwin, A. L. (1992, February). *Redefining teacher education: A model for comprehensive reform.* Paper presented at the annual meeting of the American Association of Colleges of Teacher Education, San Antonio, TX.

Dewey, J. (1929). *The sources of a science of education.* New York: Horace Liveright.

Glickman, C. (1981). *Developmental supervision: Alternative practices for helping teachers improve instruction.* Alexandria, VA: Association for Supervision and Curriculum Development.

Grant, C. A., & Secada, W. G. (1990). Preparing teachers for diversity. In W. R. Houston (Ed.), *Handbook of research on teacher education* (pp. 403–422). New York: Macmillan.

Lortie, D. (1975). *Schoolteacher: A sociological study.* Chicago: University of Chicago Press.

Mitchell, D. E., & Kerchner, C. T. (1987). Labor relations and teacher policy. In L. S. Schulman & G. Sykes (Eds.), *Handbook of teaching and policy* (pp. 214–238). New York: Longman.

Snyder, J. (1993). Perils and potentials: A tale of two professional development schools. In L. Darling-Hammond (Ed.), *Professional development schools: Schools for developing a profession* (pp. 98–125). New York: Teachers College Press.

State University of New York. (1992). *Amendments to the regulations of the Commissioner of Education,* Sections 207, 305 and 3004 of Education Law. Albany, NY: New York State Education Department.

Zumwalt, K. K. (1988). Are we undermining or improving teaching? In L. N. Tanner (Ed.), *Critical issues in curriculum: The eighty-seventh yearbook of the National Society for the Study of Education* (pp. 148–176). Chicago: University of Chicago Press.

CHAPTER 6

Elementary Teacher Education Program at University of California, Santa Barbara

Jon Snyder

Elementary teacher education at the University of California, Santa Barbara (UCSB) offers a combined master's–credential program serving approximately 45 candidates each year. The program requires three contiguous academic quarters and three summer quarters to complete. Since it is possible for candidates to complete two summer quarters in one 3-month period, many candidates complete the program in 13 months. Others return to UCSB to complete their master's degree during a summer session after they have been teaching full time for a year or more.

Program candidates tend to be high academic achievers as a result of a combination of rigorous standards for admission to a University of California graduate school and state content knowledge requirements for teachers. Recruitment efforts and fellowships for bilingual candidates as well as an admissions process that provides "value added" for life experiences make for a more diverse candidate cohort than typical in University of California graduate schools, but the cohort is still less diverse than the classrooms and schools in which candidates will serve.

The state of California offers three multiple subject credentials for elementary teachers: the traditional credential, the Cross-cultural Language and Academic Development Credential (CLAD), and the Bilingual Cross-cultural Language and Academic Development Credential (BCLAD). The base of the CLAD credential is the same as the traditional credential with a set of additional requirements designed to prepare teachers with the knowledge, skills, and dispositions to work effectively with the diverse linguistic and cultural populations that attend California's public schools. The base of the BCLAD credential is the CLAD credential with a set of additional requirements designed to prepare teachers with the knowledge, skills, and dispositions to work effectively in the primary language of children who are learning English as a second language. Candidates who meet UCSB requirements meet state requirements for the CLAD authorization. Historically, approximately 20% of UCSB elementary teaching candidates were preparing for bilingual teaching. In the past several years that number has dropped to approximately 10%. This reduction can be partially attributed to a state political context that abolished affirmative action, reduced social services (including education) for immigrants, and outlawed bilingual education in the schools. In addition, cohort demographics have been affected by the state's response to shortages of qualified teachers in certain subject areas and communities which allows over 30,000 people to enter the classroom as instructors of record without any preparation for the role. College graduates can receive a paying job as an instructor of record and have their teacher education expenses subsidized by the state. This serves as a disincentive to learn something about teaching prior to being responsible for the education of children.

The program works closely with seven partnership schools in the two districts that serve the local community. A group of educators representing the local districts, local schools, the teachers' union, and the teacher education program collaboratively developed the responsibilities of the partner schools and the university, as well as the criteria and process for selecting partnership schools. School-based educators from the partner schools helped design the program and continue to redesign it through multiple forums. School-based educators also participate in enrollment decisions, teach or coteach courses, and equally share the responsibility for recommending candidates for licensure. In addition, each partner school has one elementary teacher serving as a paid in-house coordinator, who is responsible for working with the on-site supervisor (a college-based educator) to coordinate the educational experiences for the cohort of candidates who spend the entire school year at their school site.

In this chapter, we will present three complementary perspectives from which to view the program:

- the values that guide the work;
- the state policy context as it relates to standards and assessments in preservice teacher education—and thus also guides the work;
- the programmatic structures that help candidates and faculty simultaneously to enact values and survive in an occasionally constraining and often less than coherent policy environment.

VALUES

Teacher education at UCSB is undergirded by a set of values. These values serve as guideposts for assessing what the program is attaining and what it wishes to attain. The values, distinctly progressive in nature, were first written in 1992 to provide a foundation for the creation of the partnership, the redesign of the program, and the development of a research agenda in teacher education. The impetus for the public statement came with the hiring of a new director of teacher education and from the university's desire to establish a research agenda and to create a recognizable niche in teacher education. The content of the values themselves had been a shared, if not explicit, basis for the program for several decades.

The school- and college-based educators who enact the program organize the values that guide its work in three categories: (1) learning in schools, (2) the preparation and support of teaching that will enable that learning, and (3) institutional accountability for the preparation and support of teaching. In the day-to-day activity, the three categories form a dynamic interaction and are ultimately indistinguishable. Together they become an explicit statement of the moral purpose of the program's endeavors.[1]

Learning in Schools

The teacher education program begins with a vision of children and families, the kinds of experiences students have in schools, and the kinds of teachers with whom they will work. The program wants all students (and their families) to be treated with trust and respect and provided with a nurturing educational environment. This vision requires teachers who:

- believe passionately that all students want to make sense of their world and have the capacity to do so;
- believe passionately that content—the knowledge, skills, and dispositions teachers have to share—will help their students make sense of their world;
- accept the responsibility to help students understand what the world means and to construct their own lives, because that is what learning is.

Preparation and Support of Teaching

To become teachers who embody this vision is a lifelong process. The goal of the program is thus, not to tell people how to teach, but to prepare them to learn from teaching (their own and others) so that they can, over time, become the teachers our children deserve and our communities require. While the program seeks to develop lifelong learners, it does not ignore its responsibility for the calibre of its graduates in their first year of teaching.

To prepare teachers who know how to learn from teaching, the program helps candidates construct knowledge, skills, and dispositions in six interrelated theme areas. It strives to weave these themes through every class, every experience, and every interaction that candidates have with the program. These themes are the following:

- *Autobiography/Philosophy of Education.* If teachers are to respect and understand how students make sense of the world, they have to understand and respect how they themselves make sense of the world and why.
- *Study of Children/Study of Schools.* To understand students and how they learn, teachers must be able to observe and communicate with them and to learn from those observations and interactions. Since most of a teacher's interactions with a student are in a school and the nature of that environment shapes the nature of those interactions, teachers must understand both the student and the school.
- *Methodological Competence.* Watching and respecting students is not sufficient. Teachers must also know how to help students learn, and that involves learning a repertoire of teaching skills and learning activities so that when they determine how to help a student, they can actually do so.
- *Diversity.* People have always been very different from each other. For many reasons there may be a greater sense today of the presence (if not always the value) of those differences than in the past. The essence of the diversity theme is to respect and understand students as individuals and as members of groups. The pedagogical component is captured by the paradox that to treat each child the same requires treating each child differently.
- *Collaboration.* There are definite limits to how much one can learn from teaching without intellectual and emotional support. Thus, teachers must be capable of working with other people if they are going to meet the needs of students or if they are going to continue to grow as teachers. Collaboration means acquiring and using the knowledge, skills, and dispositions required to be a member of multiple learning communities and involves working within schools and outside of schools to support their clients.
- *Reflection.* While collaboration is a requirement for growth, so too are those hard, personal looks at oneself. Reflection is believing in the importance of looking critically at oneself, the possession of skills that enables that process to happen, and the wisdom to change what one can to improve oneself.

Institutional Accountability

Members of the Santa Barbara partnership represent different institutions who share a common set of beliefs about what it means to support professional practice. The change is from a controlling, distrustful bureaucratic model of accountability to a professional accountability that seeks to enrich the capacities of people within the institution. Thus, the program attempts to grow and sustain institutional environments in which experienced educators embody, and neophyte educators are initiated into, the following four commitments:

- A primary commitment to our clients (children, their families, our student teachers)—not state, district, or institutional policies and regulations;
- Because our clients deserve the best, a commitment to use the best of existing knowledge and practice;
- Because knowledge and practice are not static, and permanent perfection unattainable, a constant commitment to create new knowledge and new practices to serve our clients and our profession better;
- Knowledge and practice do not work in schools; children and adults do. Therefore, a commitment to prepare people capable of providing the education all our children deserve and supporting those already in schools to continue to be so capable.

STATE POLICY CONTEXT— STANDARDS AND ASSESSMENTS

Perhaps the essential challenge of any teacher education endeavor is how to enact closer approximations of its values within the nested environments in which it conducts its work. These environments include the state, the university, communities, districts, schools, and classrooms. In this section we discuss several state environmental conditions that have pushed the program to consciously confront the challenge of enacting its values.

Over the past several years, the Santa Barbara program has had the opportunity to be involved in two statewide standards and assessment processes. Neither has significantly altered the program's core belief systems. Both have influenced the work of the program as well as making those belief systems more public. As a result, our values have become more open to scrutiny—from ourselves as well as from others.

The first of these processes chronologically was the adoption by the state of the California Standards for the Teaching Profession (CSTP). Over the course of 5 years, the state developed and then validated a description of the domains and elements of quality teaching. Given their point of origin within programs designed to support the development of beginning teachers and the professional and educative forums in which they were developed, the standards view teaching as contextual and complex and treat teachers as professionals.

In the CSTP process, the state engaged school- and college-based educators in the development of the standards and authentic assessments of those standards. Locally, partnership members were intricately involved in writing the new standards, conducting the validity study of those standards, and writing descriptive narratives of the standards at different levels of teacher development. In addition, the program used the new standards in its experimental program design and in its redesign of candidate assessment processes. What program personnel learned from their engagement in the effort, in turn, fed into the creation of new state standards for program review and for teacher assessments. The CSTP process contained an inherent reciprocity between state-level policymakers and professional educators. For instance, the state wanted a study of how the new standards could be used to support the re-creation of pre-service teacher education. The program wanted to use the new standards to reenact its values as well as to study its graduates. In exchange for a promise to conduct a systematic research study on its graduates, the state granted the program the right to build a program around its values (as embedded in state standards for the teaching profession) rather than around the traditional accreditation input standards. In effect, the CSTP development process followed the kind of professional model of accountability the program values. Thus, state and local interests and needs matched at both the values level and the pragmatic level.

As a result of this agreement with the state, UCSB redesigned its work to create a program where candidates and program faculty have multiple opportunities for learning, practicing, and assessing their development in the six domains of the CSTP. This includes opportunities for:

- reading about the standards including the theoretical frame and research base from which they are derived;
- experiencing learning strategies that model (at the appropriate skill and maturation level) the standards within their college classes;
- linking college course work with field experiences through assignments (i.e., lesson plans, literacy assessments, unit plans, child observations) that must be carried out in classrooms and supported by both school- and college-based educators;
- practicing the standards under the watchful eye of multiple professional educators in their field experiences;
- individually and collectively reflecting upon the standards and their growth towards meeting them in small supportive cohort groups.

The second state standards and assessments process, which took place in 1998, consisted of a legislative mandate without any input by, or influence from, professional educators. The legislation viewed teaching as mechanistic and teachers as subservient and compliant workers. The specific mandate regarded the explicit systematic teaching of phonics. In a highly charged, ideologically based debate, whole language was blamed for abysmal scores on standardized tests of reading ability. As a result, the legislature mandated the following specific content to be taught in all preservice teacher education programs:

> The study of organized, systematic, explicit skills including phonemic awareness; direct, systematic, explicit phonics; and decoding skills. For the purposes of this section, direct, systematic, explicit phonics means phonemic awareness, spelling patterns, the direct instruction of sound/symbol codes, practice in connected text, and the relationship of direct, systematic explicit phonics to [any other components of a reading program]. (Assembly Bill 3075)

The state used a five-year deliberative process with multiple opportunities for feedback from the public and the profession to develop the CSTP. In sharp contrast, the phonics policy changes were all in effect at the local level (school and college) in fewer than twelve months from the passage of the legislation. To assure speedy compliance, the State Board of Education made it illegal to use state funds for textbooks that were defined as literature based or to use state funds for staff developers who had ever been associated with whole language.

Based on a controlling, distrustful bureaucratic model of accountability consisting of a definition of outcomes and a standardized test as the single source of evidence of those outcomes, the phonics policy initiative process consisted of tightly coupling all state-level policy levers including:

- state standards for students and teachers,
- the use of state funds,
- state curriculum adoptions aligned with the legislative mandate,
- state accreditation reviews (including a session-by-session review of college courses, instructors, and texts),
- certification requirements (e.g., state certification now requires passing a standardized examination aligned with legislative mandates).

Because of the tight coupling of policy levers, the phonics initiative significantly impacted the classrooms where candidates are placed for field experiences—especially in districts that did not use the limited flexibility provided to them. One of the participating partnership districts interpreted the phonics initiative to mean that teachers had to follow a single basal text in the sequence and chronology outlined in the teacher's manual. Attempts by program candidates to be learner- and learning-centered professionals were viewed as an act of insubordination. The same was true when the program requested space for its candidates to exercise professional expertise in the service of their students. For instance, this particular district's definition of a lesson plan is the page from the teacher's manual whereas the program's definition includes collecting assessment data, how to use that information to adjust instruction immediately and in long-range planning, and reflections on how to improve the lesson in the future.

A third state policy change, the passage by the electorate of Proposition 227, June, 1998, did not directly address teacher education programs, but did drastically alter the classrooms in which candidates practice and assess their skills. Proposition 227 fundamentally banned bilingual programs and mandated a nebulously conceived pedagogical approach that the proposition entitled English Language Immersion. In this instance, candidates experience an environment where their program maintains the requirements for the BCLAD (the equivalent of a bilingual teaching license) while the school policy prohibits the use of the knowledge, skills, and dispositions learned in that program.

THE STRUCTURAL CONTEXT

In the midst of this turbulence, the program was still responsible to its candidates and to the students whom they would serve. In this section, we outline the structures by which the program attempts to simultaneously enact its values and meet state demands so that it can continue to remain open for business. A thorough rendering of the balancing act is beyond the scope of this chapter, but the following program description embeds brief narratives that link several of the structures to program values and provides examples of where the program and its candidates experience the conflict between their values and the policies surrounding them.

Admissions Criteria and Process

The program stipulates two sets of entry criteria: content knowledge criteria (established by state) and dispositional–experiential criteria (established by the program). Candidates meet content knowledge criteria prior to admission either by completing a state-approved sequence of courses or passing a state-approved standardized achievement test. The partnership developed the following dispositional–experiential criteria through a collaborative process with cooperating teachers:

- respect, understanding, and interest in children and adolescents (this is an inviolable criterion as the program believes such respect kindles the humanity that is the flame of the profession);
- presentation of self—enthusiasm, poise, articulateness, persuasiveness;
- knowledge of schools, experience with teaching;

- social presence and performance—listening skills, empathy, social appropriateness, cooperation;
- strength of convictions informed by ethical principles;
- cultural sensitivity— recognition and appreciation of differences due to cultural, linguistic, ethnic, socioeconomic, and gender diversity;
- quick and flexible thinking;
- knowledge of subject matter—content knowledge and pedagogical content knowledge.

In addition, the phonics initiative requires candidates to pass a standardized test of knowledge of linguistics and reading in order to receive a credential. Although not an admissions requirement as such, the potential to pass the examination plays a role in admissions because failure means not receiving a credential. As early as admissions decisions, then, program values come in conflict with state policy. The program's admissions standards, aligned with its values, often place the program in a position where it must choose between its values and state requirements. For instance, while the program values diverse life experiences, the passing rates on the state content and reading examinations mirror the disproportionate failure rates of candidates of color on nearly all standardized tests. From 1992 to 1997, 71.4% of white (non-Hispanic) candidates passed the elementary subject matter knowledge test on their first attempt while in the same time period 25.7% of African American candidates did so.

Students develop an admissions (showcase) portfolio consisting of documentation of meeting entry criteria (state and institutional) and potential to meet our exit criteria. This portfolio lays the groundwork for the admissions interview—a 3-hour process involving a combination of group and individual activities. Each interview panel includes school- and college-based teacher educators and current credential candidates.

PROFESSIONAL PREPARATION PROGRAM

Once admitted into the program all elementary candidates share a set of experiences and learning activities that occur over the course of one summer session and three contiguous academic quarters. A CLAD emphasis requires a second summer session. In addition, over 95% of elementary candidates complete requirements for a Master's in Education that involves a third summer. Thus, the basic UCSB program consists of three academic quarters and three summer sessions.

Summer One (August–Mid-September)

The official first summer session begins the first week in August. All summer session courses are cotaught by school- and college-based teacher educators.

Until public schools open, candidates attend classes on campus from 8:00–5:00 daily. Once public schools open, they are in classrooms daily. As is true of all of the program's course work, each of the summer courses has a direct link to program values. During this time period, candidates take four courses:

- Writing Project Approaches to Teaching Composition (to explore themselves and the world through writing);
- Seminar in Cross-cultural Education: Concepts and Theories (to begin to understand better their own cultures, cultural differences, and how those differences can play out constructively and/or destructively in classrooms and schools);
- Issues in Human Development (to understand children);
- Ethnography (to learn how to collect information that sheds light on children and schools).

Fall Quarter

Field experiences and supervision. Candidates join the school communities on the first teacher duty day of the school year and are included in whatever professional development activities the schools or districts provide for experienced teachers. Prior to the beginning of college courses in late September, candidates spend the entire day in public school classrooms. From the start of college courses until the public school's winter break, candidates are in their classroom placements from the beginning of the school day through lunch. The course schedule provides one afternoon a week for candidates to plan with their cooperating teachers. Completion of this fall field experience requires a successful four-morning takeover where they are responsible for the full school program.

Candidates have two placements over the course of the year—one in a primary and one in an intermediate classroom. The program places candidates in classrooms where they have to consciously plan, implement, and adjust instruction based upon differences in language, gender, socioeconomic status, cultural and ethnic backgrounds, and learning and behavioral challenges. All candidates have at least one placement in classrooms with second-language learners. Until the passage of Proposition 227, which fundamentally banned bilingual education, bilingual candidates had one placement in a bilingual classroom where content instruction occurred in the students' primary language.

Candidates are placed in supervisory cohort groups. Cohort members remain together as a group at a single site throughout the entire school year. The cohort meets weekly for a 3-hour seminar on professional issues. The seminars are collaboratively planned and enacted by college- and school-based teacher educators. Issues that arise include lesson planning, assessment, and other pedagogically focused material as well as ongoing work with child and school studies. These seminars provide students with regular facilitated opportunities to reflect on teaching and learning as well as to test theory in practice and practice in theory in a collaborative setting.

Course work. Candidates take six courses during the fall term: (1) Reading/Language Arts; (2) Psychological Foundations of Education in the Elementary School; (3) Multicultural, Social, and Linguistic Factors in Teaching ESL; (4) Teaching Strategies: Bilingual Cross-cultural Education; (5) Computers in Education; (6) Professional Credential Seminar—Introduction to Exceptional Children. Professional credential candidates from elementary, secondary, administrative, and school psychology programs take the professional credential seminar in which they work in mixed cohort groups on school-based problems. Other students take a more traditional, yet still problem-based, special education course.

Though they do not appear as courses in the fall, candidates are introduced to methods and procedures in math, social sciences, and science. In both fall and winter terms, candidates have single-discipline-oriented models and procedures sessions as well as integrated sessions. They also participate in courses that provide learning experiences in domain-specific pedagogical content knowledge as well as integrated pedagogical content knowledge. As the partnership studied itself, it discovered that in order to integrate instruction, candidates needed background knowledge, skills, and dispositions in each of the disciplines. Thus, in the fall, the emphasis is on content-specific pedagogical knowledge. In the winter, the emphasis in on integrated pedagogical content knowledge.

Winter Term

Field Experiences and Supervision in the winter term follow the same process as in the fall. January is primarily a college-based month. Communication among student teachers, partner schools, and cooperating teachers takes place in two forums: (1) through a school service project (part of the social foundations course) and (2) in assigned individual discussions between student and cooperating teacher to facilitate the mesh between methods and procedures and placements. For instance, students must develop an integrated curriculum unit in collaboration with their cooperating teachers. In February and March students return to the fall model, spending mornings in public school classrooms and afternoons and evenings at the university.

Course work. Candidates take seven courses during the winter term: (1) teaching strategies: Bilingual Cross-cultural Education (required for bilingual candidates only), (2) Reading/Language Arts, (3) Math Procedures, (4) Social Science Procedures, (5) Science Procedures, (6) Multicultural, Social, and Linguistic Factors in Teaching ESL, and (7) Social Foundations of Education.

The social foundations course is comparable to traditional courses with inclusion of a site-based school service project as an assignment for the course.

The goals of the school service project are to help candidates develop leadership skills, to learn about school change and the role of the teacher within school change, to become more fully participating members of the school community, and to support the changes the schools are making.

All methods and procedures courses are integrated during the winter term. The five instructors (along with the computer education instructor) coplan and coteach the activities. In this way, candidates have the opportunity to learn how to plan and enact integrated lessons and units. In addition, the program is able to mesh reading, language arts, and second-language-learner issues (i.e., English Language Development, Specially Designed Academic Instruction in English) into all methods and procedures courses. Each week also contains studio time when candidates develop integrated curriculum units with instructors and supervisors available for consultation.

Spring Term

In the same classroom as during the winter, candidates spend all day every day in public schools. With a reduced course load, candidates become full members of the school community in which they student teach. Completion of this experience requires a successful two-week takeover of the classroom. During the spring, the content of the weekly Professional Seminar becomes more site-specific and more student-specific as the candidates explore their own passions; this will ultimately lead to their M.Ed. portfolio project. The only course that candidates take during the spring term is Teaching Strategies: Bilingual Cross-cultural Education.

The student takeover provides a specific example of the challenge of enacting one's values in a policy context that does not share those values. These preservice teachers find themselves in a program caught in the middle of competing state policies. The culminating assignment for the courses that constitute integrated studies is to teach and then assess the effectiveness of the integrated curriculum unit developed during the winter term. From the perspective of the program, this assignment aligns with its values and with its accreditation arrangements with the state. High-ranking district officials, however, believe this assignment lets candidates do whatever they wish in district classrooms and flies in the face of district policy that stipulates that teachers spend a precise number of minutes each day following basal text manuals, which do not on the whole tend to support integrated curriculum units. As in any partnership of parity, both parties have options. In this instance, they can either dissolve the partnership or choose to negotiate.

Due in large part to the trust and respect of school-based educators which has developed over the previous decade, the teacher education program would rather not dissolve the partnership and start all over in another district. On the other hand, the program would clearly rather not deprive candidates of the learning opportunities they need in order to develop into the kinds of teachers all children deserve. So school-based educators are banking their minutes-per-basal-text to allow candidates the time needed to teach the integrated curriculum. And candidates are attempting to balance their own values, their credential requirements, and their desire to be hired in the district.

Postpreparation Summer Sessions (June–July)

In the first summer following the professional preparation year, candidates have the option of completing their CLAD requirements or their master's requirements. The CLAD requirements consist of two courses: Linguistics for Teachers and Seminar in Language, Culture, and Literacy. The master's requirement is to complete the M.Ed. portfolio outlined briefly in the following section. Whichever set of requirements candidates do not complete in the first postsummer, they may complete in a subsequent summer. Once candidates discovered it was possible, if not conceptually advisable, to do so, a large majority began taking the two CLAD courses in the summer prior to their professional preparation year.

The Portfolios

In addition to the experiences outlined above, the program uses two portfolio processes as key integrative learning, assessment, and evaluation activities—the Credential Portfolio and the Master's Portfolio. The Credential Portfolio is a key element of the program's accreditation agreement with the state and is based upon the California Standards for the Teaching Profession (CSTP).

The credential portfolio. For this portfolio, candidates collect artifacts, primarily from their professional preparation year, documenting their growth over time in each of the six domains of the CSTP. They have ongoing opportunities to share their emerging portfolio contents weekly in supervisory seminar groups (from September through June) as well as in October at their first 3-way meeting with their cooperating teacher and supervisor; in December at the end of their student teaching placement in a second 3-way conference; in late January as an introduction to their second student teaching placement, again in a 3-way conference; and in a summative evaluative format in June, once again in a 3-way conference.

In the final presentation in June, the cooperating teacher, college-based supervisor, and the student sign off to verify that all agree that the collection of artifacts provides compelling evidence that the candidate has met all state outcome standards. Thus, the purpose of the credential portfolio is fundamentally accountability—assessing the knowledge, skills, and dispositions possessed by candidates in order to assure the state (and the program) that they are capable of working with children and their families in a responsible and responsive manner.

Briefly, the credential portfolio embeds three essential conceptual assumptions. First is the notion of multiple sources of evidence. Candidates must include test and test-like events, observations, and samples of performance or work. The second assumption is that accurate information for assessment purposes requires that data be collected over time. The development of a candidate's work, as well as the candidate's thinking about that work, is charted and reflected upon throughout the course of a candidate's professional preparation. The third conceptual assumption embedded in the matrix is that it is appropriate to use externally defined categories (e.g., state standards) as the criteria of good teaching. The program adopted the standards used for licensure in California, the state to which it is held accountable. The program decided, not without rambunctious debate, that these standards provide articulate learning outcomes for teachers and credential candidates and are therefore appropriate for use as the bases for the credential portfolios. In addition, the program felt it fair to candidates to let them know in advance the criteria by which they would be evaluated. Thus, within the first week of courses, candidates receive the state's written explanation of the standards and engage in activities designed to help them construct their own understandings of those standards.

The M.Ed. Portfolio. This portfolio is a candidate-driven inquiry developed over the course of at least eleven months.[2] During the August ethnography course, candidates begin developing their ability to collect data in natural settings. By December, most candidates have identified an inchoate passion about some element of teaching and learning. Through a series of workshops and field-based experiences, they refine and focus their questions, moving between questioning and reflecting upon the concrete artifacts they have been collecting in their field experiences and in their course work. The data they collect may include articles from the research literature and other readings on the topic, analyses they have conducted through research papers and through data collected in their school or classroom, reflections on observed events that bear on the topic, and examples of their own teaching efforts and outcomes that bear upon the topic.

By March students form self-selected support groups and are assigned a facilitator. These support groups meet regularly so that members can inform one another of their thinking and practice regarding their issue along with the evidence they have selected to document the outcomes of their inquiry and their learning and growth over time. These conversations, like those that accompany the construction of the credential portfolios, provide multiple perspectives on the topic, raise new questions, and provoke deeper thinking. In the summer (June–July) following their full-time student teaching experience, they complete the M.Ed. Portfolio.[3]

Successful completion of the M.Ed. portfolio involves two checkpoints. First, the group facilitator and every student member of the group must give his or her approval to the document. Once approved by the group, students schedule a public conversation where they receive feedback on their portfolio from five critical friends. Candidates select their critical friends to include a school-based educator who knows the candidate well (i.e., a cooperating teacher), a school-based educator who does not know the candidate well (i.e., a principal or another teacher), a university-based educator who knows the candidate well (i.e., the supervisor), a university-based educator who does not know the candidate well (i.e., a content expert or researcher), and someone whose primary intersection with the school is as a parent or as a school board member or a social service professional in the community.

Several of these public conversations occur simultaneously in a large room, somewhat like a poster session for the American Educational Research Association. Critical Friends arrive prior to the session and review the entire document without the candidate present. The conference then is not a 2-hour presentation of the work, but rather a 2-hour conversation among professional educators about a topic of mutual concern in teaching and learning.

One goal of the inquiry and its assessment is to develop and evaluate skills of investigation and analysis. In addition, the project is structured to encourage moving between levels of abstractions—using theory to inform practice and practice to inform theory. Finally, the process of evaluation is organized to ensure multiple perspectives on the question, including those of parents or community members, and feedback from various sources. The goal is the development of a professional educator who has tools to inquire into and address problems of practice throughout his or her career.

NOTES

1. Though too lengthy to be presented in this chapter, for each category the program has articulated a set of action principles that it believes must be followed in daily decisions and interactions to support closer approximations of its values.

2. This discussion draws upon Snyder, Lippincott, and Bower (1998).

3. Some students postpone completion of the M.Ed. portfolio, electing to give themselves another year in the belief that additional experience and reflection will enrich their portfolio, their teaching, and their students' learning. The program holds a series of Saturday workshops through the subsequent year to support the growth of these students. Despite the logistical problems and the unpaid time and labor demanded by this model, it remains the preferred choice of the program faculty who work with these first-year teachers.

CHAPTER 7

What We Learned From Site Visits

Jon Snyder, A. Lin Goodwin, Sarah Jacobs, Ann Lippincott, Tanya Sheetz, Anne Sabatini, Alexandria T. Lawrence, and Karen Siegel-Smith

As the dyad team observed, thought together, and interacted over the course of the three years of the Leading Edge Project, we were struck by the different contexts in which our work is embedded. We witnessed the results of three different policy mechanisms for deciding what teachers need to know and be able to do (standards) and of different structures and processes for assessing teacher candidates' abilities to meet those standards. The University of California, Santa Barbara (UCSB), operated within two such policy structures: the California Standards for the Teaching Profession (CSTP) and the Reading Initiative. Teachers College (TC) was guided by one longstanding state policy—a relatively accommodating and flexible state program-approval process. Perhaps not at all surprisingly, we found that who decides, and how, what a teacher should know and be able to do influences the shape of learning opportunities

The dyad team consisted of school-based and university-based educators from both sides. The UCSB members included Tanya Sheetz, a classroom teacher, Pat Morales, an elementary school principal, and college-based teacher educators Ann Lippincott, Sarah Jacobs, and Jon Snyder. The TC members were Karen Siegel-Smith and Robyn Ulzheimer, both of whom were serving as clinical faculty with the TC Preservice Program in Childhood Education and as classroom teachers at PS 87, the TC PDS, and Martha Erickson, Anne Sabatini, A. Lin Goodwin, and Alexandria T. Lawrence, all instructors in the Preservice Program.

for teacher candidates and thus what beginning teachers actually do know and can accomplish.

We divide the rest of this chapter into three sections. In the first two sections we offer vignettes of practice from the perspective of three distinct policy contexts in order to show the varying teacher education experiences that can result from different guiding principles. In the third section, with the three policy contexts as a backdrop, we discuss key issues that influence the nature of learning opportunities for teacher candidates, the inherent dilemmas that naturally arise in the professional education of teachers, and explore how these issues and dilemmas play out differently within each of the policy arenas we identified.

PART ONE: SITE VISITS AT TC AND PS 87

The Search

> Dear Karen and Martha—
>   Although today was hard, I'm looking forward to tomorrow and the little moments with individual students that remind me to think of the whole experience and all of the dimensions of our class. Martha, you wrote about how I might think of learning from the students, and Karen, you also reminded me to see the kids as resources. Thank you. They really have been my teachers in this experience.
>
> —Eleanor (Intern Journal, June 13)

We Santa Barbarans[1] went to New York City in search of teaching standards. Rather than look at the Preservice Program in Childhood Education in its entirety, we had been asked to focus our search on the five participants in the TC/PS 87 Intern Program. These participants are not teachers of record, but rather are a subset of TC teacher education candidates who stay longer, assume greater teaching responsibilities, and have a more tightly coupled student teaching experience at PS 87. By coming to know these interns as beginning professionals, we hoped to see if—and if so, how—a focus on standards and assessment had influenced their preparation. Our three research questions were What standards are there? What are the opportunities for learning, practicing, and assessing development in the standards? What professional development opportunities are there for teacher educators?

Our first data collection trip was in the spring of 1997. Martha, the Leading Edge point person for TC, met us at our hotel upon arrival. Her warm hug was followed by presenting us with a canvas bag bulging with stuff she said would provide context for our experiences over the next few days. Most compelling to us was a stack of three-way dialogue journals kept between interns, cooperating teachers, and Martha, who served as supervisor to interns during their extended time in classrooms. The interns wrote in the journal daily, reflecting on their classroom experiences and responding to observation notes and questions posed by Martha and their cooperating teachers. From issues and challenges highlighted by interns themselves, to three-way problem-solving conversations, the journals authentically documented the interns' initiative and growth. They also made visible the awesome challenge both neophyte and mentor teachers undertake in striving toward deliberative practice. As we finished our reading, we looked forward to meeting the people behind the words, but were left with more questions than answers, particularly in relation to our standards search. Nowhere in the journals, or in any of the other artifacts, was explicit reference made to teaching standards.

Our first face-to-face encounter with the TC/PS 87 partners took place at the Shining Star Breakfast Diner. Seated around the long table were the Preservice Program codirectors, two college supervisors, the coordinator of teaching seminars conducted on site at PS 87, the two clinical faculty members and several cooperating teachers. Meeting with this group for the first time, we Santa Barbarans were struck by the enthusiastic energy of the professional conversation. Players at all levels were engaged participants. As the time for school to begin drew near, Martha gave us an observation schedule and a list of people to interview. Together we walked the block to PS 87.

Over the next several days, we spent significant chunks of time documenting the interns in action. They opened their classrooms to us saying they were used to "being under the microscope." In follow-up discussions, they eagerly shared educational philosophies and thinking. Knowing that the 10 Interstate New Teacher Assessment and Support Consortium (INTASC) standards were being considered for use in New York State licensure, we looked at our collective observation and conversation data in relation to them. We found convincing evidence for entry-level competence in each of the 10 INTASC categories, and we wondered about the role these standards may have played in supporting the interns' development. We also conducted individual interviews with members of the TC/PS 87 partnership and held a roundtable with interns. The New York team had provided us with an interview protocol designed to facilitate formative assessment of the intern program. We added a question about the INTASC standards to the protocol.

Responses to the standards question varied. Martha and the clinical faculty spoke of contact with the INTASC standards through a Leading Edge meeting where they had toyed with ideas for using them to assess the internship. One cooperating teacher told us that she and a colleague from the college were redesigning the TC student teaching evaluation form using the INTASC standards as their rubric. The rest of the cooperating teachers and all of the interns claimed never to have heard of them. One of the program codirectors, Lin, told us that she was actually participating in the development of new teacher tests driven by the INTASC Standards. She highlighted the fact that in New York State, and nationally, TC is a reputable educational institution. As a result of this stature, TC faculty are often invited to add their voice in relation to public initiatives. Her counterpart, Fran, began her response to the question with, "We are supportive of the standards at a policy level, but we are also not afraid of raising questions about whose purposes they serve and who benefits." She went on to say that the values underlying the INTASC standards were consistent with program values; however, she and her partner had designed their program, which was "sensitive to the primary goals of teacher preparation," long before the emergence of INTASC. She said:

> I wouldn't want to pretend that our program didn't have standards, they just aren't the INTASC Standards. Our programmatic standards are articulated by the five domains of knowledge of teaching: personal, contextual, pedagogical, sociological, and organizational. These knowledge domains play along with two themes—teacher leadership and cultural diversity—which interlace throughout the program.

The interview with Fran enlightened and advanced our standards search. Her remarks discredited our hunch that INTASC had directly influenced the interns' professional preparation. She also helped us to see that issues of language had obscured our search. At TC, the faculty spoke of underlying values rather than standards. However, using the language of standards, Fran had identified as TC program standards five domains of knowledge: personal, contextual, pedagogical, sociological, and organizational. We came to see that whether called "standards" or "values," both terms represented a conceptual framework for the program's beliefs about what teachers should know and be able to do.

After learning of TC's knowledge domains, we found two program documents that made explicit the essential role played by these standards. We found the first within a folder given to cooperating teachers—a one-page graphic organizer that defined the five knowledge domains, aligned them with student teaching assignments and activities, and outlined their practical applications. The second document was the syllabus for the spring Preservice Seminar. The preface articulated the role the knowledge domains, or knowledge standards, played in shaping college course work:

> In keeping with the goals of the Preservice Program to build teacher leadership through linking the domains of knowledge, we will integrate what we have learned throughout the year through completing culminating projects and presentations.

The syllabus preface made visible another set of program standards. Across the year, all preservice experiences were filtered through the lens of three questions:

During the fall term we explored the following questions: What do children need? How do we know what children need (and by whose authority do we derive that knowledge)? How do we organize to address children's needs in the classroom? In attempting to answer those questions as individuals and within groups, we examined such topics as child development, lesson planning, management, organizing the learning environment, and understanding classroom and school communities.

The interns' ongoing investigation of these questions necessitated a child-centered approach to teaching. Nested within the knowledge domains, these three questions do not define a rubric for teacher knowledge and practice, but rather serve to inculcate an underlying set of values about teaching and learning.

We went to New York in search of teaching standards and had to look beyond surface features and issues of language to find them. Like the veteran teacher whose deftness makes her job look simple, the TC standards were so deeply embedded in program structures that they were invisible to the uninitiated eye. But they were there, two sets of them. The three questions embodied a values-based set of standards. The five domains represented a complementary set of knowledge-based standards.

They All Say the Same Thing

Once the dual program standards were identified, we moved forward in documenting their impact on the interns' preparation. This became the focus of our second documentation year, September 1997 through July 1998. The INTASC standards provided a vehicle for this documentation.

Martha and the clinical faculty's "toying around" with the INTASC standards as a tool for evaluating the interns' program eventually matured into an interview questionnaire. The questionnaire, administered to interns in November, consisted of a series of ten questions based on the ten INTASC standards. Interviewed individually by cooperating teachers other than those with whom they were working, interns were prompted to ground their responses in educational philosophy and classroom experience.

Martha transcribed audiotapes of the interviews and collated the data, removing names. She gave a copy of this summary to each intern and cooperating teacher and sent a copy to Santa Barbara. Our perusal of the collated responses confirmed the match Fran had indicated between program values and those underlying the INTASC standards. It also provided evidence from verbal sources that the interns met both program and INTASC standards. But we had expected these outcomes. What jumped out from the data was a marked consistency in the language of the interns' responses.

Our next visit to New York coincided with discussions of the INTASC questionnaire results. In meetings with both cooperating teachers and interns, we heard that they had also noted consistency across responses. Robyn, a cooperating teacher, noted:

> When I went through the collection I couldn't believe the glaring similarities. I thought to myself, "The brainwashing at Teachers College is coming through." In answering question number 1, which asked about making content matter meaningful to students, almost every one of the interns talked about building on student interest. They all mentioned the student directly: "How this relates to whom I am teaching." In the second question, about how knowledge of child development supported planning, they all referred back to "What do I know about these kids? How can my own life experience and knowledge of child development help me design curriculum accessible to students?" In answering the question about taking the needs of diverse learners into consideration, they all identified the variety of learners and learning styles within their classrooms, and said that they had to look at things through different approaches.

Robyn's analysis revealed evidence that TC's values standards were indeed guiding the interns, as all of their responses addressed the three questions: What do children need? How do we know what children need? How do we organize to address children's needs in the classroom?

She went on to make a connection between the experiential grounding of the interns' responses and their TC program:

> I wonder how much of their answers play from the TC course work? They do cooperative learning in the Models of Teaching class, and they are required to teach a cooperative learning lesson. I think they referred to those strategies because they were comfortable with them.

An additional read-through of the fall preservice syllabus confirmed Robyn's hypothesis; there was a match between the practical examples the interns used to anchor their responses and the knowledge and experience derived through course work.

In response to Robyn's comments about TC's influence on the interns, the college-based supervisor, Martha, credited the field placement: "What is so cool is that you started by saying this is TC's influence on them, and I was thinking just the opposite. I'm reading all of this and thinking this is your [Robyn's] influence on them." In the interns' analysis of the collated data they also noted similarities, and several mentioned what they referred to as "the TC talk." One said:

> I was surprised by the similarities in our answers, and that I agreed with what other people said. I don't know if the PDS experience has made us learn this,

or if it's because we are a pre-selected group. I felt like I had heard all of the questions and answers before. I knew what to say. I think we learned to talk a talk at TC.

Bottom line: the collated responses to the INTASC questionnaire revealed that interns had adopted language consistent with the TC standards.

Structured Opportunities for Reflection

During the 1997–98 school year we explored the second question driving our inquiry: What opportunities do TC interns have to learn, practice, and assess standards? The graphic organizer of the knowledge domains and the fall and spring preservice syllabi articulated a set of structures and processes in place at TC and PS 87 designed to integrate program standards into the work of interns. We used a case study approach to help us understand how these structures and processes were operationalized during the interns' experience. At Martha's suggestion, we documented the work of one intern, Cara. Toward the end of the year, we asked Cara to send us copies of preservice assignments she felt had contributed to her professional growth. The hefty package of papers we received cost $7.49 in postage. The contents revealed a series of structured opportunities for reflection.

A paper titled "Taking Stock" became our telling case; it was a reflection upon her entire body of work within the fall semester. In this one document we found evidence for all five knowledge standards, as well as the values standards. Her introduction to the paper began:

> This portfolio is the culmination of my written work during my first experience in an elementary school classroom as a student teacher. This collection has been arranged to illustrate my growth within the classrooms of PS 87 and those at Teachers College. These writings challenged me to respond to public critique of education and use my own ideas and experiences to develop my opinions. These papers guided me through an examination of the environment where I taught and the effects of these surroundings on the students in my class.

Here Cara acknowledged the importance of the course assignments, which were integrally linked to her field experiences. She gave evidence for her understanding of the contextual, organizational, and sociological knowledge standards of teaching. Later in Taking Stock, she referred to an assignment that addressed the personal knowledge standard: "My autobiography illustrates the events of my past which have been pulled into focus under the lens of education."

The pedagogical knowledge standard was taken up when she wrote about her lesson plans, the journals she was asked to keep, and interactions with her supervisors and cooperating teachers. In this document, Cara also talked about another assignment, the child study project, for which she observed one student over time, assessing her academic, social, and emotional needs. This project explicitly addressed the program's values standards. In the conclusion to Taking Stock, Cara summed up her fall experience, putting the dual program standards in a nutshell:

> As a whole, the fall written assignments allowed me to explore and express my thoughts surrounding education: starting with an intense look at one child, opening the discussion to the learning environment within the individual classroom, then broadening the boundaries of learning to take advantage of the community at large.

In addition to Cara's own writing, structured opportunities for reflection came in the form of feedback she received, which further supported her professional development in relation to program standards. Stapled to the back of Cara's Taking Stock was a xeroxed two-sided sheet titled "Reflections on Teacher and Teaching," covered with handwritten feedback on the various components of her fall student teaching portfolio. The comments had been written by Cara's reader, Celia. In response to one of Cara's papers, "Critique of a Teaching Episode," Celia affirmed Cara's use of the three-question lens: "Your decision to focus on a child and your emotional connection to her whole person speaks volumes about your belief in the teacher's role in the classroom." In reviewing the papers Cara had sent us, we found written comments on all of them, penned in a variety of hands including that of Celia, peers, cooperating teachers, supervisors, and other instructors. Much of the feedback came in the form of questions and suggested readings related to the teaching issues Cara was addressing.

A third opportunity for structured reflection was identified by the interns who talked about how much they had learned from their cooperating teachers and supervisors. Cara said: "I get a lot out of the conversations we have after an observation. My teaching mentors always let me take the lead, but also ask probing questions, and push me to come up with my own solutions." In a postobservation conference with Martha in November, after a lesson she described as "my worst teaching experience ever," Cara said, "What do I think that I did well? Other than not fall apart? I learned I can reflect on my teaching and identify what I did wrong. That's positive. I can figure out what I need to work on."

As Cara talked through her lesson, she addressed the values standard, "How do we know what children need?" She based her judgments on her knowledge of the children in her classroom and how they typically respond to questions.

Only three of them were raising their hands, which is atypical. I've been in there enough to know at what time in the lesson kids are going to start raising their hands, and that didn't happen. That was a cue, too, but I just couldn't step back and figure out what to do. . . . So I went on.

Martha then posed questions with the intent to push Cara's thinking and cause her to apply what she was learning at the college to her work in the field placement. She asked, "What might you do in the future, if you found yourself being that directive—doing all the talking?" and "What are strategies that give children ownership?" Embedded in Martha's questions were the values standards as well as the pedagogical knowledge standards. After being prompted by Martha, Cara continued by suggesting remedies for what had gone wrong in her lesson:

I could pass the lesson back to them, have them act out the steps, let them lead it. I could work from their ideas rather than putting out mine. The kids could make up problems in cooperative groups and then swap with each other. And in some of the examples they could be involved in acting out the problems.

Here she addressed the questions, "What do children need?" and "How do we organize to address children's needs in the classroom?" As early as the first field placement in the fall, Cara's thinking was being shaped by the questions asked of her. The lasting influence was evident toward the end of her spring field placement when she reflected on another lesson, saying, "I feel like I'm getting better at looking at the needs of individual children and figuring out the best approach for each." Consistent in her teaching was a reliance upon the knowledge, skills, and dispositions developed through the program.

In addition to asking questions to guide Cara's reflective thinking, Martha also used feedback as a way to reinforce program standards. After observing a letter-writing lesson, Martha wrote in Cara's three-way journal:

You have such a gentle manner with the kids. It's clear that you understand each one, and know how to reach out to each one in a way that causes them to want to respond. You focus them on the task at hand. You guide them to stretch. You help them take small steps so each is successful. Watching you deal with Galen was instructive. Never did you label him in a negative way. He was having a hard time, but was still an okay person. That's so hard to do and so important.

Martha's journal entry gave evidence of Cara's ability to teach in a manner consistent with the program's values standards and knowledge standards. Cara had grown a lot in the seven months since the postobservation conference concerning her self-described "worst teaching experience." She was stepping up to the pedagogical challenges that had stymied her earlier.

In looking at all of our data, we began to see that program experiences provided interns with both opportunities and obligations to integrate their learning through decision making, experimentation, and reflection. Our documentation showed how all three processes were modeled for interns in multiple contexts. College-based and school-based teacher educators acted in ways that were consistent with the philosophy of the teacher education program, by teaching the interns to think and act in particular ways, and by modeling their own professional interactions.

Our observations of a weekly faculty meeting illustrated how integral the standards were in the practices of teacher educators in this program. At the meeting were the two codirectors, several college-based instructors, as well as the two clinical faculty members (who are also cooperating teachers at PS 87). Teacher education partners discussed the past week's core course session and planned for the next week. Guiding the meeting agenda were the program values represented by the three questions: What do students in the teacher education program need? How do we know what they need? How do we organize program structures to address their needs? Grounding their interaction in assessment of students' participation, the faculty reflected and proposed adjustments, and they discussed individual students and how to provide appropriate support to meet their particular needs.

Observations and conversations with Cara's intern cohort showed all to be meeting program standards and to be capable beginning professionals. We could see how the alignment between program standards and assignments had helped to facilitate the development of this capacity. We began to look for other matches.

A Match Made in . . .

At the end of the 1997–98 preparation year, we asked several of the interns to talk about their philosophies of education and how they had changed over the year. For the most part, they talked about how they had entered the program with a philosophy already attuned to the program philosophy. They credited the teacher education program with giving them language tools and teaching tools that matched their philosophies. As one intern articulated:

> When I sat down to write my philosophy of education for my master's project, I realized I had already written it when I wrote my autobiography before the program started . . . I've definitely learned . . . I have names for things now, like cooperative learning and child-centered classroom. But my views about teaching were pretty much there before I came.

Another match, this one between TC and PS 87, emerged when we asked Cara and her teacher education partners to articulate their notions of what constituted good teaching. Cara said that good teachers were observant and aware of their students, created a safe and comfortable learning environment for children, made connections between the curriculum and children's daily lives, made students feel in control of their education, worked collaboratively with colleagues, and were innovative, resourceful, reflective, and passionate lifelong learners. When we asked the same question of the professional educators with whom she worked (cooperating teachers, site administrator, and college supervisor), each expressed more than half of the ideas contained in Cara's definition. All definitions were consistent with the standards of the program. One of the program codirectors, when asked the same question, provided a more global framing: "I hope teachers exit this program not with how-to's, but with tools for invention; with the ability to study a situation and make more, rather than less, appropriate decisions." Across the data was evidence that Cara, in fact, did not perceive teaching to be a series of how-to's. Rather, she was thinking through and reflecting upon her work with children.

In summary. Looking for answers to our research questions, we discovered that the TC program was driven by a dual set of standards. We learned that these standards were embedded in the work of the interns through an aligned set of assignments and activities. Influencing the interns' experience was a three-way match between the values underlying program standards, the philosophies of education with which interns entered the program, and the philosophies of education held by PS 87 partners. Our exploration of these matches led us to a complementary two-way flow of influence between interns and their educators, the college and PS 87, and colleagues within PS 87 and the preservice seminar faculty at TC. We went to New York in search of teaching standards and found them rooted in structured opportunities for reflection enhanced by the multiple matches of philosophy among and between college-based faculty, school-based teacher educators, and the candidates.

Questions

Our data and analysis clearly document that the interns from the TC Preservice Program placed at PS 87 experience a theoretically and logistically coherent set of opportunities for learning that support their development as exemplary beginning professionals. Our work, however, does raise several questions regarding the TC program as well as the state policy context in which it evolved.

We have two sets of questions for the program. First, what of the non-intern candidates who are not afforded extra time in the classrooms of a carefully matched school and exquisitely prepared and supported cooperating teachers? From the TC program's experience with the internship, what lessons have been learned that can support program-wide improvement? What lessons for other teacher education programs can be learned? The second set of questions regards the linkages between the preservice seminar block (including the PS 87 intern experience) and the other opportunities for learning in the TC Program. We were simultaneously struck, for instance, by the overwhelming number of times interns referred to their learnings from the preservice seminar block and conversely by the very few times interns referred to other elements of the TC Program. Why was this so? Might there be communication and coordination efforts that would build greater complementarity and cohesion that would enhance even more the knowledge, skills, and dispositions of the interns?

We also have two sets of questions about the nature of the relationship between the program and the state. To this point it appeared to us that the nature of the relationship was more TC communicating with the state than the state communicating with TC. That is, because of the combination of the professional status and expertise of TC (not to mention the caliber of their graduates) and the flexibility of the state's program-approval process, TC is granted generous leeway in defining and enacting their vision of the teaching professional within the parameters of state requirements. Yet, in today's climate where standards for teachers and teacher education are suddenly the favorite political strategy of officeholders across the country, might this generosity be withdrawn? How would this affect the TC program? Might it result in greater permeability between state and program to the benefit of both TC and the rest of the state? Or might it severely constrain the professional autonomy of the program?

At the heart of this second set of questions is the nature of public education in a democracy. Frankly, as teacher educators, we think we should be allowed to define our own standards and assessments. Still, in the case of TC, their graduates are not just receiving a degree from a private institution, they are receiving a license to practice in the public schools. A lawyer, for instance, receives a degree from a law school, but must pass a state examination to practice law. The comparison breaks down on a number of levels, but the core issue of a state's legal and ethical responsibility to the children it compels to attend schools remains. Just as there will always be differences of caliber among doctors and lawyers, so will there always be differences among teachers. Some of those differences may result from the quality of opportunities for learning provided by their educating institution. Regardless, it is the state, not the institution, which licenses teachers. How does a state balance granting institutions appropriate professional discretion with its legal mandate and ethical responsibilities to assure children the teachers they deserve? How does it do so in a way that raises the floor without hindering programs, like TC's, that are constantly creating higher ceilings?

> I am glad it was not easy. Somehow it wouldn't have been such an initiation had it been easy. (Michelle, Intern Journal, June 14)

PART TWO: VIGNETTES FROM UNIVERSITY OF CALIFORNIA, SANTA BARBARA

Julia's Box

In July, 1997, we[2] made our first documentation trip to Santa Barbara, in an effort to familiarize ourselves with the Teacher Education Program at UCSB. Arrangements had been made for us to meet with Julia, a graduate from the program who had just completed her first year of teaching. Julia began by describing the path she took to become a teacher. She related that she had received an M.S. degree in marine biology, inspired by "an incredible tenth grade biology teacher, Miss Bauske." During graduate school, Julia worked as a volunteer in local public schools, teaching children about tide pools. She continued:

> Rather than going on to get my Ph.D. in Marine Biology, I finished my master's degree and took a job as an instructional aide in a bilingual third grade classroom. The class was composed of children from both English-and Spanish-speaking homes, and the teacher was unlike any in my experience. My mother is Chilean and my father is American, and throughout my schooling we moved between the United States and South America. My teachers had always taught in either English or Spanish. This teacher, Mr. Cordova, used both languages for instruction, and powerful learning was taking place for all children. It was in this classroom that I realized I wanted to become a teacher. As a teacher I felt I could motivate children to learn, as Miss Bauske had done for me, and at the same time honor their culture and language, as Mr. Cordova did. That spring I applied to the same teaching program he had attended, the one at UCSB. I received my bilingual multiple subject teaching credential in May of 1996. This past June, I completed my first year of teaching and my M.Ed.

Julia confirmed that she had come to the UCSB program with a well-formed idea of good teaching. She explained that her basic educational philosophy had not changed as a result of having attended the credential program. Rather, her experiences in the program had expanded her previous educational values by providing a language and a way of thinking that enriched what she knew and already believed.

What Are the Standards? Julia came ready to talk with us about her experiences and brought with her a box containing artifacts she had collected during her teacher education program. The box, she explained, represented the labor and learning she had put into, and gained from, her professional preparation year. Ann, an instructor in the program and a member of the Leading Edge team, clarified that the contents of Julia's box were from her credential portfolio. Each candidate, Ann explained, constructs a credential portfolio over the course of the preparation year. The credential portfolios are not only for purposes of high stakes evaluation (i.e., recommending candidates for licensure), but are also a key element in the program's accreditation agreement with the state.[3] Julia, like her colleagues, built her portfolio around the six California Standards for the Teaching Profession (CSTP), which Ann recited from memory: (1) engaging and supporting all students in learning; (2) creating and maintaining effective environments for student learning; (3) understanding and organizing subject matter for student learning; (4) planning instruction and designing learning experiences for all students; (5) assessing student learning; and (6) developing as a professional educator. Ann's comments, as well as the organization of the artifacts in Julia's box, provided an answer to the first of our three shared research questions: What standards are there? Further exploration of Julia's box provided insights into the second and third shared research questions: What are the opportunities for learning, practicing, and assessing development in the standards? What professional development opportunities are there for teacher educators?

What Are the Opportunities for Learning, Practicing, and Assessing Development in the Standards? Julia described the contents of her box as a representation of what she had accomplished during her time in the program. As she lifted items from the box, she talked about how each artifact illuminated her understanding of the six California standards, and how these six standards provided a frame for her reflections upon and learning from her teaching.

The first artifact was a map she had drawn of the neighborhood surrounding the partnership school where she had completed her field placements. Accompanying the map was an analysis of the possible influences home and community might have on children's learning in school (e.g., neighborhood play space and sidewalks, crowded apartment complexes). She also discussed her findings regarding the lives of the children whom she was teaching. Many were recent immigrants to this country who were learning English as a second language; some had few books in the home; many were living in intact, extended, and supportive family environments. Because one must know one's students to engage and support them, these artifacts provided evidence of her understanding of the first standard, that of engaging and supporting all students in learning.

Her management plans for her 1-week takeover in the fall placement, as well as those for her 2-week takeover in the spring, showed her attention to issues embedded in the standard, *creating and maintaining an effective environment for student learning.* These plans included diagrams of the classrooms in which she had taught, as well as analyses of the implications of different classroom designs and arrangements for student learning. Julia then shared the integrated curricular unit she had co-authored with two other kindergarten student teachers, built around the themes of community and interdependence. This artifact, accompanied by voluminous documentation such as analyses of student learning, and post hoc critiques of lessons, demonstrated her development in the standard, *understanding and organizing subject matter knowledge for student learning.* Her lesson and unit plans for the takeover periods allowed us to assess her developing skills in and understandings of three other domains of the CSTP: *understanding and organizing subject matter for student learning, planning instruction and designing learning experiences for all students,* and *assessing student learning.* Julia's write-up of a parent–teacher–student conference in which she and the cooperating teacher used student work samples to talk about the child as a learner offered further supporting evidence of her growing knowledge and skills in assessing student learning.

The program requires credential candidates to audiotape and videotape themselves working with children in classrooms. The program believes that these can serve as tools that enable beginning teachers to examine their own teaching. Also included in Julia's portfolio were context-specific answers to questions about her objectives and how she communicated them to students, about how students responded to the work, and about the consistent and inconsistent messages she might be sending to students. As she described both types of artifacts, pointing out the ways in which she could measure and define her growth over time, she commented, "We are required to reflect on all our work, both course work assignments and student teaching." These reflections provided empirical evidence of Julia developing as a professional educator.

Julia's portfolio box showed us that she had been given multiple opportunities for learning about and practicing the six domains of the CSTP. Our exploration of her portfolio addressed, in part, our second research question. But we were still uncertain of the structures and processes in place that enabled Julia to learn further from her portfolio and allowed the teacher educators to assess her work. Furthermore, what opportunities existed for the teacher educators to continue their own professional development?

Julia reached deeper into her box and pulled out a 2-inch binder containing three credential portfolio write-ups—one from the late fall, one from the winter, and one from the spring—and 4 three-way assessments of her work as a teacher. She told us that each assessment documented a three-way conference involving herself, her cooperating teachers, and her university supervisor. Two of the conferences occurred during the first placement, and the other two in the second. She said:

My supervisor described the first three-way in the fall as a "strength and stretch conference." Before this meeting, each of us wrote down three of my teaching strengths and three areas for growth. We all had to support what we said with concrete evidence from my teaching. At the conference, I was the first to share. Next, my cooperating teacher shared what he had written, and last came my supervisor, Sarah. The three of us had talked a lot during Sarah's regular visits to the classroom, so I wasn't that surprised by the similarities in our assessments. At the end of the conference we set goals for the rest of the placement, and talked about what each of us could do to support me in meeting them. Finally, Sarah connected our goals and strengths and stretches to the California Standards for the Teaching Profession.

Credential candidates, throughout their professional preparation year, conduct self-assessments, integrating evidence of growth from multiple sources. Their self-assessments, coupled with the assessments of university- and school-based teacher educators, help to initiate candidates into the process of collaboratively determining areas of and for professional growth. Apparently, the series of three-way portfolio conferences provide opportunities for student teachers and teacher educators alike to learn more about the CSTP. Julia said, "We both really learned a lot about [the CSTP] during this conference. My cooperating teacher even mentioned at the end that she had learned as much as I had about the standards." The three-way portfolio conferences, which link standards and classroom experiences, serve as opportunities for teacher educators to grow professionally. Of her second three-way assessment conference Julia said:

The second assessment conference took place at the end of my fall placement. This time I was expected to select three of the six standards and use them as a framework for talking about my strengths and stretches. In preparation for this conference I sorted through my collection of work and selected those artifacts which best represented my development as a professional over time. To the conference I brought two or three artifacts for each standard, maybe a lesson plan and samples of student work, and then photographs. I also brought a short write-up explaining what each artifact demonstrated about my teaching, and how it related to the standard. This was the start of my credential portfolio. For the final two portfolio conferences, one which served as my introduction to my second cooperating teacher and the other which occurred after my two-week takeover of the classroom in the spring, I presented artifacts that showed my professional growth in relation to all six standards, and set new goals.

Julia's narrative made it clear that, as the year progresses, candidates become increasingly responsible for using the CSTP as an assessment tool to gauge professional growth and to set goals. In a parallel process, the teacher educators who work with credential candidates become increasingly responsible for using the CSTP as both an accountability measure and a frame for documentation over the course of the year. The formative assessment episodes facilitated by the ongoing series of credential portfolio conversations become opportunities for candidates and teacher educators to learn from each other as they work together on realizing the standards.

We asked Julia what other kinds of support, beyond the three-way portfolio conversations, she received. She responded that she received feedback from multiple sources. "We get feedback on every assignment, and from different perspectives: instructors, supervisors, cooperating teachers, other people at the school site, and from our peers." She went on to say, "I particularly liked the feedback from other student teachers in my weekly support group." She elaborated on the power of peer feedback by describing a small group seminar in which candidates shared videotapes of their student teaching:

> In each placement my supervisor came into the classroom and videotaped while I was teaching. First I watched the tape alone at home, using a reflective guide to write down my thoughts. Then I picked a five-to-ten minute section of the tape to show to three of my peers. Before showing them the clip, I told them what my lesson objectives had been, and why I had elected to show this section. I told my colleagues the things that I wanted them to look for. For example, I asked them to focus on how I was actively engaging students during the instructional part of my rain forest lesson, including the types of questions I asked. Then they took notes while watching the clip, and afterwards gave me feedback on what I had asked them to watch for, and other stuff they had noticed.

Julia's comments helped us to see how collegial exchange during these small group seminars could potentially support her growth in all six of the CSTP. In this case, the feedback she asked of her colleagues clearly centered on the standard, *engaging and supporting all students in learning.* We asked if addressing specific standards was part of the assignment. "No," she told us, "our own identification of teaching issues came first, not the standards. What I learned through the program was that knowing the standards could help me to focus my thinking and to talk about my teaching. But I always started from my own issues."

Video analysis and debriefing explicitly support credential candidates' professional talk about and reflections on teaching practice, key components of the standard, *developing as a professional educator.* For example, Julia shared one video session which particularly "influenced me because it provided me with input from people who were experiencing classroom management problems, too. My peer, Celia, had some good ideas on organization that I had not considered. And Mark impressed me with his honesty and his perspective on letting kids make their own rules." Evidently, while candidates bring their own issues to the table, the standards give them a common language and the program creates a space for feedback and dialogue. Candidates are afforded the opportunity to practice collegial and professional norms that hopefully will define their future work.

With the box completely unpacked, its weighty and colorful contents splayed about her, we asked Julia to consider the impact the box has had on her as a teacher. She responded by saying that its contents symbolized her growth during the credential year and the way that she thought about teaching.

> The UCSB lesson plan format burns in my head. We did about 120 [lesson plans], and [the format] serves as the mental framework I use when planning. All of the reflecting we did on our teaching, and the expectation that we would use our observations of children to help guide our instruction—these activities represent the values about teaching and learning that guide my work. The box is not static. Like myself, its contents grow and change in response to my experiences with children, new research, interactions with colleagues, and changing district and state standards.

Julia's walk through her credential portfolio helped us see how state standards provide a shared language for what constitutes good teaching. Julia also helped us realize the multiple levels at which the standards guide the teacher education program at UCSB. Course work, student teaching experiences, workshops, supervisory group seminars, and assignments are all designed to provide candidates with structured opportunities for learning, practicing, and assessing development in the standards. The standards provide an intellectual frame as well as a language candidates and teacher educators can use to contemplate and learn from their practice. The standards also serve as evaluation and accountability mechanisms. We discovered that university faculty, cooperating teachers, student teachers, and university supervisors, through continuous reflection and deliberative collaboration in a variety of carefully constructed forums, use the standards as opportunities to develop professionally. In this way, the program and the standards are recursive, each supporting the other; the creation and sharing of knowledge is not linear but circular around and among the people and the structures that comprise the teacher education program partnership.

Mentoring and Supervision Workshop: CSTP

This idea of professional learning through continuous reflection and collaboration was again apparent when we returned to Santa Barbara in the fall of 1998 and attended an all-day workshop on mentoring and supervision. This workshop, repeated five times over the course of the year, was sponsored by the teacher education program partnership. The partnership offers these workshops in order to support school- and university-based teacher educators in their understanding of the standards and to enhance skills that support the learning of teachers. Participation in the workshop lent further dimension to our understanding of opportunities for learning, practicing, and assessing standards within the Santa Barbara Partnership. Concomitantly, it provided evidence for our third research question, addressing the professional development opportunities for teacher educators. Most critically, what emerged from the workshop, and was articulated over and over again, was how the standards have provided California educators with an opportunity for professional dialogue about their work in an institutionally neutral language with which to converse, think, and reflect.

Lynne, one of the university-based teacher educators facilitating the workshop, and also the director of the local Beginning Teacher Support and Assessment (BTSA) Project,[4] opened the day by talking about the role of the cooperating teacher:

> Because we know that the cooperating teacher is absolutely fundamental to the success of the student teacher, what we are looking at is . . . what are the key areas to think about in preparing professional educators. . . . Many of you have been doing this for a lot years, others not. So today is about seeing what you are doing and if we have a couple of ideas that might work for you.
>
> It is really important for cooperating teachers to be interested in working with adult college graduates. Not everyone is comfortable . . . talking with other adults about ways of teaching—especially in this program when, in some cases, they are older than you. There is nothing easy about being a cooperating teacher.

Referring to an overhead transparency, she reiterated that the role of a cooperating teacher is "a complex blend of mentoring, instructing, collaborating, and encouraging as the student teacher develops in each of the six California Standards for the Teaching Profession." She reminded us that the overhead was a copy of the first page in the handbook for cooperating teachers that had been collaboratively conceived by school- and university-based educators. Going over the agenda for the day, Sarah, Lynne's copresenter (and Julia's college-based supervisor), said workshop participants would have the opportunity to think about the California standards in depth, and to become familiar with documenting observations, interactive journaling, and leading pre- and post-observation conferences to facilitate reflection and deliberative action. On this particular morning, sixteen cooperating teachers, supervisors, and administrators from local districts assembled. All were committed to helping student teachers enter the profession. All were also interested in their own professional development. Although they would receive their daily wage for attendance, all were sacrificing a sunny Santa Barbara Saturday.

At the onset of the workshop, participants were asked to reflect silently on the act of teaching and to record on post-it notes their notion of what an effective teacher should know and be able to do. Participants formed small groups and categorized their post-it notes on a graphic organizer that displayed the six standards as headings. In doing this activity and sharing ideas, participants highlighted three critical points:

- understanding and organizing subject matter for student learning, and creating and maintaining effective environments for student learning were the most commonly tabbed standards;
- many elements could be placed under more than one standard domain;
- several essential elements (dispositional issues such as flexibility, empathy, sense of humor, liking children, and experiencing joy in learning) seemed to fall outside the six standards.

After grappling in small groups about where to place these seeming outliers, the entire group decided to place them dead center on the organizer, indicating possible flow in any direction. Lynne wrapped up the conversation by noting that overlap and flow were natural and by design:

> The beauty of the standards is that, although they have been divided into six categories, there is phenomenal overlap . . . because the whole act of teaching involves all six at the same time. It is not that you plan a lesson and you are not thinking about assessment, not thinking about engaging students, not thinking about the environment. But what this does do, especially when working with beginning teachers, is to give you a way to think very specifically about the areas they are working on and to zero in on an area you want to focus on for the next eight weeks with the student teacher.

Lynne then directed the group to relate each standard to classroom practice and to indicate specific evidence of each. She emphasized, "If this standard were going on, what kinds of things would teachers be saying and doing? What might the students be saying or doing? Think of examples from your own experience." In small groups, we rotated to each of six standards posters, recording our recalled examples. Rich data emerged. For example, engaging and supporting all students in learning took the shape of children working together in a cooperative group, each with a clearly articulated role. In effect, by being forced to tap tacit knowledge, the activity imposed a heavy responsibility on participants to recall and articulate what they know and do daily. We had to make explicit our craft and professional artistry, both of which may be even more difficult to talk about than to enact. The activity reminded us that it is not easy to make visible to beginning professionals the tightly interwoven threads that comprise the tapestry of teaching. We discussed how challenging it is to be a mentor capable of bringing out a beginning professional's voice while maintaining one's own.

In the next activity, called the "reflective conversation," we explored how such conversations can help the student teacher find his or her voice while providing an opportunity for experienced teachers to realize their own "ah ha's" and refine their own voices. Sarah said:

> Just because you are an experienced, skilled classroom teacher does not mean you have expertise in the area of facilitating another person's growth. There really are skills and strategies to be learned in relation to that . . . such as inviting the conversation, making the time for it, and building from where the person is ready to start and going from there.

Watching a videotaped problem-solving interaction between an experienced teacher and a first-year teacher reminded us of the importance of active listening and deft responsiveness. Postvideo discussions revealed authentic dilemmas that occasionally occur in classrooms with beginning educators. Among the questions raised were: What happens when the responsibility to support student teachers is lost because the opportunity for structured conversation does not exist in a particular school? What happens when the student teacher becomes defensive or simply does not hear (or want to hear) the mentor's voice of experience?

The group discussed and debated these difficult issues and shared possible strategies for addressing them. We talked about how politics, personal perspectives, and diversity of developmental and philosophical stances influence how we enact our responsibilities. We wondered how these factors influence the work we do with credential candidates, with beginning teachers, and with each other.

As the workshop closed, one participant talked about how the standards not only showed newcomers the way but also gave experienced professionals a picture of themselves. Standards can provide a process for professionals to share understandings and, more importantly, provide teachers at all levels with an opportunity to recreate daily the big picture of teaching. Standards can provide a frame from which professional educators can rethink their work with students in their classrooms and their work within the contexts of given school cultures. We discussed how we must first be able to see what is already there before we can grow and make changes (or consciously determine that changes may not be appropriate). In talking about the standards and sharing what we do in our own teaching worlds, we had the opportunity to think anew about what we do. The mentoring and supervision workshop suggests that the Santa Barbara Partnership approaches the professional responsibility for establishing and enhancing standards of practice as an opportunity to learn about and alter the nature of a relationship. Every opportunity, however, equally implies an obligation to learn about that which we do as professionals.

A Day in the School

Our work to this point in the fall of 1998 documented that the six domains of the CSTP matched the values of the teacher education program regarding good teaching. The definition of teaching, the understanding of learning, and the recognition of the roles of teacher and family that undergird the CSTP also undergird the UCSB teacher education partnership. In addition, the mentoring and supervision workshop indicated that school-based educators agreed that these standards not only were tools for teacher candidates, but represented opportunities for their own professional growth.

In continuing to expand our understanding of the Santa Barbara Partnership, one member of the TC team visited the school where Julia was now beginning her second year of teaching and prepared the following report:

It was 9:00 a.m. on a warm Wednesday when I arrived at Victoria Elementary School.[5] School had been in session for 30 minutes and most students were in classrooms. A few stragglers ran up the sidewalk. My tour started with a brief walk through many of the classrooms. We began with the first grade. As I entered the classroom, I could see children sitting in the rug area facing the teacher who was seated on a chair in front of them. On her lap rested a teacher's manual—the mandated teacher's manual for the skills-based reading program adopted by the district. The teacher was reading from the manual a story about a pig which was designed to serve as an introduction to the sound represented by a letter of the alphabet. When she finished reading the story, the teacher asked a series of questions printed in the manual. She asked the first question, got a response, and then glanced down at the manual to see what the next question was. After a few minutes, I moved on to another first grade. As I entered this classroom, it was as if I had not missed a beat from the previous classroom. The teacher was reading from the same manual and asking the identical questions. She was perhaps 2 or 3 minutes behind the teacher next door. In a third first grade classroom, the same scenario was repeated. As if listening to monophonic music from three different speakers, I was hearing the same words from all three teachers while they performed the same movements.

As I moved through the school on my very brief tour, I realized that the same lesson was taking place at the same time at every grade level. The classrooms I visited were those in which the teacher education program placed students teachers. Many of the cooperating teachers were graduates of the UCSB teacher education program. Some of the teachers who spoke to me expressed frustration with a series of school board decisions to (a) adopt a prescripted, skills-based language arts program and (b) dismantle the bilingual education program and implement an English-only policy. They went on to say that the manner in which they were being required to teach language arts was inconsistent with what they knew about helping children learn to read and write.

After my classroom visits I entered the school auditorium where a training session for the prescripted reading program was being held for upper grade teachers. The audience included numerous seasoned practitioners and a few teachers beginning their careers. The building principal was also present. The program trainer, who had used this reading program in her own classroom for many years, was explaining how the program should look in a classroom. She began by telling the teachers how they should schedule their day and what to assign for homework. The trainer then modeled how to read a story with the class. She detailed a fully prescribed outline. First, one child must read a few sentences aloud to the rest of the class, without having already read it silently. When the child finished, she was to ask another student to summarize the paragraph, and then that student would ask another student to explain what the paragraph meant. The trainer emphasized that the students, not the teacher, must call on each other. She offered no explanation or rationale for this inviolable rule. The group practiced by role-playing the procedure, with the trainer acting as the teacher and the teachers as students. In their roles as students, teachers were admonished for waiting for the trainer to call on someone rather than remembering to call on another student themselves.

After several minutes of practice, the trainer commented that they would be spending more time on some stories than others. A teacher in the audience asked, "If John's class needs four days for a story and my class only needs two, can I move my class on to the next story?" The principal jumped in, saying, "I really want everyone to stay together at the same place at the same time." She also made it clear she wanted the grades to plan together. She wanted them to all be in the same place when they came to their weekly planning session.

Unlike the CSTP workshop, this felt like a training session for technicians expected to implement a teacherproof curriculum. The message I heard was, "We are going to read the directions to you and then have you practice reading them back to us." From their earlier comments to me, I knew that not all of the teachers agreed with the rigidity of the program and some were uncomfortable with both its content and pedagogy. Regularly throughout the training, the teachers sought permission to take differences into account, if not individual student differences at least group differences. They asked questions centered around adapting the program to meet the needs of their students. Each time they received the same response: follow the manual exactly. The implicit message seemed to be, "No professional judgment required. Teach as we say. Do not stray from our formula and your students will score well on our tests." In addition to the underlying assumptions about teaching embedded in this message are underlying assumptions about learning: If all children get the same input, they will all produce the same output—the same learning at the same pace and rate.

My experience at the elementary school site seemed antithetical to what we had seen earlier in Julia's work and at the mentoring and supervision workshop where the CSTP had been emphasized. The trainer at Victoria Elementary did not mention the six standards. The only standard, or value, I heard was that teachers were to follow the prescribed program without questioning it.

Language Arts Methods and Procedures Class

The following day, unnerved by the discrepancy between the inservice workshop at the school site and what we knew about the Santa Barbara Partnership and its work with the CSTP, and more than a little bewildered by how the school- and university-based educators could cope with the values clash, we made our way to the campus in order to observe a reading/language arts methods and procedures class.

It was Tuesday afternoon and credential candidates were running from their student teaching placements to attend this required class. The class was cotaught by two instructors, Sabrina and Ann, each with extensive experience as bilingual elementary classroom teachers, as instructors and supervisors in the UCSB teacher education program, and as researchers. As the students entered the classroom and found space at a table, they quickly glanced at the questions projected on the screen at the front of the room. They carried on their greetings and conversations as they took their seats and began copying the four multiple-choice questions and one constructed-response question in which they were required to address an issue presented through an abbreviated study. An example of one of the multiple-choice questions is: "One of the more difficult phonemic awareness activities is: (a) sound addition and substitutions, (b) rhyming, (c) segmentation, (d) counting phonemes in spoken words."

The class schedule written on the board told us what they were doing was called RICA REVIEW. Sabrina told us that RICA is the commonly used acronym for the recent state-mandated Reading Instruction Competency Assessment, a test all elementary credential candidates must now pass prior to state licensure. She told us this use of 30 minutes of class time was new to the language arts class. Prior to the RICA requirement (a different kind of standard) instructors opened each class session by reading a book with the candidates and leading them through several skills-based instructional strategies that could be used with the text.

The stress among the credential cohort was palpable, even though this was not an actual test. Most of them would be taking the state examination, RICA, for the first time in December, just 6 weeks away. They knew that to receive their credential, they must pass this assessment.

As their copying finished, conversation began to fade. What were the questions really asking? How could they gather all they had learned, both in the language arts class and from their field placements, and pull out the one piece of pertinent information needed to answer the multiple choice and case study questions? The students discussed and debated the questions. "I know the Phonics Law says this, but in reality . . ." They reminded each other that reality was not necessarily what was required for passing most exams. Part of the test consisted of multiple-choice questions with one right answer. Several students had a hard time with this because they had been learning specific observation and evaluation tools (e.g., miscue analysis) to help make professional decisions about appropriate approaches and next steps to help a child develop competence in reading, writing, and oral language. They were experiencing difficulty reconciling RICA right answers with the CSTP, their course work, and their experience with children.

Sabrina called the class to order and all eyes turned toward her. The remaining questions elicited possible answers, well-defended, from all sides of the room. The candidates knew how to do well on exams. They had scored well on several to get into a University of California campus, on several more for entry into the UCSB Teacher Education Program, and on still others to meet state content requirements for teacher credentialing. They sought to utilize what they had learned in the past about test-taking in order to determine the most appropriate responses.

After the discussion, Sabrina read the "right" answers. Grimaces emerged on faces around the room. Students started asking "But what if" questions. Anxious to move from test preparation to the instructional agenda of the class, Sabrina did not let the discussion continue too long. She did, however, answer questions and provide quick descriptions because she and other faculty felt obligated to get their students through the test.

Sabrina also had little choice because the state legislature had mandated that every teacher education program document that they taught to the RICA exam. The instructors had to assure state monitors who reviewed their syllabus that "the teaching strategies presented are . . . consistent with the Reading Instruction Competency Assessment." The addition of the RICA REVIEW was one of the more obvious adjustments Sabrina and Ann had made to their extensive curriculum. They also worked to make explicit to student teachers which parts of their curriculum pertained to which parts of the RICA standards: "This is something that addresses standard two on RICA and you want to be thinking about that." In addition, Sabrina and Ann tried "to infuse the class with 'politically correct' literature." At times this meant going against what they might agree with philosophically. Ann commented, "One change we made in our reader was in the section addressing the teaching of spelling. The articles that addressed the teaching of high frequency spelling words were replaced in keeping with the state directions and directives." She continued:

> Yes, [the RICA standards] changed our curriculum. For example, I find myself more aware of what I say, and what I do, and how it is perceived. . . . I'm finding myself being more cautious than I've ever been in my class. . . . Tensions have already begun to arise between dealing with the RICA standards and making changes to the language arts course. For example, in order to make room in the syllabus for *more* attention to phonics instruction, we deleted the teaching of the Language Experience Approach. A balance between paying attention to RICA standards and sharing what we believe is good teaching has, at times, been difficult. . . . I struggle between knowing that the students are expecting to pass the test [RICA], that they must be prepared for the test, and also knowing in my heart of hearts that I need to prepare them to teach language arts to children with different needs and different learning styles.

At the conclusion of our fall 1998 visit to Santa Barbara, we wondered what changes in the curriculum, based on legislative mandates such as RICA, would mean for the future of the program. Would instructors feel the need to compromise their philosophical and professional beliefs in order to prepare students for standardized tests? In response to our question, the director of the program commented:

> As the year continues and the program finds out how our candidates do on the RICA and, more importantly, how they do in classrooms, we will gain an empirical perspective on how many changes really need to be made; which changes are beneficial and which detrimental, and for which purposes.

It seemed that the teacher educators at UCSB had not given up the fight, but were maintaining a quiet confidence in themselves and their students until results proved them wrong. Partisan ideology notwithstanding, the program personnel believed that the combination of their students' test-taking expertise and the program's integration of content, pedagogy, and understanding of children would create a situation where UCSB candidates passed the RICA examination *and* learned how to support children's development in the language arts. They believed quality professional education would ultimately outperform sequences of test-preparation workshops—both on the test and in the classroom with children. (As of June of 1999, all candidates who took the RICA passed; two candidates had not yet taken the exam.)

Meeting with Credential Candidates: Frustrations Expressed

Because of the partnership, the district climate strongly influences the university. The district Board of Education mandated the skills-based reading program because of their belief that a prescripted program would improve student tests scores.[6] We noted that this philosophy contradicted the CSTP and UCSB philosophy. The philosophy of the credential program is based on the premise that teachers are professionals who must adapt curriculum to meet the needs of individual students and provide children opportunities for learning through various instructional strategies, and that standardized test scores are only one of the multiple sources of evidence needed to assess and support student learning. UCSB credential candidates, at times, felt caught in the middle between the stance taken by the district administration and the philosophy of the program.

Like Julia, many student teachers entered the program sharing the teaching and learning values of UCSB. A student teacher who was doing her field placement at Victoria Elementary School defined good teaching as:

> Knowing your students and being able to do what you think is right for your students and providing the curriculum. And sure, I think phonics is very important, but I don't think that you need a textbook to definitely go by—teach this lesson specifically on this day because all of the first grade should be on this same lesson on the same day. Even between the different first grade classes the students are all different. It is a different dynamic in each class. I think teachers should . . . know their students and know what is right for them and how to teach them.

This student teacher's philosophy, or beginnings of one, is consistent with the university's philosophy of what constitutes good teaching. It is compatible, too, with the six domains of CSTP. It is in direct contrast, however, to what the cooperating teachers are mandated by the district to do in their classrooms. It was not simply that the student teachers were frustrated by being told to read directly from a textbook; they perceived the district's mandates as prohibiting adapting instruction to students' individual differences. They were implementing a curriculum that did not agree with their professional commitments to children. As one student teacher put it, "I just do not think it supports the learning of the students."

Our one visit to Victoria Elementary School in October 1998 confirmed this dissonance. At that point in time, some student teachers felt they lacked opportunities for practicing and assessing their development as teachers: "I am a little frustrated because the prescribed phonics-based reading program is such a big part of our student teaching experience. . . . All the tools I gained over the last several months in the program mean nothing in my student teaching."

This sentiment typified the feelings of some student teachers about the discrepancy between their work in local classrooms and their courses at the university. According to the candidates, the language arts instructors asked student teachers to consider children's strengths, interests, and needs. But they seldom saw in their classroom placements strategies that were directed toward individual strengths, interests, and needs. Said one student teacher:

> I just came back from an inservice about the reading program. I find that this district and our school have adopted something that goes against a lot of what we learn in the program. It is really frustrating for me to go through all these great classes that I enjoyed and get into the classroom and not be able to apply that knowledge and all those ideas.

All teacher education programs, but especially those programs with close and sustained relationships with partner schools, depend upon student teaching placements to help students see the enactment of theories and strategies presented at the university. As of our visit in early October, the opportunity to practice multiple pedagogical approaches in the service of one's students was not immediately evident. Given that experienced educators were having great difficulty understanding the value conflicts, let alone how to resolve them constructively, it is not surprising that beginning professionals were becoming frustrated. They made their discontent clear: "We are not learning content (in the student teaching placement), we're not learning things, we're not learning lessons. All we are learning is how to do the same thing everyday."

As the year progressed, many of the cooperating teachers understood the frustrations felt by the student teachers and went to great lengths to manipulate their teaching schedule so that student teachers had opportunities to enact practices congruent with the philosophy of the program and the CSTP. They created space in their classrooms for the student teachers to enact a variety of pedagogical approaches designed to account for the strengths, interests, and needs of individuals and groups. Assignments from college courses were to design lessons covering the content of the mandated curriculum that reflected the CSTP values about teaching and learning—not an easy task. For example, in planning for their 2-week takeovers, the student teachers, in coordination with their cooperating teachers, were required to develop an integrated curriculum unit addressing the district's expectations and incorporating ways of thinking and practicing that they had learned in their university methods courses. If the cooperating teachers had not created these spaces, sacrificing the few daily moments of professional discretion allotted to them by district policy, the student teachers would not have had the opportunity to enact their college-based learnings in their student placements. In this way, the district permitted the Santa Barbara Partnership to construct creative and context-specific solutions so that credential candidates could learn and practice.

Summary

We focused our visits to Santa Barbara on our three research questions about standards. We discovered two sets of standards. Although both sets of standards operate at the state level, they differ considerably in how the state created and defined them. One set of standards, the CSTP, was created through a process that primarily involved professional educators. The UCSB teacher education program explicitly wove these standards into the fabric of every preparation experience. We saw clear evidence of these standards in the work of the credential candidates, in both school and university classrooms, and in the efforts of the school- and university-based faculty. We also saw multiple opportunities for student teachers, classroom teachers, school-based administrators, and university faculty to learn, practice, and assess their growth in those standards. These opportunities for learning provided spaces for professional development.

We were then struck by the disharmony of the second set of standards, the RICA standards, which were created through a partisan process that excluded professional educators. This disharmony was particularly evident in the way the statewide reading initiative played out in local districts. These standards appeared to us to clash drastically with much of the UCSB philosophy and with the CSTP. As we sought to uncover ways in which the teacher educators in the UCSB Partnership reconciled the potentially immense gap between the two sets of standards, new questions emerged: (a) What does a teacher education program do when a school district mandates and monitors a curriculum that is not aligned with the values and ways of thinking about teaching and learning promulgated by the program? (b) Whom does the program support—the student teacher, the cooperating teacher, the district administration and board of education, the university-based faculty? How? And in what balance? (c) Should teacher educators compromise curriculum content to satisfy standardized test requirements? If so, how? Although the dilemmas inherent in a clash of professional values could not possibly be resolved in the time period we observed, if at all, we were able to realize that through the struggle to overcome the apparent mismatch, the program partnership engaged in further and deeper exploration of their definition of good teaching. They transformed an obligation to change into an opportunity for learning.

PART THREE: CONCLUDING THOUGHTS

All three of the policy mechanisms influencing the sets of vignettes presented involve state level decisions. They varied widely, however, on who should decide what teachers should know and be able to do and *where* that should be decided.

In the case of the CSTP, the state of California engaged school- and college-based educators in drafting standards and in validating and revising them.

Because the resulting standards are a product of the profession, we call the CSTP policy initiative an external-professional approach. ("External" calls attention to the fact that the standards were derived external to individual teacher education and induction programs.) Perhaps because of the engagement of the profession in the determination of the standards, the assessments of those standards will be embedded in classrooms, will possess a balance between support and evaluation, and will be conducted by educators.

In the case of the Reading Initiative, the state of California used a legislative mandate to decide the standards for teaching. In an overtly ideological manner, the state legislature engaged in the reading wars and phonics won. Because partisan leaders considered the profession to be the problem—it was the profession that had embraced the villainy of whole language—the legislature systematically excluded the profession from their deliberations. Thus, we term the Reading Initiative an external-partisan approach. The resulting assessment of candidates for certification is a purely evaluative paper-and-pencil test developed from the legislature-mandated standards by a psychometric corporation 2,500 miles from a California classroom.

The development of the CSTP standards and assessment process

- engaged program faculty in significant and difficult conversations about the nature of good teaching and, therefore, about the nature of a good teacher education program;
- made visible program structures and processes that had previously just been "the way we do things here";
- opened conversations and relationships on an equal footing allowing the reciprocal participation of all school- and college-based teacher educators;
- resulted in significant additional efforts and program improvements evidenced by graduates' perceptions of their preparation;
- constituted exemplary professional development as evidenced by survey and interview data of program graduates as well as statewide data on the Beginning Teacher Support and Assessment Project that uses the CSTP.

The Reading Initiative process explicitly excluded professional educators (who, as long as they used, or advocated using, literature to teach reading, were seen as the cause of the problem). Therefore, it shut down internal communication, demeaned the value of teacher education and teaching, and decreased candidates' opportunities for learning, practicing, and assessing the CSTP. In the case of RICA, for instance, in the review of the program, course-session by course-session, approval depended upon proving that the program served as appropriate preparation for the examination. The document the program submitted to prove it met state mandates trivialized both the program design and the caliber of UCSB candidates' opportunities for learning. A local district using this external-partisan policy exacerbates the effects. For instance, one local school board in the Santa Barbara area overturned the textbook recommendation of the district's reading-language arts committee, which consisted of teachers and parents. One Board member explained his reasoning by stating, "It is time we stopped listening to educators." Instead of the educator-endorsed selection, the Board imposed the prescripted, skills-based basal series mentioned earlier.

UCSB's experience with CSTP and RICA suggests that the act of making standards and assessments explicit, coupled with a professional model of accountability, is a powerful mechanism for educational change. This held true even with the highly centralized statewide adoption of CSTP. When the act of making standards explicit is imposed on—rather than developed with—the people doing the work and is then coupled with a coercive and bureaucratic model of accountability (as in the Reading Initiative), the power of standards as a mechanism for educational change is diminished.

In the case of the accreditation process in New York, the state traditionally has allowed individual teacher education programs a great deal of flexibility in establishing their own goals and their own assessments, as long as these goals respond appropriately to state requirements. We call this an "internal-program" approach since each program internal to itself, can decide what teachers should know and be able to do, and how to determine if candidates meet those standards.

A process like New York State's has its advantages and problems. An advantage has been the flexibility afforded to institutions to define good teaching as long as they responsibly acknowledge the requirements outlined by the state. This freedom could be interpreted as the state's trust in education professionals to "do the right thing" and create programs which conform to state policy and are professionally defensible and intellectually rigorous. The advantage of this approach is also its greatest potential problem: are the programs' definitions of good teaching good enough? Do they satisfy the state's need for high quality teaching?

As a professional school of education that prides itself on its long history as an innovator in the field, TC sees itself as a full-fledged partner that has something of value to offer national conversations about good teaching. The Preservice Program's status as a TC program has probably helped open up a negotiating space with the New York State Education Department (NYSED) where issues of professional preparation can be collaboratively discussed and mutually agreed upon. Of course, the program has also worked hard not to betray the trust of the state. One could say that its insistence on always going beyond minimum competencies is its way of earning and sustaining state trust. The fact that its graduates are successful undoubtedly bolsters the state's trust. This fact, coupled with the program's reputation for rigor, is extremely important today, given the reregistration process that NYSED is currently initiating whereby every teacher education program is undergoing serious revision in order to meet new state guidelines. These guidelines are far more prescriptive than in the past and include, for example, the requirement that by 2001, at least 80% of a program's candidates pass the New York state teacher examinations if it is to receive state approval. Programs that do not meet NYSED mandates risk being shut down. TC is working hard to respond to the new requirements and has adopted a proactive rather than a reactive stance. Even while it is figuring out how to respond to state prescriptions, TC is communicating frequently with the state and exploring options and alternatives. Thus, the TC experience indicates that even within a system that appears to be changing from internal decision making to include more external directives, teacher certification decisions are not totally closed to outside influence, nor, conversely, to internal influence.

Where to Decide: Centralized and Decentralized Decision Making

One issue related to where decisions regarding standards and assessments should occur plays out in the interplay between centralized and decentralized decision making. The preceding sets of vignettes portray the inherent dilemmas in the uneasy relationship between state- and program-level responsibility for the professional preparation of teachers. Certain states, such as New York, historically have made a conscious effort to distribute responsibility to the program level, but most states, in reality if not in rhetoric, assume significant state-level responsibility.

There are at least three compelling reasons for the state to assume a significant responsibility for the preparation of teachers. One is legalistic in nature. The state, through its elected officials, owes an accounting to its citizens for the money they forward to teachers. We are not talking of minuscule amounts here—well over half of every state's budget funds public education and a vast majority of that funding goes to teachers' salaries. A second reason is ethical in nature. Because the state, by law, compels parents to send their children to school, it is responsible for the caliber of care and of educational opportunities children receive. If a child has a teacher—with a license granted by the state and with a paycheck from the state—who physically, emotionally, or educationally abuses him, the state is guilty of putting that child in harm's way. A third reason, both legal and ethical, is more social in nature than the first two. We citizens have agreed that public education is necessary for the welfare of a democratic society—and for the individual child's future, liberty, and pursuit of happiness. With our votes and our pocketbooks, we have agreed that public schools are both a social necessity and a protection of a child's inalienable rights—rights upon which our country's existence is premised.

Despite a convincing case for state responsibility, we know (and if we do not, by now there is certainly no excuse) that those external to teacher education programs cannot do the work of preparing teachers. Teacher preparation occurs in school and college classrooms in the moment-to-moment efforts of teacher candidates and school- and college-based teacher educators who interact with them daily. There is scant evidence that a teacher candidate has learned anything solely because a state legislature decreed it.

The lack of a direct relationship between legislative intent and effects on the preparation of teachers is a consequence of a series of false assumptions. Legislative mandates hope to find the "one best system," (Tyack, 1974) codified by law and specified in regulations, by which all prospective teachers may be educated. They assume that (a) teacher candidates and teacher educators will respond in identical and predictable ways to the treatments devised by policymakers, (b) sufficient knowledge of which treatments to prescribe is both available and generalizable to all educational circumstances, (c) this knowledge can be translated into standardized practices, which in turn can be maintained through regulatory systems, and (d) university administrators and school- and college-based teacher educators can and will faithfully implement the prescriptions for practice (Darling-Hammond & Snyder, 1992). The validity of each of these assumptions is questionable at best, as the history of educational policy enactment makes abundantly evident.

Ultimately, states cannot ignore the basic fact that the work of teacher education takes place in teacher education programs (of one form or another), but neither can teacher education programs (no matter their form) ignore the influence of state accountability efforts on their work. States' efforts to achieve accountability (such as standards for teachers, assessment decisions, and program accreditation processes) profoundly influence the nature of the work that candidates and teacher educators do. State-level decisions regarding credentialing policies and curriculum monitoring profoundly influence who, and whose ideas, are even allowed in those programs.

Concerning the perplexing balance between centralized and decentralized decision making, UCSB's experience with two different centralized decision-making policy mechanisms suggests that the influence of where a decision is made interacts with who makes those decisions. We take up that issue in the following section.

Who Should Decide: Trust

The question of who should decide teacher education policy is intricately related to public trust in the profession of education. Professions are, by definition, exclusive; only those who possess specialized knowledge in relation to specific work are permitted membership and allowed to practice. As a consequence of their specialized knowledge and skills, the public affords professionals the discretion to make decisions about their work and enters into an implicit agreement to abide by their expertly informed judgments and actions. Public trust in a profession determines professional self-governance. The more the public trusts the profession the greater discretion it grants. This relationship between trust and discretion is extremely delicate and depends always on the public believing that (a) a profession is doing good work, (b) said work cannot be done by nonprofessionals, and (c) the work produces satisfactory and visible results.

The field of education has not historically enjoyed, and does not now enjoy, the consistent and full trust of the public.[7] Public trust in education and educators has waxed and waned, and the level of discretion permitted educators has waxed and waned accordingly. Currently, education is under public scrutiny. Well-publicized stories about new teachers' dismal passing rates on licensing exams, students' standardized test scores, state takeovers of low-performing schools, vociferous debates over instructional methods, and the often poor achievement of American students compared to students in other countries have fueled public concern about the quality of the work of professional educators. This concern has resulted in more restrictions being placed on educators, more prescriptive mandates, and more public control. As public mistrust increases, the discretion granted to educators decreases.

Our work together in Leading Edge over the past 3 years portrays the differences that arise in different contexts of public trust in the education profession. The two programs are quite similar. They hold reputations as effective programs. They share common beliefs about what constitutes good teaching and about the purpose of schooling. They enact these shared beliefs through similar methodologies, and they work with students who demonstrate strong achievement. Similarities notwithstanding, the two programs enjoy different levels of professional discretion that have little to do with program quality. Rather, they are a consequence of the state and local contexts in which each program operates, and how, by whom, and where people in these contexts believe standards for the work should be decided.

The vignettes reveal the complex nature of the relationship between public trust and professional discretion and the issues that can support or undermine that relationship. Although New York currently grants TC greater professional discretion than California grants UCSB, the positions of the two institutions could easily be reversed if changes in context and political climate should occur. Our study, therefore, offers insight into how UCSB or TC or any other group of education professionals should respond when public trust is withdrawn. They can choose to ignore or give lip service to public dissatisfaction and continue on as they were. They can fully comply with and succumb to state and local mandates; in essence, give in. Or they can see new obligations as opportunities to reexamine their practice and transform themselves.

In a context that is less than amenable to professional decision making, UCSB chose to recast obligations as opportunities for development. Using public criticism of the field as lenses for self-reflection, program faculty looked deeply into what they do and why and searched for ways to connect what they value to what a powerful segment of the public demanded. This does not mean that they accept the public's criticism or deserve the public's mistrust. It does reveal, however, that their sense of professional responsibility leaves them open to change and supports their work with the public, despite differences in knowledge as well as values. They elected to use conflict constructively and to harness its energy to support their own growth. Their response demonstrates that professionals are defined not simply by their specialized skills and knowledge but by the choices they make when those skills are called into question.

The UCSB experience with the external-partisan policy which excludes the knowledge base of the profession limits professional discretion and affects the learning opportunities of students. Therefore, the program must strive to reach some compromise between what it professionally knows and what the ideologically driven legislation prescribes as educationally sound. In contrast, TC's position within an internal-program policy context means that TC possesses the discretion to determine the nature, scope, and goals of its work. This professional discretion, although informed by and relevant to the collective wisdom of the field and the desires of the public, is not controlled by educational stakeholders external to the program. Thus, TC's discretion is simultaneously a function of its long-standing legacy as an exemplary school of education and the political climate in New York State. State legislation codifies the public's trust in the education profession at TC.

The different policy mechanisms documented in this study not only illuminate the symbiotic relationship between public trust and professional discretion, but also suggest three key issues surrounding this relationship: (1) values match and mismatch, (2) negotiating space, and (3) open systems: permeability.

Values Match and Mismatch

TC's values align with those currently codified in state accreditation policies. In the absence of philosophical conflict, it is easy for the state to trust that TC will produce the kind of teachers the state needs. It is important to note, however, that TC faculty did not "close their doors" but rather participated, and continue to participate, in the public conversation regarding educational policy. Indeed, like UCSB's participation in the development of the CSTP, their participation in state and national policymaking on educational issues enhances the possibilities of a close fit between the program's and state's values.

Conversely, in the context that gave birth to the Reading Initiative, UCSB must accommodate to values to which it does not fully subscribe, values that run counter to professional knowledge regarding effective teaching and meaningful learning. Because it must continue to live up to its responsibility to students— that is, prepare them for state licensure—its teacher educators must "find them- selves" within these values (and practices that support them). The challenge to the program becomes how to maintain professional integrity while mediating multiple rub points—between the program and the district, between the students and cooperating teachers, and between school- and college-based educators. Thus, the contrasting policy mechanisms reveal that (a) public trust is more likely when the public and the profession share values governing the work, and (b) pub- lic mistrust quickly transforms into demands that the work be done differently in order to achieve better results—most likely creating a values mismatch.

Negotiating Space: Constructive Communication

A mismatch in values does not, in isolation, indicate or generate public mis- trust. Various constituents are more likely than not to hold distinct ideas about norms, goals, practices, and assessments in education (or any other field). Dif- ferent perspectives, roles, and needs all influence what one sees as important. Value mismatches are not inherently destructive. Like all conflict, they can re- sult in constructive outcomes when separate constituents build bridges across seemingly disparate ideas and agree to live by mutually agreed upon resolutions. Bridge building requires negotiating spaces where conflict can be constructively resolved, where ideas can be shared and debated, and where all involved seek to understand the values and needs underlying all parties' positions prior to con- demning those positions as the prime source of evil in the world. Such under- standing opens communication and enhances a healthy balance of public trust and professional discretion because both sides agree to negotiate through dis- agreements, rub points, and values mismatches.

Mutual respect between conflicting parties and the belief, on the part of each side, that the other has something valuable to offer supports constructive negotiating space. The participation of TC faculty in state policymaking and TC's adherence to state certification requirements represent a negotiating space between the two entities within an internal-program policy context. The work of each is informed by the knowledge, perspectives, and values of the other and the dialogue around professional practice flows in both directions. In Califor- nia's development and use of the CSTP the same held true. With the Reading Initiative, however, negotiating space was in limited supply. The legislature did not invite educators to participate in the development of the initiative, and sys- tematically excluded educators who might not agree with the state mandates. Instead of constructive conversation among the state and education profession- als, there was instead a one-way flow of mandates and prescriptions. The flood of directives from state to educators suggests that an external-partisan approach creates a closed system where the resulting policies are immutable—open neither to evidentiary informed discourse or improvement.

Open Systems: Permeability

Constructive conflict resolution among differing educational stakeholders requires a commitment to continue the relationship which, in turn, necessitates an open or permeable system. In an open system, the state, local programs, and the profession influence one another. Ideas flow in multiple directions; thus the ideas from the state's set of perspectives, roles, and needs can penetrate local programs and the values of professional educators—and vice versa. Openness and permeability engender constructive communication; constructive communication fosters openness and permeability. A lack of trust between state- and district-level politicians and bureaucrats on the one hand and professional educators on the other often creates closed and impermeable systems at all levels. Communication channels shut down and conversation withers as one side exerts pressure on the other to conform. In the case of California's Reading Initiative, our study documents the deleterious effects on the preservice program created by such a closed and impermeable system of policymaking. In the case of New York State, the study documents the benefits to all educational stakeholders of constructive communication within an open and permeable system.

NOTES

1. Though all members of the dyad team participated in the conceptualization of this set of vignettes, they are told from the perspective of the UCSB members of the team.

2. Though all members of the dyad team participated in the conceptualization of this set of vignettes, they are told from the perspective of the TC members of the team.

3. UCSB had developed a state-approved experimental program, built around the six CSTP. Furthermore, embedded throughout the program were the standards for Cross-cultural, Language and Academic Development (CLAD). This experimental program included a research component, as well.

4. BTSA is a state-funded induction program for first- and second-year teachers that uses the six California standards as the center of its support and assessment processes. The Santa Barbara Partnership has made a concerted effort to align professional preparation with BTSA , hoping to articulate pre- and in-service professional education.

5. Fictitious names have been substituted throughout.

6. As of June of 1999, the end of the first year of full implementation of the program, preliminary results from the state standardized test showed an increase from the 46th percentile to the 48th percentile in reading test scores for K–6 students. This was the second year the same test was administered. Because of errors beyond their control in categorizing students, the district could not analyze the gains by student population (e.g., English Language Learners, native English speakers).

140   SNYDER ET AL.

7. An in-depth discussion of the reasons for this lack of trust is beyond the scope of this chapter. The reasons are familiar: the dependence of schools on public moneys, public (i.e., nonprofessional) license to participate in policymaking, the perception of teaching as women's work, debates about what constitutes the knowledge base for teaching, the lowering of standards to allow those without specialized knowledge to do the work, and products/results that are perceived as unsatisfactory. For a more complete discussion, refer to Darling-Hammond & Goodwin (1993). "Progress toward professionalism in teaching," G. Cawelti (Ed.), *Association for Supervision and Curriculum Development 1993 Yearbook* (pp. 1952), Alexandria, VA: ASCD.

REFERENCES

Cal. Assembly Bill 3075, Chapter 921 (1996).

Darling-Hammond, L., & Goodwin, A. L. (1993). Progress toward professionalism in teaching. In G. Cawelti (Ed.), *Challenges and achievements of American education. 1993 yearbook of the Association for Supervision and Curriculum Development* (pp. 19–52). Alexandria, VA: ASCD.

Darling-Hammond, L., & Snyder, J. (1992). Framing accountability: Creating learner-centered schools. In A. Lieberman (Ed.), *The changing contexts of teaching. The 91st yearbook of the National Society for the Study of Education Part 1* (pp. 11–36). Chicago: University of Chicago Press.

Snyder, J., Lippincott, A., & Bower, D. (1998). The inherent tensions in the multiple uses of portfolios in teacher education. *Teacher Education Quarterly 25*(1), 45–60.

Tyack, D. (1974). *The one best system. A history of American urban education.* Cambridge, MA: Harvard University Press.

CHAPTER 8

Beyond Standards:
Creating Depth in
Teacher Education Reform

Amy Otis-Wilborn and Marleen C. Pugach

"Preparing them to work with diverse learners needs to be in there. But what do we mean by diverse learners, anyway? We're all diverse learners. When we use that word, what are we saying? Who are we referring to? What do we *really* mean? Can we just not use that word anymore?"

Despite burgeoning attention to the potential of standards as a means of improving the preparation of teachers, it is well recognized that any teacher education institution whose faculty is interested in accomplishing reform cannot stop at the adoption of standards. Instead, standards are better conceptualized as "tools for inquiry"; they serve as guideposts for local change (Darling-Hammond, 1997, p. 213). This widespread acceptance of standards-based teacher education as a vehicle for reform—both with respect to preservice teacher education students meeting standards like those promulgated by Interstate New Teacher Assessment and Support Consortium (INTASC, 1992) and institutions meeting standards associated with the National Council for Accreditation of Teacher Education (NCATE) accreditation process—renders the standards themselves as nearly nonnegotiable. Their broad-based consensus and appeal make them analogous to motherhood and apple pie. So it should come as no surprise that it is what happens at the level of local practice once standards are adopted that signals how extensive and long lasting reform actually turns out to be.

To move from standards to action that can support reform, it is generally accepted that what counts most is engaging in local, reform-minded dialogue. In fact, Moss (quoted in Darling-Hammond, et al., 1998) contends that this is one of the fundamental purposes of standards. Moss wisely reminds us that, in the absence of such dialogue, the generality of standards can actually conceal significant differences among the local players—making real local reform less likely. The ideal, she argues, is to establish an ongoing process of dialogue about standards that is informed by local experience as well as by concrete examples from local assessments. Reform itself, then, is a work in progress; it is a constantly evolving process.

However, unmasking significant differences through dialogue and building consensus from an ongoing understanding of what differences actually exist represent complex dynamics—and we are rarely privy to what these dialogic negotiations look like within institutions that are grappling with teacher education reform. We know that the adoption of a common set of values can and does occur through the NCATE process. Similarly, teacher preparation in the states that are participating in INTASC aligns expectations around the 10 broad-based standards. We know that standards can and should generate ongoing dialogue that is informed by assessment. But we are also sensitive to a comment one of us heard recently at a professional meeting that went something like this: "We've done the standards thing—we've met, we've talked, we've changed our syllabi to be consistent with each other. But it's still not happening." We believe this is a much more common situation than most of us in teacher education would like to admit. It is one that is especially problematic given the fact that contemporary calls for reform in teacher education are now well over a decade old, if the first Holmes Group report, *Tomorrow's Teachers* (Holmes Group, 1986), is used as a marker. Bridging the distance between standards and reform, it seems, continues to be a significant—and worthy—challenge.

In higher education, the prevailing norms—both institutional and individual—are so powerful that to fail to address them deliberately and at multiple levels might easily derail even the best-intended teacher education reform efforts. Our differences are hidden—often tacitly—behind classroom doors. We might agree, for example, that inclusive education is a good thing. But we may never stop to think how we actually convey what it means to work effectively with students with special needs as we teach in our individual courses, or how we ask our students to demonstrate support for inclusive education in their practice as teachers. In this chapter, we move deliberately from the general level of standards to our own local efforts to redesign teacher education with specific emphasis on precisely this issue: What kind of dialogue and action cycle is necessary to get to the level where our differences are no longer masked? What do these dialogues actually look like? At what levels must we articulate the details of agreed-upon standards and values if we are really to have coherent, integrated programs of teacher education? How do we move from the almost safe and neutral territory of standards into the contested territory of real, deep-seated program reform and reject pseudodiscussions (Barnes, 1992) that so often stand in for real dialogue?

Our experience suggests that these recursive cycles of dialogue and action, cycles which permit a progressive unmasking of differences, must occur in multiple dialogue spaces designed specifically to counter prevailing norms in teacher education. We use the term *dialogue spaces* to signify the multiple levels in which faculty must interact on a routine basis to reach the goals we set out for ourselves—and thus, for our students—as we work collectively to prepare teachers for urban schools. Dialogue spaces are the various locations in which our commitments take on meaning, where those meanings are interpreted and reinterpreted, and where we do the hard work of redesigning our pedagogy and our assessments in light of these agreed-upon, but progressively refined, meanings. They are the sites of active, recursive discussion among faculty who have responsibility for different parts of the program.

Specifically, dialogue spaces are the places that allow us to move from a general level of commitment—represented by national standards as well as by our locally defined core values—to a specific level of definition that pressures us to think more complexly about how each of us interprets the standards and values to which we are bound and how well our students are demonstrating in their practice what it means to teach from this framework. And the meaning we as faculty members have most control over—but may think least about and discuss least—is the meaning that is conveyed in our everyday talk when we teach, out of the reach of a list of standards or core values whose importance we already have conceded. Multiple dialogue spaces, entered on a regular basis, move us out of the realm of rhetoric and into the necessary danger zone of real disagreement, which is typically where the complexity of the values and concepts reveals itself. After providing some context for the dialogue spaces in which we work, we offer several very specific examples of the complex territory we entered when we chose to create and participate regularly in these reform-oriented interactions.

THE LOCAL CONTEXT

Perhaps what set us apart most from many other institutions as we embarked on reforming teacher education is that the large group of faculty members who have been driving this effort at the University of Wisconsin–Milwaukee (UWM) were already in agreement about several fundamental values when this work began. Prior to this time, our teacher education programs were like those at most other institutions, made up largely of stand-alone courses (good courses, but loosely coupled), minimal field experience, a full semester of student teaching, and a fairly traditional approach to assessment. And, as in most programs, a lot was left to chance in terms of how our students understood and acted upon their approach to teaching and their conceptions of themselves as teachers. Historically, we had assumed that our students would do the work of linking what they were learning and experiencing and would create a unified view from their preservice work with us. As we recognized that this was not occurring, we accepted the challenge of needing to unify the programs, to link them deliberately, and to grapple collectively and publicly with what it means to prepare teachers for urban schools.[1]

When UWM's reform efforts began in earnest, we did not have to argue, for example, about whether to emphasize a constructivist approach to learning, or an inclusive approach to special education; we already agreed on the importance of these ideas. We also held a fairly consistent set of beliefs about teaching literacy, one that clearly favored comprehension as the primary goal but that did not eschew the teaching of phonics. And most important, we were all committed to preparing our graduates for working in urban schools and to continuing our strong relationship with the Milwaukee Public Schools as the primary field site for our programs. This commitment to urban schools already had set our programs apart from others in the local metropolitan area. But at UWM, we clearly shared a sense of urgency about reforming our own practice in the context of this fundamental and increasingly compelling commitment.[2]

Agreement on these issues existed generally across faculty in early childhood, primary, middle, and special education. This meant that our starting point lacked the discord we were aware existed in many other schools, colleges, and departments of education. So when we began to voice what we believed to be our common core values, there was remarkable agreement on what they should be, even when faculty in special education and primary and middle level education met separately to draft initial sets of core values prior to developing a shared set of values. There was also agreement that we should adopt the INTASC standards, which actually were published after we had developed a common set of core values. The movement from standards and core values to action is represented best by describing the dialogue spaces we constructed and how they operate.

COCONSTRUCTING KNOWLEDGE AND ACTION THROUGH DIALOGUE SPACES

Operating out of Vygotsky's and Dewey's theoretical perspectives on social constructivism, many educators place the dialogic process at the center of classroom learning (see Barnes, 1992; Britton, 1970; Wells & Chang-Wells, 1992). Wells and Chang-Wells characterize dialogue as "the essence of education" (p. 33), while Barnes (1992) contends that "education *is* dialogue" (p. 90). The goal of dialogue within the context of social interaction is to develop, elaborate, and transform knowledge structures. This perspective on the value of dialogue emphasizes its role in the coconstruction of knowledge through a democratic process which serves as the basis for action.

The role and value of dialogue, however, are without question applicable beyond the classroom. Fernando-Balboa and Marshall (1994) argue that a dialogic pedagogy for preservice as well as for practicing teachers is critical to creating a democratic society. They remind us of the distinction between learning through *monologue,* or the traditional transmission of ideas, and learning through *dialogue,* or the construction of ideas with others. Specifically creating structures and opportunities for dialogue provides a means for the influence of multiple perspectives in the educational context. We argue that this same dialogic process plays an important role in the learning and action associated with the design and implementation of the Collaborative Teacher Education Program for Urban Communities.[3]

We focus here on dialogue in which speech is the medium of communication. While speech is not the same as thought, it is considered as close a reflection of thought as we have available (Barnes, 1992; Wells & Chang-Wells, 1992). In a social context, speech is an intellectual tool that makes ideas accessible to others, opening them up for scrutiny. If speech is the medium for reflecting ideas, language serves as the symbol system that represents and gives them meaning. Therefore, paying attention to the words we use to label our ideas and our values is pivotal to their interpretation by faculty peers, preservice students, and classroom teachers alike. Talk is an important reflection of our knowledge and can also serve as the fuel for our actions.

The dialogue spaces that we have constructed as the structure for the Collaborative Program permit us to analyze and understand the role that dialogue plays in the process of reconceptualizing and restructuring the teacher education process at UWM. Drawing upon social constructivist theories and models that place dialogue at the center of learning, we have based our interactions on three aspects of a dialogue and action cycle that are intimately connected with our program development and reform. The three parts of the process include: (1) generating the rhetoric that represents big ideas and key concepts, (2) engaging in extensive exploratory talk, and (3) developing belief structures that influence our expectations for action.

In the first part of the process, rhetoric represents what individuals as well as the field of education have proffered to the conversation. During the course of the current wave of teacher education reform, an identifiable language has emerged. Key concepts or ideas establish the themes; like mantras, they are repeated in the literature and in talk—private talk, small talk, talk in classes, and professional talk. *Multiculturalism, equity, empowerment, literacy, collaboration, partnership, "All children can learn,"* and *inclusion* are examples of ideas that have gained prominence. Such words represent the rhetoric assigned to these big ideas and are full of meaning, meaning that individuals as well as groups hold. Rhetoric represents the level of generality that Moss (as cited in Darling-Hammond et al., 1998) referred to when she noted that standards—which are an instance of rhetoric that subsumes these big ideas—can mask differences. Most of the time when we use this kind of rhetoric we assume there is large-scale agreement on what these keywords, big ideas, and standards mean. This rhetoric, however, is more valuable when it is used to initiate the dialogue and to move us out of the relatively safe, broad territory that the rhetoric defines.

Fernando-Balboa and Marshall (1994) characterize the vital process of "problematizing dialogue and opening it up for scrutiny and discussion" (p.178). In the second part of the dialogue and action cycle, we refer to Barnes's (1992) notion of *exploratory talk*. During exploratory talk we unpack the rhetoric and examine it in its complexity. Exploratory talk serves several functions. For individuals, it is an opportunity to be explicit about old ideas and test out new ones. Bruner (1966) describes this process as telling ourselves what we know, or working ideas out in our own words. "It is as if the talking enables us to rearrange the problem so that we can look at it differently" (Barnes, 1992, p. 19). Such talk is as much for the group as it is for individuals. This joint exploration of ideas sets the stage for constructing new ideas using the various meanings brought by group members. Wells & Chang-Wells (1992) identify this coconstruction of knowledge as the "hallmark of the collaborative talk" (p. 82).

When knowledge and ideas become part of our sense of purpose, used toward specific ends, then they have been integrated into our belief structure. The extent to which this new knowledge affects the action of individuals and groups demonstrates the real value of dialogue. Barnes (1992) characterizes this kind of knowledge as action knowledge:

> Insofar as we use knowledge for our purposes . . . we begin to incorporate it into our view of the world, and to use parts of it to cope with the exigencies of living. Once the knowledge becomes incorporated into that view of the world on which our actions are based, I would say that it has become "action knowledge." (p. 81)

The concept of action knowledge is useful in describing a third part of the cycle of dialogue and action—the part that translates the results of our exploratory dialogue into action. Action, in our experience, may take a number of forms, which include (a) clarifying, modifying, and/or strengthening beliefs and values, (b) continuing the dialogue with ourselves and others in formal and informal ways, and (c) taking specific steps toward defining and meeting collaboratively established expectations for performance. A good example of the connection between dialogue and action is reflected in how students in Education express key concepts and ideas both within and outside of the university classroom. This sort of spontaneous, informal talk is a powerful type of performance that reveals students' integration and use of new or emerging concepts and ideas, often in school-based settings with cooperating teachers, parents, or other professionals. As teacher educators, we too demonstrate performance in our own talk during teaching and, in a similar way, reveal the impact of dialogue on our own construction of ideas behind the rhetoric of reform. If our subsequent talk does not change as a result of our dialogues, it is more likely that there has been little impact.

During all three parts of the dialogue and action cycle, the knowledge base for program development becomes more refined and expectations for our students' performance more explicit. In the various dialogue spaces that we have constructed, faculty associated with the development and implementation of the Collaborative Program move back and forth among these three dialogic parts to define and redefine the meaning of the local values we developed. The process is not linear, however; conversations occur simultaneously and in a variety of contexts, and topics of conversation are transported from space to space. Rhetoric serves as the starting point and sets into action the recursive cycle of exploratory dialogue and action that helps us as individuals and as a group define and act on our beliefs about what it means to prepare teachers for urban schools.

CREATING A STRUCTURE TO SUSTAIN MULTIPLE DIALOGUE SPACES

Early on in our reform efforts we entered into a period of thinking that realigning departments within the School of Education would be significant for the reform of teacher education. We quickly came to realize that the work of program reform had to go on no matter what the departmental configurations were, and that the time we spent haggling over whose office would be next to whose was a distraction from the real task of redesigning the programs themselves.[4] Once we came to terms with this, we began to create a structure which had as its major purpose supporting the interdepartmental and interdisciplinary character of what would come to be known as the Collaborative Program. We needed a way to preserve the newly developing habit of jointly participating in formative development and assessment of our program through a recursive cycle of dialogue and action. In short, we needed to define the dialogue spaces that could set the cycle in motion. We also needed to keep up the momentum of reform and sustain the voluntary energy needed to reach the stage of implementation within a reasonable time frame and with consistent support. Figure 1 represents this interactive organizational structure.[5]

Formal dialogue spaces include regular meetings of three groups: (1) the entire program faculty; (2) meetings of block team faculty (including school-based instructors) who are responsible for a given semester's program and who typically represent at least two and sometimes three disciplines or departments;

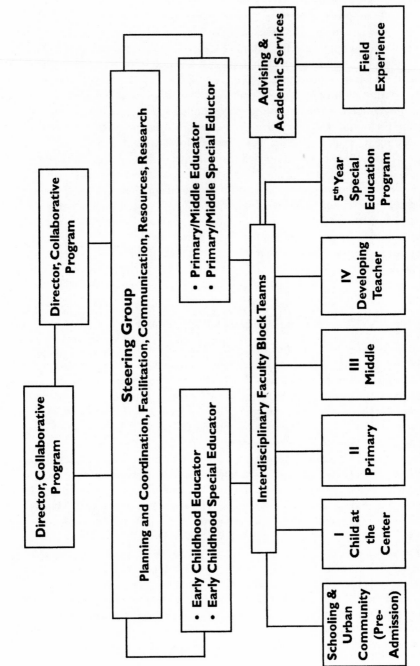

Figure 1. Collaborative Teacher Education Program for Urban Communities, organizational structure.

and (3) the steering group of the Collaborative Program, which includes a representative from special education, two from primary/middle level education, and the Assistant Dean of Advising and Academic Services. Faculty block teams exist for both the special education and primary/middle level education programs, but cross-program dialogue occurs at all levels.[6]

Because each of these groups meets on a regular basis, there is a continuous interactive cycle of dialogue and action across blocks within a program and across programs. Block teams are in various stages of program development, implementation, and revision at any given time. At full collaborative program meetings, faculty who work on these teams are in a position to reflect upon and share their actions, thus feeding directly into the dialogue in which other block teams and the Steering Group engage. The program director moves among block teams to carry an understanding of each block's actions to faculty in other block teams, which represents yet a different kind of dialogue space. Some dialogue spaces are created on an ad hoc basis to deal with specific issues. For example, the working groups for making the transition from the old to the new program and for developing the initial plans for assessment and monitoring of student progress met intensively during the formative phase of the program. Most important, there are both very public and much more intimate dialogue spaces available and the work that goes on in them is shared extensively, which is critical to sustaining the conversations that move the program forward. But the substance of the dialogues that take place in each of these spaces, whether small or large, whether within or across departments, is continually made public and is a source for future discussion and problem solving. The goal of sharing the substance of dialogues among all groups raises the expectations for all meetings to be focused on the program, the students, pedagogy, and assessment.

In addition to providing sustained opportunities for interdepartmental interaction at multiple levels of dialogue and action, this structure also assists us in (a) making sure that the formal governance structure works to support the program, (b) providing direct support to program faculty, and (c) linking university and public school staff to support our students' experiences in the field.

What actually takes place in these varied dialogue spaces changes over time depending on where we are in a given stage of program development, implementation, or refinement. What is critical is that the expectation has been firmly established for in-depth discussion of program and pedagogy as a regular part of our work rather than as a single exercise in reform.

EXAMINING DIALOGUE IN MULTIPLE SPACES

We turn now to examples of dialogue that have taken place in these spaces as we moved through various phases of program reform. Our intention is to highlight different ways the dialogue occurred and how, through our agreement to hold recursive conversations and continually revisit our work, we moved from rhetoric to exploration to disagreement to agreement—each occurring in relationship to specific actions we took in program development and implementation and each informed by the results of those actions.

From Rhetoric to Exploratory Talk: Defining Local Values

The rhetoric of teacher education reform framed our early exploratory dialogues and initiated the identification of core values, or principles, which would become the framework for program redesign and would drive the development of the program, its standards, curriculum content, and performance assessments. Terms such as *urban teaching, diversity, inclusion, constructivism,* and *child-centered education* are a few examples of the rhetoric we considered during this phase, in which faculty generated language that represented the ideas they considered central to the preparation of teachers for urban schools. Individuals made explicit their views within the social contexts that had been structured to facilitate our working together, which originally consisted of large group dialogue spaces only. In this way, ideas held by individuals became accessible to the broader group.

Exploration is aimed at answering the question, "What does this idea mean . . . to me, others, and to us as a community?" In our experience, the elaboration of meaning came from individuals collectively; the perspectives reflected a broad range of experience and expertise in teacher education and represented at least four departments and multiple disciplines. At times we all seemed to be using the same words to mean the same thing, but at other times different words were used to represent what appeared to be similar ideas. At still other times we did not mean the same thing and needed to clarify and lobby for various issues to be placed on the table. The actual dialogic process engaged participants in a variety of interactive patterns of talk that reflected revisions in thinking, reconstruction of ideas and meanings, and a reconceptualization of the larger ideas.

As an example, in our numerous dialogues around the concept and practice of constructivism, the conversation often relied initially on formal definitions within the literature. We all used these definitions as a way to help us begin to move away from the safe territory of other people's ideas and into our own. We restated or rephrased each other's explanations before adding another perspective or new examples. And while our conceptions of constructivism continue to deepen, the dialogic process helped us to create shared understandings and ownership of a collective definition. This would be important as the various committees moved into the dialogue explicating what a beginning teacher needs to know and do and the action associated with the assessment of a teacher's performance using a constructivist teaching/learning paradigm.

The continuation of our dialogue encouraged an elaboration of larger concepts. New key ideas were introduced, for example, a focus on families as serious partners in the educational process. We finally agreed on a set of eight core values as a starting point for program development.[7] The original list was revisited and revised during the initial stages of implementation of the primary/middle level program. The revised list that forms the conceptual umbrella for the entire program appears in Figure 2.

These revisions occurred because the original statements did not serve our purposes as well once we began to implement the program as they had during the planning stages. For example, as a result of continued deliberations informed by initial program implementation, we strengthened the value related to content preparation. We also decided to dedicate a core value to the education of students with disabilities, which originally had been integrated with a

---

The foundation of the Collaborative Teacher Education Program for Urban Communites are the seven core values. All students must reach satisfactory levels of performance in these seven areas to complete the program. Semester-by-semeter assessments provide students with a continuous measure of their performance and ongoing feedback to foster their growth and development. These seven core values are:

- **Advocating and providing equitable education** to all children, but particularly for children in urban schools.
- **Placing the developing learner at the center of the act of teaching;** teaching is child-centered.
- **Teaching based upon sound solid content knowledge** in all academic areas forming the foundation for learning.
- **Teaching based on sound pedagogical content knowledge** and sound knowledge about creating and sustaining effecting learning communities in the classroom.
- **Advocating for and educating students with disabilities** in inclusive educational settings.
- **Working closely with families and the community** as partners in the educational process.
- **Demonstrating professionalism** in all interactions with teachers, staff, administrators, and family members and in relationship to their own professional development.

Figure 2. Core values for the Collaborative Teacher Education Program for Urban Communities.

broader value on equity. By revisiting our local values on a regular basis, we gave ourselves permission to continue to raise them in public dialogue, and to question ourselves repeatedly about how we are interpreting the values in our teaching as we implement the program. Most important, we are disciplining our dialogue with an eye to how our practice is affecting our students' conceptions of their work—and their performance—as prospective teachers.

We soon discovered, however, that, like standards, core values too exist as rhetoric, as a credo of sorts. Although they represent another level of specificity in relationship to the INTASC standards (and we were able to nest our core values comfortably within the INTASC framework), it is only at the stage of implementation that they too take on meaning. Even with an initial level of prior high agreement as a factor that distinguished our starting point, we recognized that it was only when we engaged in ongoing discussion regarding how each of us treats the issues in our day-to-day work with students that we really began to understand how the meanings we personally assign to these values differ and need clarification. It is only when we revisit issues that we get to the level of saying, "This is how I talk about it in my class" or "This is what I tell my students," and talk in ways that allow us to hear each other as our students might hear us. Our work must include, on a regular basis, uncovering these nuances—that is, how we are conveying issues that are related to or represent our core values—so that we can identify the differences we hold. It is to some of these differences we now turn our attention.

Talk as the Indicator of Dissonance

Bakhtin (1981) points out that in order for dialogue to be useful in creating new ideas, a necessary characteristic is dissonance among the voices. Dissonance represents the tension that is created when participants hold different views or present dissenting opinions as part of the process of coconstructing meaning. And exploring the dissonances—rather than letting them sit unresolved because it may be uncomfortable to confront them directly—represents the occasion for greater understanding of the values that guide the program.

Example 1: Dissonance in framing children's needs. One instance of such dissonance focuses on how we address the needs children might have as a result of their living in poverty. We worried collectively about reinforcing the stereotypes our preservice students might hold in this regard. During a meeting of the full program faculty, one member said that she just tells all of her students to focus on the children as individuals and in this way they will be able to meet any needs due to any situation or cause, including poverty. Her meaning was clear: "If you frame your teaching from the perspective of children as individuals, you should be able to do your job well as a teacher." She said this without great solemnity; it was her perspective and it seemed to be sensible and realistic. The unspoken assumption was, "Isn't that how everyone else talks about it?"

In contrast, others immediately raised concerns about how the social context of urban education, urban poverty, and the complicated conditions that lead to high levels of failure for students in urban schools interfaces with the "meet individual needs" approach. Meeting individual needs was fine, and necessary, but in a teacher education program that values a serious understanding of teaching in urban schools, it seemed crucial to nest the notion of individual needs within the larger social context of institutionalized racism that also impacts children's needs and, in many cases, represents an indisputable factor in how those needs came to be in the first place. And finally, it was critical to us that our students did not equate individual needs with deficits. As prospective teachers they should recognize, actively seek to identify, and value their students' strengths as a fundamental starting point for learning.

Although we had worked for months to reach consensus on our core values, this particular slice of conversation, fraught with contradictions and cross-purposes, required clarification. Engaging in this dialogue led us all to rethink how we represent, in our own language, the way we talk about meeting children's needs and how we want to represent the interaction of the individual with the larger sociocultural context in which all individuals live. It is not that aspiring to meet the needs of every individual student is problematic in and of itself. But this view always has the potential to be problematic if our students have not yet figured out what the relationship is between children's individual needs and the sociocultural context of their lives, a context that needs at once to be honored and understood in relationship to those needs. Teasing out this complexity first for ourselves and then assessing our students in relationship to that complexity becomes paramount.

Example 2: Dissonance in how we think about disability. A second example of dissonance involves revisiting the core value related to meeting the needs of children with disabilities. From the outset, our redesign was predicated on an unusually strong linkage between special education and early childhood/primary/middle education; we had a strong history in this regard and close, longstanding working relationships among faculty in both departments. We continue to agree on a view of disability that is based on a commitment to inclusive education as well as to addressing the persistent overrepresentation of minority students in special education. So it was not surprising that our early exploratory dialogues included substantial discussion of issues related to disability. We addressed working with students with disabilities in several of the initial core values, including those related to equity, collaboration, and diversity, but chose not to develop a separate core value related to working with students with disabilities. Further, block faculty teams for the primary/middle program were constructed to include faculty from primary/middle and special education in all

phases of program development and across all four professional semesters to assure that the regular conversations in which our students were engaged provided
multiple examples, and applications, related to students with disabilities.

When we revisited the core values less than one semester into the program
pilot, it became clear that we needed to reconsider whether or not to devote a
core value to the issue of disability. The discussion focused on the degree to
which students who graduate from our program should view teaching students
with disabilities as a fundamental part of their role. If this were one part of the
program that distinguished the preparation of our students, we might argue
that this needs to be communicated through the core values, much in the same
way that we agreed that families needed a separate core value to elevate the
issue in our own minds and those of our students.

During this conversation, one faculty member, who voiced opposition to a
separate core value, stated matter-of-factly that disabilities are another "ism"
and should be handled in the same way that we present racism and sexism. The
tone echoed the one heard earlier in the dialogue about individual needs,
namely: "Isn't this the way we all talk about it?" At this point, others presented
the notion that rather than thinking of disability as another equivalent "ism,"
it might be more appropriate to see it as embedded in children's sociocultural
and socioeconomic contexts (see Pugach & Seidl, 1998). From this perspective,
the whole issue of how we talk about disability becomes more complex, and it
becomes critical to see how it fits within the core values of our program in
terms of how we address race, class, and ethnicity as well as how it is unique.
This is a dissonance that had been veiled in our earlier exploratory dialogue.
We all had agreed on the importance of disability as a theme in our work, but
the importance of exploring these subtle nuances did not surface. Initially, this
was enough; as we moved along, however, it was not sufficient.

Ultimately we chose to retain the separate core value at the same time we
continued to stress the linkages between disability and each of the other core values. However, the issue of how we address disability continues to be revisited. For
example, we are trying to identify exactly how much we address disability in our
course sequence as well as how we address it in required courses—not as an identified place in course syllabi, but rather as informal slices of conversation that have
come to be so important in our classes. We find we need to revisit the issues in
block faculty meetings to see what various instructors are actually talking about
and when, and how we can build on concepts in a way that makes most sense to
our students. One challenge has been to make sure that within each block our
Linking Seminars, which to date have been taught by special education faculty
(albeit those with clear interdisciplinary expertise and sensibilities), are not perceived as special education courses. Coteaching this seminar with school-based
instructors who are not special education teachers is one way we have conveyed
the broader nature of this experience. Once again, the challenge is to figure out

how to help our students construct a multilayered, complex understanding of the issues in relationship to their practice as teachers—without shortchanging the real knowledge they must have about disability to be the kinds of teachers that fit with the program's purpose.

Example 3: Dissonance in how we think about diversity. The quotation opening this chapter characterizes part of a recent conversation we had about our commitment to preparing teachers for urban schools. As we revisited the initial set of core values, we were in essence revisiting how we communicate this commitment in our value statements and in our teaching. What is it that the terms we readily (and often too glibly) use in relation to urban teaching actually convey? As we talked again about terms like *equity* and *diversity*, one of our colleagues expressed her frustration with the term *diversity*, reminding us that when people use the phrase *diverse learners*, they are often referring to minority students alone—and often minority students from low socioeconomic levels. It was in this context she asked if we could refrain from using the term *diversity* altogether.

In essence, we were being asked to consider more deeply how we talk about our urban mission. It is not the case that none of us had thought about the glib use of the term *diversity* and the ease with which it can connote things we might not wish it to, in particular a deficit model of students in urban schools. We do not believe any of us wishes to convey this, but we have not all thought about it sufficiently or collectively, however deep our commitment to the urban schools of Milwaukee (in which all of us are involved). It is the case that, under the umbrella of a program that holds a very public commitment to preparing teachers for urban schools, we continue to need to be vigilant about conceptions of urban teaching that we present across the program and in every experience our students have.

CATCHING THE DISSONANCE IN INFORMAL TALK

We have found that it is important to view our dialogue spaces as opportunities to catch the dissonance in our own conversations and be quick enough to address these dissonances as they naturally occur. In a sense, each time dissonances surface in our natural talk, they represent teachable moments in the reform process and as a group we must be ready to address these dissonances immediately. It is in such contested dialogues that we begin to expose how what we say conveys what may actually be discrepant representations of values upon which we thought we had agreed.

Habitual responses and regularly used verbal representations become fair and necessary game for discussion as a means of helping us push ourselves to deeper levels of complexity about the values we appear to share. We find that we must have these discussions in both small and large dialogue spaces, over time, to make sure we have regular opportunities to critique our own practice of teacher education in relation to these issues. If we fail to revisit major themes and major commitments, we run the risk of sending mixed messages to our students about some of the most important foundations of the program. We do not ask of ourselves that we each attempt to become experts in each core area; rather, we are trying to achieve a deeper level of agreement based on more substantial understandings of these issues.

As we move back and forth from considering our own practice to assessing our students, informal class talk on their part becomes a form of on-demand performance assessment that we must also catch and address. Just as we are learning to monitor our own talk as a means of clarifying our own thinking about complex issues, we also need to consider how the talk our students present in university classes and in the schools represents their own growth and development in these areas. What does a student mean, for example, when he or she consistently talks about being prepared for "diverse schools"? Are we, as faculty, willing to push the conversation with students to clarify this meaning? What conceptions of disability and inclusive education do students reveal when they talk about "the LD kid in my room," and do not talk about the child first rather than the disability label that has been attached? Do faculty members use this same language? What is implied by it?

Viewing talk as on-demand performance also obliges us to identify the stock phrases our students use that clearly signify that they have not progressed in a given area. We all have personal favorites, we find, related to our various areas of expertise. Collecting and sharing these phrases heightens our awareness of the role of talk as it represents practice. Our task, then, is to reflect on how we can better assist our students in acquiring new conceptions of the issues through their work in the field and in our classes—and then to act on those reflections. However, because we all have different areas of expertise, we need to share what these stock phrases represent and why they are problematic, thus also sharing our more complex explanations and ways of moving our students' understandings ahead. Dialogue, then, when it occurs over time in multiple spaces, becomes a form of ongoing faculty development. And faculty development, we believe, is one of the most shortchanged areas in the reform of teacher education.

DIALOGUE AND ACTION IN THE PRESERVICE
SPECIAL EDUCATION PROGRAM

Reform is a complex process when dialogue is persistent and cyclical with action. The postbaccalaureate certification program in special education illustrates this complexity as it works to develop and implement its part of the Collaborative Program. A departmental faculty team is responsible for coordinating the primary/middle special education program. As our team addressed issues specific to special education, faculty were mindful of the rhetoric that framed initial decisions regarding the relationship between special education and general education within the larger Collaborative Program. We expressed the need for the general education curriculum to have an overall greater presence and influence for students with disabilities. Additionally, there was consensus that special educators needed to be prepared to make unique contributions to educational teams supporting students with disabilities (Hains et al., 1997). Our long-term challenge was to identify what special educators needed to know and be able to do that fit with our collective conception of their role.

Faculty in the Department of Exceptional Education were active participants and coconstructors of the core values that serve as the framework for all early childhood, primary, and middle level teacher education programs and they shared dialogue spaces during the entire process. However, as faculty entered dialogue spaces associated with the special education program, dilemmas arose when attempting to align the core values, standards and assessments, and teacher education pedagogy with traditional philosophies and practices in special education. Specifically, the adoption of a constructivist paradigm as a program-wide core value stood in stark contrast to special education's historical grounding in a behavioral and technical orientation to teaching and learning. Our dilemma is not unique and represents a "tension of fundamentally different concepts of knowledge and reality" as the field of special education moves from a modern to postmodern era (Kromley, Hines, Paul, & Rosselli, 1996, p. 88). In special education, the contradiction between constructivism and behaviorism is often most salient when the question, "What do special educators need to know and be able to do in the area of literacy instruction?" is raised. Constructivist orientations have influenced all aspects of reform in teaching and learning but particularly in the area of literacy, where reading and writing instruction is connected with the broader context of communication for various purposes and audiences. In contrast, behavioral orientations prevalent in special education characterize reading and writing as a set of skills that develop in prearranged sequences disconnected from broader contexts in which reading and writing are used to satisfy needs and get things done (Searle & Dudley-Marling, 1991). The challenge was reconciling these contradictions so that the program could reflect new and consistent conceptions of teaching and learning for special educators.

While the team's conceptual and philosophical discussions continued, dialogue became driven by the need to engage in the day-to-day implementation of the teacher education program; dialogue spaces were now associated with the faculty team's collaboration around joint tasks and decision making. Specific tasks included selecting texts and materials for campus-based courses, identifying placements for teaching experiences, designing field-based projects for performance assessments, and advising and supporting preservice teachers in their work with pupils in field-based teaching experiences. As the team worked through each of these tasks, the cycle of dialogue and action drew faculty back to the need to clarify the relationship between core values and how the particular expertise of special educators would be defined.

Selecting Textbooks and Materials

One of the most salient reflections of a program's philosophy can be found in the textbooks and materials used in course work. The faculty team decided that texts and materials students would use throughout the course of the certification program should be jointly selected. Our goal was to identify a set of materials that would serve not only as teaching tools for faculty but also as useful references for preservice teachers during and beyond their teacher education program. This process of reviewing materials engaged the special education faculty in a dialogue that enabled us to reconsider what we meant by constructivist approaches when teaching students with disabilities. In particular, we had to clarify the information and experiences that preservice teachers needed to learn through course work and field experiences about how to teach reading and writing from a constructivist paradigm.

The values-based rhetoric associated with the Collaborative Program that focused our conversations on literacy included key words such as *student-centered, strengths-based, equity,* and *inclusion,* all of which we considered important elements of our view of constructivist approaches. In contrast, the rhetoric we found in the special education texts we reviewed included concepts like *individualized, deficits,* and *program alternatives.* We did not frame our dialogue by the rhetoric of typical textbooks in special education and, thus, felt free to make decisions which were more closely aligned with our established program reforms. Because we continually expanded our dialogue to include the core values and our own standards and performance expectations, we reaffirmed our belief that special educators who are certified through our program must be able to situate children with disabilities within the context and expectations of the general education curriculum.

In the area of literacy, we adopted textbooks with detailed descriptions of reading and writing development, framed instruction within balanced literacy models (e.g., Leslie & Jett-Simpson, 1997), and situated assessment and instruction in authentic literacy tasks. This framework serves as the basis for developing constructivist approaches to teaching students with disabilities and requires that preservice teachers understand and utilize the knowledge and experiences that students bring to literacy learning. We found most of our textbooks and materials in literature that addressed the needs of struggling readers and writers as well as portions of texts that addressed specific reading difficulties that students with disabilities might display.

Faculty regularly revisit the consensus-building process to confirm beliefs about what is important for students to know and to be able to do to provide consistent and ongoing support for learners' literacy development. Our approach to literacy instruction has become grounded in a process of helping learners solve problems that confront them during the reading/writing process as opposed to the application of specified procedures, or strategies, which all too often have no contextual support. To put this approach into practice, course work and teaching experiences are designed to develop students' abilities to (a) observe and document in detail reading and writing performance and strategies, (b) identify potential barriers to development by examining not only the disability but also the context in which literacy is taught and learned, (c) align expectations for achievement with typical developmental patterns, and (d) assess development within meaningful reading and writing tasks.

As we continue to review, discuss, and select materials as a faculty team, we find evidence that the dialogic process facilitates the presentation of a clear perspective to students. It provides faculty a means to articulate the ways they see the core values and standards integrated into course work and the supervision of preservice teachers. However, because of our differences in backgrounds and experiences in special education, faculty come to the task with various and developing notions of what constructivism means and looks like in teaching. Our disagreements and confusions become part of the discussions that are shared with preservice teachers as well. The process of building consensus in the midst of multiple perspectives is one that is important to preservice teachers as they, too, are faced with multiple perspectives in the field.

Unique Expertise: Conflicts in Pedagogy

But what of the instructional lessons we have accumulated from traditional empirical research based upon a positivist orientation? How do we reconcile the conflicts in orientation that historically have been the basis for much of our practice? As the faculty team focused discussions on specific pedagogical methods special educators should know and be able to use, the team faced another layer of conflicts and contradictions.

In the second year of the program, we incorporated into our team meetings the program instructors, field experience supervisors, and others who were in direct contact with our preservice teachers. Additionally, faculty increased their time in schools and classrooms, meeting with administrators and cooperating teachers and observing and talking with preservice teachers about their work with pupils. The dialogue in the team meetings, therefore, reflected an even greater urgency to prepare teachers to meet the needs of students with disabilities in urban schools because participants had built direct connections with the needs of classrooms and students. These experiences also continuously reminded us of the complexity and tensions in the field of special education, particularly with respect to pedagogy.

Our closer connections with the field fostered dialogue about issues of pedagogy that previously, in the absence of alternative perspectives, were resolved in the university-based program because faculty had control over the content of methods instruction. We were all of like minds—or so we thought. When reviewing one preservice teacher's difficulty in constructing an effective approach to reading instruction, her field experience supervisor, a new faculty member, advised the student to "get DISTAR." Other supervisors at the team meeting offered their own testimonies regarding the success of *Reading Mastery* with certain children—with some reluctance.

For faculty, *Reading Mastery* (formerly DISTAR; Englemann et al., 1988) represented the most significant contradiction to constructivist approaches to teaching students with disabilities. This instructional program embodies the strictest of behavioral principles, including scripted texts for teachers in order to assure fidelity of instruction. For many years, this program has been a staple in special education classrooms and heavily used in urban schools with students characterized as "disadvantaged." Our concerns were not only the prescribed, scripted nature of instruction; we also were concerned with the limited perspective presented to teachers and students regarding the nature of reading and writing as tools for meaningful communication and for empowering students. As an instructional approach, reading and writing mastery programs seemed more oppressive than liberating.

Several practices, programs, and strategies that are integral to the research, literature, and practice in special education are based on a philosophical framework and were developed and validated according to theories that contradict those of constructivist approaches to teaching reading. But the question we continually asked ourselves was, "Do we have to buy the philosophy with the practice?" "Are they so entwined as to prohibit our accessing these practices in ways that fit our beliefs about how students learn to read and write?" "How do the practices from the traditional experimental research base in special education that address specific needs of students with disabilities fit into the constructivist approaches we are fostering in preservice teachers?" "At the same time, how do we reconcile these practices with our core values and program standards that, on the surface, present obvious conflicts?" It is sometimes the case that the goals and process of inclusive education conflict with the need for supplemental curricula and unique instruction required for some students.

These were the questions we willingly revisited on many occasions within the team meetings and in private dialogues with students and other teachers. What emerged was our need to find ways to transcend the paradigmatic contradictions. Our decision was to reemphasize our beliefs about teachers as reflective practitioners and to support them in developing an inquiry-based approach toward accountability for student learning. Each of these is key to the core values of the Collaborative Program and to the standards within the special education program. In coming to this decision, we were reminded of Delpit's (1995) concern that practices often take precedence over children.

Our action focused on identifying ways that preservice teachers could integrate a strong sense of accountability for the methods they chose for students with disabilities based upon evidence of student learning. One of the projects in practice developed to link preservice teachers' course work and classroom teaching experiences is to design a system for monitoring student learning (Winn & Otis-Wilborn, 1999). The project requires that preservice teachers identify key indicators of learning and development for their students in the area of literacy and probe regularly for student growth in authentic reading and writing contexts. For preservice teachers, this creates the dynamic link between instruction and student learning. Hilliard (1995) stressed the need to provide increased benefits to children with disabilities stating that "children must gain significant benefits from professionals' services or there is no need for those services" (p. xi). In order to find instructional strategies that "add power to ordinary successful teaching . . . and justify special assessment and intervention" (p. xiv), we are all obliged to continue a dialogue that is open to justifiable instructional strategies but also leads to accountability for success.

CONCLUSION

In this chapter we have clarified the role that national standards can play in changing teacher education, serving as guideposts and tools of inquiry. We have also acknowledged that unless these standards are interpreted in the context of local values and local practice, they remain unexamined, surface-level rhetoric. We are not interested in reproducing knowledge that has failed and continues to fail many children and families in urban schools. We want to construct knowledge and action that have the potential to positively impact urban schools and promote learning and social change (Weiner, 1993). To do this, however, we must make concerted efforts to dig deep to understand what it is we are all talking about in the name of reform.

We have found dialogue to be a non-negotiable aspect of program reform at UWM. The rewards of this process have been a progressively closer alignment of what we say, what we know and believe, and what we do as participants in teacher education. The dialogue spaces that support various parts of the dialogue and action cycle are not temporary solutions; rather, they are an integral part of our re-normed professional life every day. As such, it is important to keep track of the meanings on which we agree as we move along—

the intellectual history of our value commitments. Because of the mobility of faculty and urban educators and the dynamic nature of professional careers, it is increasingly important to document dialogue, decisions, and actions to assist us in maintaining momentum toward the larger goal of improving the preparation of urban teachers.

Assuming leadership roles is another important way of maintaining momentum. Leadership serves many functions, not the least of which is facilitating consistent and shared communication; dilemmas, decisions, and conflicts must be kept out in the open for public dialogue. Additionally, leadership requires raising questions about issues that are sensitive and uncomfortable but important to push beyond the level of rhetoric; for example, what we really believe about urban teaching and how we express our commitments to it. Leadership also requires that individuals take responsibility for keeping alive the exploration of key issues in the various dialogue spaces in which we work. Leadership, however, is not the responsibility of a single individual but a role that we all play in the process of reform.

We see a distinct link between dialogue, action, and performance assessment. The ways in which we talk about our work are an important aspect of our performance. It is often in what our students say about teaching—not in a formal paper or a prepared presentation, but in daily dialogue in class, talk in schools, informal conversations, and informal writing—that signals what their beliefs are and whether they are shifting over time. Also, it is in their talk that we better understand our own performance—what we have accomplished and where we need to look harder at ourselves and the talk that reflects what we believe. Performance can be assessed in many contexts; however, talk is perhaps one of the most revealing among them.

The power of dialogue in reform rests with our ability to support the individual's sense of reality—confirming the fact that what each of us says and understands means something—and creating a shared reality through solidarity in the values and meanings we collectively adopt. Most important, however, the power of dialogue rests with our willingness to link our talk with our actions—actions that pose the most promising potential for improving education for students in urban schools.

NOTES

1. For a history of teacher education reform and the structure of our new programs, collectively known as the Collaborative Teacher Education Program for Urban Communities, see Hains et al., 1997 and Pugach, Winn, Ford, & Jett-Simpson, 1997.

2. Irvine (1992) contends that if we are to be successful in preparing teachers to support learning in the growing number of students from diverse cultures and backgrounds, teacher education programs must reconceptualize, that is, develop and act on

new knowledge rather than depend upon the old knowledge that has failed children in urban schools in the past. We were prepared to rethink how our programs could move away from this old knowledge.

3. Known simply as the "Collaborative Program."

4. See Hains et al., 1997, for a description of this shift in emphasis.

5. Groups within this structure are related to formal governance units such as departments and schoolwide committees; decisions regarding curriculum changes for teacher education must, for example, go through the traditional route of the School of Education's Curriculum Committee. However, because the number of faculty who participate in the Collaborative Program is large, there is usually adequate representation on major committees and in departmental decision-making meetings so that the needs of the program and the needs of the departments and other governance structures mesh well.

6. Membership on the Steering Group changes depending on the players; for example, when one member took an administrative position in the School of Education, she dropped off the group. However, it is always interdepartmental and interdisciplinary.

7. The original list of core values appears in Hains et al., 1997.

REFERENCES

Bakhtin, M. M. (1981). *The dialogic imagination: Four essays by M. M. Bakhtin.* Austin, TX: University of Texas Press.

Barnes, D. (1992). *From communication to curriculum.* Portsmouth, NH: Heinemann Publishers.

Britton, J. (1970). *Language and learning.* Portsmouth, NH: Boynton/Heinemann.

Bruner, J. (1966). *Toward a theory of instruction.* Cambridge, MA: Belknap Press.

Darling-Hammond, L. (1997). *The right to learn: A blueprint for creating schools that work.* San Francisco: Jossey Bass.

Darling-Hammond, L., Diez, M. E., Moss, P., Pecheone, R., Pullin, D., Schafer, W. D., & Vickers, L. (1998). The role of standards and assessment: A dialogue. In M. E. Diez (Ed.), *Changing the practice of teacher education: Standards and assessment as a lever for change* (pp. 11–38). Washington, DC: American Association of Colleges of Teacher Education.

Delpit, L. (1995). *Other people's children.* New York: New Press.

Englemann, S., Bruner, E., Hanner, S., Osborn, J., Osborn, S., & Zoref, L. (1988). *Reading mastery.* Worthington, OH: Science Research Associates.

Fernandez-Balboa, J. M., & Marshall, J. (1994). Dialogical pedagogy in teacher education: Toward an education for democracy. *Journal of Teaching Education, 45*(3), 172–189.

Hains, A. H., Maxwell, C B., Tiezzi, L., Jett-Simpson, M., Ford, A., & Pugach, M. C. (1997). From individual and ambiguous to collaborative and explicit: Reform in urban teacher education at the University of Wisconsin–Milwaukee. In L. P. Blanton, C. C. Griffin, J. A. Winn, & M. C. Pugach (Eds.), *Teacher education in transition* (pp. 180–206). Denver, CO: Love Publishing.

Hilliard, A. (1995). Foreword. In B. Alexis Ford, F. Obiakor, & J. Patton (Eds.), *Effective education of African American exceptional learners.* Austin, TX: Pro-Ed.

Holmes Group. (1986). *Tomorrow's teachers.* East Lansing, MI: Author.

Interstate New Teacher Assessment and Support Consortium (INTASC). (1992). *Model standards for beginning teacher licensing and development: A resource for state dialogue.* Washington, DC: Council of Chief State School Officers.

Irvine, J. J. (1991). *Black students and school failure.* New York: Praeger.

Irvine, J. J. (1992). Making teacher education culturally responsive. In M. Dilworth (Ed.), *Diversity in teacher education* (pp. 79–92). San Francisco: Jossey-Bass.

Kromley, J., Hines, C., Paul, J., & Rosselli, H. (1996). Creating and using a multiparadigmatic knowledge base for restructuring teacher education in special education: Technical and philosophical issues. *Teacher Education and Special Education, 19*(2), 87–101.

Leslie, L., & Jett-Simpson, M. (1997). *Authentic literacy assessment: An ecological approach.* New York: Longman.

Pugach, M. C., & Seidl, B. L. (1998). Responsible linkages between diversity and disability: A challenge for special education. *Teacher Education and Special Education, 21*(4), 319–333.

Pugach, M. C., Winn, J., Ford, A., & Jett-Simpson, M. (1997, March 25). *The University of Wisconsin-Milwaukee's Collaborative Teacher Education Program for Urban Communities.* Paper presented at the Annual Meeting of the American Educational Research Association, Chicago.

Searle, D., & Dudley-Marling, C. (1991). *When students have time to talk.* Portsmouth, NH: Heinemann.

Weiner, L. (1993). *Preparing teachers for urban schools.* New York: Teachers College Press.

Wells, G., & Chang-Wells, G. L. (1992). *Constructing knowledge together.* Portsmouth, NH: Heinemann.

Winn, J., & Otis-Wilborn, A. (1999). But, how do I know my students are becoming better readers and writers? Monitoring literacy learning. *Teaching Exceptional Children, 32*(1), 40–47.

CHAPTER 9

Visions and Outcomes: Developing Standards and Assessments in Wheelock College Teacher Preparation Programs

Mieko Kamii and Susan Redditt

Plant in the land of children whatever you wish to be put into the life of our time.
—Lucy Wheelock

In 1888, the year kindergarten became part of the public school program in Boston, 31-year-old Lucy Wheelock opened Miss Wheelock's Kindergarten Training School. Her curriculum was based on the writings of Friedrich Froebel, father of kindergarten education, and G. Stanley Hall, father of the child study movement. A year later, she graduated her first class of six women (Miller & Silvernail, 2000). Over time, "Miss Lucy's school," as neighbors would affectionately call it, became a college known for its program in early childhood education. Wheelock College gradually expanded its programs and currently prepares professionals at the undergraduate and graduate levels for the fields of education, social work, and child life (work with children in hospitals and other medical settings). Thus for 112 years, Wheelock's mission of improving the quality of life of children and families has found fertile ground. This mission continues to guide the college's programming and to attract faculty, students, and staff who want to make a difference in the lives of children and families.

As a result of reflecting on the school's history, appraising the needs of the surrounding community, and looking to the future, the Wheelock community has embraced high quality education in urban communities as a focal point of its work. After holding a year-long conversation recently, the campus commu-

165

nity articulated its vision for the first decade of the new millennium: Wheelock is a diverse learning community that educates students in the liberal arts and sciences; prepares students to work with, and to teach, all of the nation's children effectively; develops in students, faculty, and staff the skills and dispositions to work collaboratively with diverse families, communities, professionals, and organizations; and encourages everyone belonging to the Wheelock community to be advocates for social justice (Wheelock College, 2000).

This mission or vision is one of four contextual influences that bear on the story we share here about developing standards and assessments at Wheelock. A second influence is the culture at the college that supports faculty inquiry into questions related to teaching, student development and learning, and educational outcomes. Two such questions are prominent in current discussions of curriculum, instruction, assessment, and standards: "What does it take to educate a group of individuals to teach all of the nation's children effectively?" and "What must prospective teachers experience so that they can become lifelong learners and exemplary teachers?" (Wheelock College, 2000). The national standards movement is a third influence. The development of national standards for teachers,[1] and accreditation standards for institutions,[2] has shaped our work on standards and assessments, as has the state's accountability-driven focus on K–12 students' learning[3] and prospective teachers' competencies.[4] Fourth and finally, Wheelock's participation in the Leading Edge network provided the impetus for Wheelock faculty members and teachers from our professional development sites to come together to develop the first set of common standards for all of Wheelock's teacher preparation programs. Leading Edge gave us an all-important forum for dialogue and discussion that brought clarity to the messy process of constructing linkages among Wheelock's mission or vision, its culture and curriculum, and Interstate New Teacher and Assessment Support Consortium (INTASC), National Board for Professional Teaching Standards (NBPTS), and National Council for Accreditation of Teacher Education (NCATE) 2000 standards and performance assessments.

This chapter chronicles our continuing journey in developing standards and a system of performance assessments at Wheelock. We weave into this account some of the lessons we have learned along the way:

- In theory, standards embody the principles which shape the curriculum and pedagogy that prospective teachers experience. The curriculum that faculty members develop for programs and in their courses, and the pedagogy that they and cooperating practitioners practice in their classrooms, enact those standards. Curriculum and pedagogy, together with academic resources and supports, ought to afford students equitable opportunities to learn and achieve high standards. Standards-based performance assessments provide evidence of what students know, understand, and can do, and show faculty members whether students' knowledge and understanding is broad and deep enough to teach children well.

- Conversations about educational outcomes per se are less contentious than discussions of how those outcomes are to be achieved, for the latter reveal competing political philosophies, competing theories of human development and learning, and competing visions of the aims of education and teaching.

- The task of achieving consensus on standards inevitably yields lengthy and unwieldy first drafts that try to accommodate the core beliefs and interests of all. When the standards are put into practice, everyone sees the necessity of reducing them into a workable system. The result is fewer and broader standards with specifics articulated in developmental benchmarks and indicators.

- External mandates in the form of regional and national accreditation standards set by professional organizations[5] as well as state policies governing educator licensure and program approval force institutions to confront contradictions and alter their policies and practices in productive as well as uncomfortable ways.

- Providing students with effective, high quality opportunities to learn requires ingenuity, hard work, and compromise on the part of faculty members, administrators, cooperating practitioners, and students. One way to persuade all parties to make appropriate adjustments is to maintain focus on the learning, development, and academic achievement of prospective teachers and children.

We begin with an account of how we approached the task of developing standards and assessments and then take up the role that external influences—national accreditation standards and state licensure and program approval policies—played in our work. Next we discuss the ways in which Wheelock's culture and curriculum influenced the shape of our standards, with their clear focus on equity and diversity. Finally, we talk about the specific ways in which our membership in Leading Edge supported this work.

DEVELOPING STANDARDS AND ASSESSMENTS

In July 1997 with support from the Leading Edge network, 12 Wheelock faculty members (including one teacher-liaison from a professional development school) volunteered to form a study group. The aim of the study group was to suggest a set of college-wide standards for all of Wheelock's graduate and undergraduate teacher education programs. Together, the members of the study group represented all of the teacher preparation programs at the college. From the outset, the group's goal was to write Wheelock's teaching program standards—not separate standards for the undergraduate and graduate programs, not separate standards for the early childhood, elementary, and special needs programs, but standards that would reflect our collective wisdom concerning what novices preparing themselves for classroom teaching should know and be able to do at the conclusion of their programs of study at Wheelock.

The group wanted the standards to focus the attention of students, faculty, supervisors, cooperating practitioners, and administrators on the urgency of providing high quality teaching and learning experiences for all children. Of particular concern to the group was confronting challenges posed for education in our multiracial, multicultural society: fostering high achievement for all children; ensuring equity of outcomes; understanding diversity and antiracist, antibias practice as a strength and promise of our society, not a criticism of it; and collaborating with families and communities to secure their engagement in children's education and to build capacity within urban communities for action.

Our strategy was straightforward. We would start by reviewing internal documents related to standards and assessments that the individual programs had been using. We would study the INTASC model standards, the materials prepared by NBPTS, and documents written by our Leading Edge partners. Since earlier studies of the NBPTS assessment process had raised suspicions of cultural bias in the assessment of teaching, we would call upon Dr. Maritza Macdonald, the first director of the Leading Edge project, to help us think through our questions and hesitations. By the end of the summer, we would send a draft of the suggested standards to our colleagues at the college and in the schools for their critical review, and during the following school year we would use their feedback to revise the standards. Simultaneously, we would tackle assessment questions. To achieve the goal of preparing excellent teachers for urban communities, we would use the tripartite framework of (1) content standards: What do we want our students to know, be able to do, and be disposed to do? (2) performance standards: What does "good" look like? and How good is "good enough"? and (3) opportunity-to-learn standard: Do students have access to resources and supports that give them a fair chance at achieving high standards?

By the end of the summer, the study group had reviewed documents and arrived at consensus. We agreed to use the INTASC model standards as a framework for Wheelock's standards, and to modify INTASC language and write additional standards to reflect our core beliefs. In the fall of 1997, faculty in the graduate school's teaching programs took the lead in drafting a set of standards that articulated our values and perspectives as early childhood, elementary, and specialized educators who were committed to principles of equity and diversity, and who wanted Wheelock's teaching programs—the courses and field experiences required of students in our curriculum—to prepare people to teach effectively all of the nation's children. The 15 proposed standards were sent to the undergraduate education faculty who reviewed and edited them, and added a standard on the use of educational technology in teaching. The graduate school's education faculty approved the revised standards the following month.

The subsequent year, 1998, was a period of turbulence at the college for reasons unrelated to the work on standards. Concerted work on these standards resumed in earnest at the start of 1999. The graduate school faculty revisited and reaffirmed as its working standards what it had adopted in 1997. (Refer to the Appendix at end of this chapter while reading the discussion that follows.)

Comparison of Wheelock and INTASC Standards

The standards adopted at Wheelock shared kinship with INTASC Core Standards, but we went beyond them. Wheelock faculty members concluded that while the INTASC standards were quite comprehensive, they fell short in areas that are important for a college that not only values early childhood and elementary education, but also focuses a great deal of attention on equity and diversity and on preparing people to teach in urban communities. We point out eight ways in which the standards differ. First, the INTASC standards are written to include high school and middle school teaching and learning and thus do not always reflect the language and tasks of early childhood and elementary education. For example, INTASC's first standard on subject matter knowledge says teachers should understand the "structures of the disciplines" they teach. This is entirely appropriate for a math teacher in high school, for instance, but less so for teachers doing number sense with 4-year-olds or fourth graders. The same point applies in the third INTASC standard on individual differences, with its implied focus on teacher-centered instruction. Early childhood educators think more broadly in terms of age-appropriate play and learning activities, and elementary educators think about learning centers, activities, and projects that provide multiple avenues to conceptual understanding for children.

Second, INTASC assumes that children's learning and development are relatively context free. Wheelock's versions of INTASC's second standard on children's development and learning, and fifth standard on motivation and behavior, contain the phrase "in a variety of familial and cultural contexts." This reflects our belief that familial, cultural, linguistic, and other contextual factors that create the historical and personal experiences, and therefore the interpretive frameworks that individuals and groups bring with them to the learning environment, are critical. They are the raw materials out of which educators must create classroom norms that support the social and academic development of each child, including the ability to listen, to be respectful and kind to classmates, and to do his or her best work. Interpretive frameworks influence not only what and how children learn and construct meaning, but how individual children manage any one of a number of developmental tasks.

These points are emphasized in Wheelock's fourth and fifth standards which have no corresponding INTASC standard. Differences in experiences and ways of understanding can be powerful sources of strength, enabling more children and families to contribute to the learning community's work. In fact, our faculty thought it necessary to state explicitly in Wheelock's sixth standard our institutional focus on multicultural, antiracist, antibias educational practices, and our strong belief that educators must foster positive learning experiences and high achievement for all children.

Fourth, in INTASC's fourth standard on teaching strategies and the corresponding Wheelock standard, it is apparent that INTASC emphasizes cognitive processes underlying rational, deductive, analytic thought. Imaginative thought or cognitive processes used in the visual and performing arts are not named, as they are in Wheelock's version.

Fifth, Wheelock's ninth and INTASC's sixth standard on communication provide another example of contrasting tasks and concerns in early childhood and elementary education on the one hand, and secondary education on the other. At Wheelock, for example, we are trying to understand what all teachers need to know to teach not only standard conventions for communicating information, but to teach reading skills in multilingual preschool and primary classrooms. The next pair of standards are similar, except that Wheelock's version recognizes that early childhood and elementary teachers must be cognizant of family and community contexts as they plan and prepare lessons.

The vast majority of students entering the fields of early childhood and elementary education, and all of their postsecondary instructors, did not use computers as 4-year-olds nor surf the Net as fourth graders. We thought it prudent, therefore, to emphasize technology in a separate standard, as much for faculty members as for teacher candidates.

INTASC's eighth standard and the corresponding Wheelock standard on assessment vary in emphasis rather than content. Wheelock highlights assessment for the purpose of making pedagogical decisions, while INTASC focuses on assessment to ensure student development. The next pair of standards on reflective practice are virtually the same, except that Wheelock uses the term *families* instead of the less inclusive term *parents*, in recognition of the fact that many children are raised by people other than their parents.

Seventh, INTASC's 10th and Wheelock's 14th standard on professional responsibilities embody differences in two ways. First, Wheelock strongly believes in collaboration as a modus operandi. The days and ways of teacher isolation and of Lone Ranger or Lady Bountiful intervention to fix other people's problems are mercifully waning. Interprofessional partnerships, teamwork, and collaboration are as critical for academic problem solving as they are for the effective delivery of services to children and their families. Second, we do not assume a singular community outside the walls of the school. Most people belong to multiple communities—the neighborhoods we live in, the professions we identify with, the leisure-time groups we join, the faith-based communities we belong to, the communities based in political action we rally around, and so on.

Wheelock's 15th and 16th standards clearly broaden the arena of teacher preparation beyond the classroom door. The INTASC standards are silent about organizational structures that influence life in the classroom in important ways—just think of the elementary school schedule, for instance—and they make no mention of being aware of legal, ethical, or policy matters that influence what goes on in the classroom and school. For example, in Massachusetts and in communities across the nation, recent changes in welfare policy have had an immense impact on children and families and therefore on classroom and school life. In short, at Wheelock, we have consciously broadened the arena of teacher preparation beyond the classroom door.

Translating Standards Into Assessments

Our original objectives with respect to drafting standards for our teacher preparation programs have been achieved. The 16 standards embody the faculty's vision of what well-prepared educators should know and be able to do. But the 16 statements also gave us pause: Is it reasonable to expect students to understand all that we say they should? Is it reasonable to expect faculty members to teach all that these standards say we should aspire to teach? How would we develop benchmarks and indicators for faculty members to use in assessing student performance, and for students to use in appraising their own work? To tackle these questions, graduate education faculty meetings were structured to make time for looking at student work that faculty members had selected as examples of how they were beginning to address the standards in their courses.

At a recent meeting of the graduate and undergraduate education faculties, an illuminating moment occurred that helped us see the merit of what we were doing, but also underscored the indispensable link between standards and assessment practices. One of our faculty brought in the syllabus for a course she was already teaching, along with materials she had prepared for her students to help them make connections between the work they were doing in her course and each of the standards, one-by-one. Her syllabus had been devised prior to the drafting of our standards, so it embodied simply her professional judgment about what her course ought to cover. But with the standards now before her, she asked herself, "What relevance does my course have to the standards?" She ended up a bit perplexed, in a way that we found quite helpful (more on that in a moment).

What was encouraging is that she was already responding to one of the two vital assessment challenges: She was assessing her own course and restructuring it (as best she could while it was underway) to reflect the new standards. Our colleague was tackling the other vital assessment task—at least in part—with the materials she had prepared for her students, explaining the link between the standards and their work for the course. Student awareness of the goals set by the standards, and the connection to course topics and assignments, is an important step in the preparation of teachers. But assessment must encompass both course inputs and student outcomes. Ideally, courses designed with the new standards in mind will include their own assessment tools—in the form of course assignments, papers, exams, and so forth—that will reveal the substantive command students have developed over the course topic as well as how deeply they have absorbed the new standards in their own thinking and practice.

Our colleague's effort to match her course to our new standards left her perplexed in a way that proved helpful. The problem, she argued, was the daunting task of keeping 16 separate standards in mind simultaneously while devising a course or a student assignment. She urged us to bring some helpful conceptual order to the array.

We decided to organize the standards into seven clusters which we derived from the NBPTS standards (1995, 1996) for early and middle childhood:

  I.   Advocacy for social justice (Wheelock standards 4, 5, and 6)
  II. Understanding of all the nation's children in their many dimensions (Wheelock standards 2, 3, 4, and 5)
  III. Knowledge of content and integrated curriculum (Wheelock standard 1)
  IV. Use of educational practices that foster learning, development, and achievement for all the nation's children (Wheelock standards 6, 7, 8, 9, 10, and 11)
  V.   Assessment in a multiracial, multicultural democracy (Wheelock standards 6 and 12)
  VI. Reflective practice (Wheelock standard 13)
  VII. Family, community, and professional partnerships in a diverse society (Wheelock standards 14, 15, and 16).

Our current task is to build deep community understanding of the meaning of the seven clusters and to develop a common language to describe and communicate that meaning. Then we will be poised to compose benchmarks and indicators, and to test the system with student work. Draft two of Wheelock's teaching program standards and assessments is on the horizon.

NATIONAL STANDARDS AND STATE POLICIES

The pioneering work of NBPTS and INTASC contributed to the development of Wheelock's teaching program standards in ways other than those described above. In articulating standards for beginning and accomplished teachers, for example, INTASC and NBPTS provide guideposts for thinking carefully about a developmental continuum from beginning to accomplished practice. The assessment systems developed by INTASC and NBPTS also provide concrete and instructive models for using multiple measures—individual performance over time (reflective portfolios and videotapes of teaching) and on-demand writing prompts at testing centers—to assess professional competence. In this section we take up the influence of another set of national standards that propelled us forward in this work, those of NCATE. We also discuss the influence of the state's agenda for educational reform in Massachusetts.

In spring 1999, Wheelock decided to seek NCATE reaccreditation under the new NCATE 2000 Unit Standards. In January 2000, the college agreed to be a pilot site for the new standards and to prepare for a site visit that would take place during the 2000–01 academic year.[6] NCATE requested that the pilot sites address in detail two standards concerning candidate performance (see Table 1), and treat more globally four standards focused on unit capacity.[7]

Table 1
NCATE 2000 Unit Standards for Candidate Performance

Standard 1. Candidate knowledge, skills, and dispositions

Candidates preparing to work in schools as teachers or other professional school personnel know and demonstrate the content, pedagogical, and professional knowledge, skills, and dispositions necessary to help all students learn. Assessments indicate that candidates meet professional, state, and institutional standards.

Standard 2. Assessment system and unit evaluation

The unit has an assessment system that collects and analyzes data on the applicant qualifications, candidate and graduate performance, and unit operations to evaluate and improve the unit and its programs.

The decision to be reviewed under NCATE 2000 was critical for the work on standards and assessments in two ways. First, NCATE insists that the education unit of a college or university have considerable autonomy and control over its own budget and operations. NCATE's sixth standard on unit governance and resources states, "The unit has the leadership, authority, budget, personnel, facilities, and resources . . . for the preparation of candidates to meet professional, state, and institutional standards" (NCATE, 2000). Until the summer of 2000, Wheelock's undergraduate and graduate education faculties belonged to different departments that held separate meetings and reported to different deans. This structure impeded regular dialogue and joint work on standards and assessments among education faculty from the undergraduate and graduate divisions of the college. The restructuring of the departments and faculties into a single education unit headed by a dean of education will allow all education faculty members to engage in common conversation about standards and to construct a performance-based assessment system for the teaching programs.

Second, the need to address in detail NCATE's first and second standards focused the attention of academic and administrative leaders who had not previously been keenly interested in performance assessment that went beyond self-assessment, course grades, and scores on state tests. The INTASC standards are embedded in NCATE's first standard on candidate knowledge, skills, and dispositions. Together, NCATE's first and second standards provided a context for better explaining to them why the sixteen standards were developed earlier, and why there was urgency in developing a performance assessment system for them. The NCATE standards underscored the utility of developing an assessment system that uses multiple measures to assess program quality. In addition to student scores on the state's teacher tests, we would use performance-based evidence of student learning and achievement for program completion (e.g., reflective portfolios, videotapes, and portfolio presentations), and gather data from recent graduates on how well their programs prepared them for the complexities and challenges of teaching (e.g., surveys).

Before NCATE's first, second, and sixth standards rose to the top of their agenda, Wheelock's academic and administrative leadership's attention was riveted on teacher testing for initial licensure. In 1998, student scores on the Massachusetts Educator Certification Tests (MECT) were reported in the press. Trustees, heads of institutions, board members of professional organizations, members of the evaluation and teacher education communities, and policymakers at the Massachusetts Board of Higher Education and Massachusetts Department of Education entered into discordant debate. Federal Title II reporting requirements of "80% institutional pass rates" on state tests,[8] the state reporting requirements of "80% pass rates for each program," and "alternative route licensure" insistently consumed leadership's attention in colleges, schools, and departments of education across the state. In the meantime, statewide testing on the Massachusetts Comprehensive Assessment System (MCAS) of students in the fourth, eighth, and tenth grades (becoming high stakes for high school students), loomed as explosive issues in the state. Discussion of standards and performance-based assessments focused on deep improvement of teacher preparation and provision of a qualified, caring teacher for each child was eclipsed in the accountability debate.

National standards for teacher education (NCATE) and national standards for teacher performance (INTASC and NBPTS) which looked developmentally rather than narrowly at teacher education, teacher quality, and teacher development provided much-needed ballast in this accountability-driven environment. Continual criticism of teachers, schools, and teacher preparation programs for having no standards could be addressed productively. And the timing of the NCATE site visit added urgency to this work. Wheelock had less than a year to restructure the education unit, prepare the Institutional Report, collect the requisite documents, and (of particular interest here) design an institutional performance assessment plan focused on student outcomes for both teacher candidates and P–12 students.

With the support of the academic and administrative leadership, the Wheelock community entered a new phase of learning about, and collaborating with, schools to develop a standards-based performance assessment system that will serve Wheelock students and their students well. Our portfolio development and assessment process, combined with the traditional tools and measures we use—grades, observation and conferences reports, self-assessments, and test scores—will give us confidence that our students are well prepared to teach all children in urban as well as suburban and rural schools.

TEACHING ALL OF THE NATION'S CHILDREN EFFECTIVELY

We noted earlier that Wheelock's mission or vision attracts faculty members who love their disciplines, value teaching and learning, and willingly participate in conversations about social justice. In fact, faculty members in teacher education programs across the country probably look in a mirror and see reflected back the image of an educator who would never seek to do harm. But as an academic community we must ask ourselves why we continue to harm urban poor children and middle class youngsters of color, however indirectly, by failing to prepare educators who can teach all children in ways that result in higher educational achievement, particularly in these groups (see Chapter 10). What does "teaching all of the nation's children effectively" look like? What do prospective teachers, the vast majority of whom are and will continue to be white, need to experience in order to become "lifelong learners and exemplary teachers?" The Wheelock culture encourages white, black, and brown people of all ages to address these issues openly in communal forums such as faculty meetings, class sessions, and discussions with guests of the college who come to share their experiences and their work with us. Our discussions continue with colleagues in hallways and classrooms and with students, cooperating practitioners, and school administrators at field sites.

The Wheelock culture and curriculum help to explain why our standards look the way they do. As a college, we have embraced multicultural education as a lens through which to learn about the experiences and contributions of people unlike ourselves. Multicultural education is also a vehicle for faculty members and students to come to grips with issues of privilege, power, and oppression.

Faculty members at Wheelock understand that to educate all children, prospective teachers must have deep theoretical and experiential knowledge about how children grow and develop, and use this knowledge to construct developmentally appropriate, culturally responsive approaches to the care and education of children. We believe students must know how children develop; how children's physical, cognitive, language, emotional, and social development is influenced by the experiences they have in their families and communities; how those experiences are shaped by the sociocultural and linguistic contexts in which they live; and how the larger policy arena affects individuals and groups differently (Wheelock College, 2000).

Faculty members believe that praxis is critical, so students have a variety of field experiences that allow them to examine both the explanatory power and the limitations of the theories and models of development they are studying. As freshmen, they enroll in a required course, Children and Their Environments, which has a half-day-per-week, community-based field placement. Students learn to explore new neighborhoods, take note of community assets, interview community leaders, and work collaboratively with one another. As sophomores, they enroll in a required year-long Human Growth and Development (HGD) course that includes two semester-long field experiences. The first is with infants, toddlers, or young children; the second is with older children, teenagers, or adults. Students gain experience in closely observing specific aspects of physical, cognitive, language, social, and emotional development, and linking their observations to developmental theory and research. They learn to record children's language and behavior carefully, and develop habits of reflecting on what they see, what they hear, and what they fail to notice. Students are encouraged to be mindful of the multiplicity of sociocultural influences, theoretical orientations, and assumptions about "best practices" that bear on their interpretations of development. HGD also takes up variations in development—racial identity development, first and second language acquisition, and sexual orientation, for example—which have salience for an inclusive multicultural society (Wheelock College, 2000).

Prospective teachers must be able to make decisions about the content of instruction in light of what they know about children. Wheelock requires prospective teachers to complete a multidisciplinary major in the arts and sciences—either in the Humanities (literature, history, and philosophy), Human Development (psychology, sociology, and anthropology), the Arts (music, visual arts, and theater) or Math/Science. The multidisciplinary majors presume that knowing and understanding interesting topics deeply (e.g., the New England Renaissance of Henry David Thoreau or the Harlem Renaissance of Langston Hughes), and solving complex problems thoughtfully (e.g., global warming or the AIDS epidemic), involves drawing on multiple disciplines. The majors, and the undergraduate curriculum as a whole, reflect an expanded canon. Students are able to study the history, culture, and traditions of historically excluded peoples, thereby developing an understanding not only of what it means to know something deeply, but how knowledge is developed, constructed, and revised within disciplines (Wheelock, 2000).

Most faculty members in the arts and sciences employ pedagogical practices that are similar to those that education faculty members want their students to develop: interactions that are child-centered, family-focused, and community-oriented; teaching that is constructivist and that encourages critical thinking and deep understanding; curricular materials that are developmentally appropriate and culturally responsive; activities that enable students with differing learning styles to succeed; and assessments that inform instructional decisions and support student learning. The convergence of multidisciplinary majors and multicultural content in the undergraduate program creates an intellectual space for considering the influence of race, social class, language, and of cultural beliefs, expectations, and practices on students' and children's development and learning.

Both undergraduates and graduate students are required to fulfill a multicultural course requirement. However, most of the graduate students enter Wheelock having completed an arts and sciences major at another institution. Because their professional preparation program lasts only 14 months, they have less time to explore their assumptions and confront their biases than do undergraduates. On the other hand, many graduate students have year-long internships at PDSs that have diverse student bodies and faculties in which issues of race and academic achievement are explicitly addressed.

In the mid-1990s, many graduate school meetings included readings that provoked conversation about multicultural education, diversity, and race. However, few of these discussions went beyond what James Banks calls an additive orientation in multicultural education, or simply adding multicultural works without altering the approach to, or questions asked about, the topic (Banks, 1995a, 1995b, 1997). In the absence of critical interrogation—examination of the perspectives from which courses or questions are framed, stories are told, events are interpreted, theories are constructed—the promise of multicultural education as transformative education could not be realized. It was particularly difficult for a predominantly white, female faculty to think deeply about issues of racism, white identity, and white privilege, and to see the ways in which their internalized and often unconscious attitudes and beliefs shaped and handicapped their ability to teach students of color effectively.

The conversation in the graduate school gradually shifted as faculty members read about racial identity development and its relevance to both student and faculty learning (Tatum, 1992); about moving beyond a tolerance paradigm (Nieto, 1994, 1996); about the difference between multiculturalism with and without an antiracist perspective (Meier & Mizell, 1996); about the threat to the pillars of the radical democratic tradition by racism in America (West, 1993); and about white discourse on white racism by academics in schools of education (Scheurich, 1993). However, there was dissonance between faculty members who focused on race and racism in discussions of diversity and members of the graduate special needs program who wanted to include disabilities in these discussions. The former argued that talking about race and racism, and disability and exclusion of the disabled in the same conversation about diversity ran the danger of circumventing the role of racism in educators' practice. The outcome, they argued, could be seen in the persistent overidentification of children of color as needing special education (Meier & Brown, 1994).

As contentious and shrill as such discussions could become, they nevertheless persisted over time. It is in the context of these developments in the undergraduate and graduate divisions that (by 1997) education faculty members from across the college were able to articulate standards that emphasize equity and diversity.

HELP FROM LEADING EDGE PARTNERS

Among the Leading Edge partners were individuals who had followed the work of the NBPTS closely. Also in the network were institutions—the University of Wisconsin–Milwaukee (UWM) in particular—that had begun to use the INTASC standards in their teacher education programs generally, and to modify them in specific programs. Wheelock College was originally paired with UWM because both institutions were committed to preparing teachers for urban schools and inclusive classroom teaching (see Chapter 10). That pairing was fortuitous not only because of the commitments we had made to matters of race and social justice directly, but because Wheelock was able to learn and borrow from UWM's example of working with the INTASC Model Standards.

Earlier we described the manner in which Wheelock used the INTASC standards as a framework and the role that the NBPTS standards played as we began to develop an assessment system. Our Leading Edge dyad partner had accomplished two things before the network was convened: UWM had added an 11th standard to INTASC's 10; and faculty members in UWM's postbaccalaureate special needs program had revised the INTASC standards to reflect teaching tasks and language of the special education community. UWM showed us that, indeed, the INTASC standards could be used in the way INTASC originally intended, and that is as a model to be modified to meet state, institutional, or programmatic goals.

More recently, as Wheelock began to design its performance assessment system, we turned once again to the system that UWM's postbaccalaureate special education faculty members had designed. Theirs is a system of broad standards, developmental benchmarks, and specific indicators that provides guidance to students about where they should be heading. At the same time, it provides common tools for faculty members to use in assessing students' progress early in the program, at the midpoint, and at the conclusion of their formal studies. The special education faculty had been developing the system over several years and was almost done. UWM once again provided a model from which we could compose benchmarks and indicators for Wheelock's teacher education programs.

The reader might reasonably ask, "Why was it necessary to expend funds to support this kind of dyadic work in Leading Edge?" As is true of difficult, complex work in many areas of education where competing perspectives and competing interests make progress extremely difficult and slow, the person-to-person assistance, understanding, and mutual support that grows out of relationships built over time make an immense difference in staying the course in stormy seas. It is an oft-repeated story in the tales of building professional development school relationships. The Leading Edge partners built relationships that helped each of us navigate the currents of our departments, institutions, and states. Our relationship with UWM helped bring us closer to the system of standards and assessments we envisioned.

NOTES

1. We refer to the Interstate New Teacher and Assessment Support Consortium Model Standards for Beginning Teachers (INTASC 1992), and the National Board for Professional Teaching Standards (NBPTS, 1990).

2. We refer to NCATE 2000, the standards and performance-based assessment scheme of the National Council for Accreditation of Teacher Education (NCATE, 2000).

3. We refer to NCATE 2000, the standards and performance-based assessment scheme of the National Council for Accreditation of Teacher Education (NCATE, 2000).

4. Prospective teachers are required to pass the Massachusetts Tests for Educator Licensure (MTEL), formerly called the Massachusetts Educator Certification Test.

5. Wheelock College is accredited by the New England Association of Schools and Colleges (NEASC), the National Council for Accreditation of Teacher Education (NCATE), and the Council on Social Work Education (CSWE).

6. Wheelock's visit was scheduled for October 2000.

7. These include field experiences and clinical practice (standard 3), diversity (standard 4), faculty qualifications, performance, and development (standard 5), and unit governance and resources (standard 6).

8. Massachusetts Tests for Educator Licensure (MTEL).

REFERENCES

Banks, J. A. (1995a). Multicultural educational and curriculum transformation. *Journal of Negro Education, 64*(4), 390–400.

Banks, J. A. (1997). *Teaching strategies for ethnic studies* (6th ed.). Boston: Allyn & Bacon.

Brandt, R. (1994). On educating for diversity: A conversation with James A. Banks, *Educational Leadership, 51*(8), 28–32.

Interstate New Teacher Assessment and Support Consortium. (1992). *Model standards for beginning teacher licensing and development: A resource for state dialogue.* Washington, DC: Council of Chief State School Officers.

Meier, T., & Brown, C. R. (1994). The color of inclusion. *Journal of Emotional and Behavioral Problems, 3*(3), 15–18.

Meier, T., & Mizell, L. (1996). Multiculturalism and anti-racism: A schemata. Unpublished document.

Miller, L., & Silvernail, D. (2000). Learning to become a teacher: The Wheelock way. In Linda Darling-Hammond (Ed.), *Studies of excellence in teacher education: Preparation in the undergraduate years* (pp. 67–108). Washington, DC: AACTE.

National Board for Professional Teaching Standards. (1990). *Toward high and rigorous standards for the teaching profession.* Washington, DC: Author.

National Board for Professional Teaching Standards. (1995). *Early childhood/generalist: Standards for national board certification.* Washington, DC: Author.

National Board for Professional Teaching Standards. (1996). *Middle Childhood/generalist: Standards for national board certification.* Washington, DC.: Author.

National Council for Accreditation of Teacher Education. (2000). *NCATE 2000 unit standards.* Washington, DC: Author.

Nieto, S. (1994). Affirmation, solidarity, and critique: Moving beyond tolerance in multicultural education. *Multicultural Education, 1*(4), 9–12, 35–38.

Nieto, S. (1996). *Affirming diversity: The sociopolitical context of multicultural education.* White Plains, NY: Longman.

Scheurich, J. J. (1993). Toward a white discourse on white racism. *Educational Researcher, 22*(8), 5–10.

Tatum, B. D. (1992). Talking about race, learning about racism: The application of racial identity development theory in the classroom. *Harvard Educational Review, 62,* 1–24.

West, C. (1993, October). Audacious hope and sense of history. Keynote address at conference of the Organization for Social Change, New York.

Wheelock College. (2000). *Institutional report: Continuing NCATE/State accreditation.* Boston: Author.

Appendix to Chapter 9

Teaching Program Standards Wheelock College	INTASC Core Standards
1. Educators understand the central concepts, tools of inquiry, and content/subject matters/disciplines they teach, and can create learning experiences that make them meaningful and accessible for children.	1. The teacher understands the central concepts, tools of inquiry, and structures of the discipline(s) he or she teaches and can create learning experiences that make these aspects of subject matter meaningful for students.
2. Educators understand how children learn, construct knowledge, and develop in a variety of familial and cultural contexts, and can provide learning opportunities that support their intellectual, aesthetic, social, and personal development.	2. The teacher understands how children learn and develop, and can provide learning opportunities that support their intellectual, social,and personal development.
3. Educators understand how children differ in their approaches to learning and create age-appropriate play, activity-based or instructional opportunities that are adapted to diverse learners.	3. The teacher understands how studnets differ in their approaches to learning and creates instructional opportunities that are adapted to diverse learners.
4. Educators understand the social, economic, cultural, and linguistic contexts from which children come and communicate respectfully, from a strengths perspective, with children and families in the learning community.	
5. Educators build on the cognitive, linguistic, physical, and social abilities that children bring with them from their homes and communities.	

Appendix to Chapter 9 (continued)

Wheelock Standards (continued)	INTASC Standards (continued)
6. Educators employ multicultural, antiracist, antibias educational practices, and foster positive learning experiences/high achievement for all children.	
7. Educators understand and use a variety of teaching strategies to encourage learners' development of critical and creative thinking and their aesthetic, problem solving, and other cognitive skills.	4. The teacher understands and uses a variety of instructional strategies to encourage students' development of critical thinking, problem solving, and performance skills.
8. Educators use an understanding of individual and group motivation and behavior in a variety of cultural contexts to create learning environments that encourage positive social interaction, active engagement in learning, and self-motivation.	5. The teacher uses an understanding of individual and group motivation and behavior to create a learning environment that encourages positive social interaction, active engagement in learning, and self-motivation.
9. Educators communicate effectively and age-appropriately within many domains (oral, written, mathematical/symbolic, nonverbal) to foster active inquiry, collaboration, and supportive interaction.	6. The teacher uses knowledge of effective verbal, nonverbal, and media communication techniques to foster active inquiry, collaboration, and supportive interaction in the classroom.
10. Educators plan instruction based upon knowledge of subject matter, children, families, the community, and curriculum goals.	7. The teacher plans instruction based upon knowledge of subject matter, students, the community, and curriculum goals.
11. Educators employ technology effectively to promote children's learning, helping them to make use of technologies to find, organize, and interpret information, and to become reflective and critical about information quality and sources.	

Appendix to Chapter 9 (continued)

Wheelock Standards (continued)	INTASC Standards (continued)
12. Educators respond to the broad range of children's abilities and learning needs and use effective formal and informal assessments to inform practice.	8. The teacher understands and uses formal and informal assessment strategies to evaluate and ensure the continuous intellectual, social, and physical development of the learner.
13. Educators are reflective practitioners who continually evaluate the effects of their choices and actions on others (children, families, and other professionals in the learning community) and who actively seek out opportunities to grow professionally.	9. The teacher is a reflective practitioner who continually evaluates the effects of his or her choices and actions on others (students, parents, and other professionals in the learning community) and who actively seeks out opportunities to grow professionally.
14. Educators collaborate with colleagues, families, and agencies in the larger community or communities of which they are a part to support children's learning and well-being.	10. The teacher fosters relationships with school colleagues, parents, and agencies in the larger community to support students' learning and well-being.
15. Educators consider how their work with children and families is affected by larger organizational structures within the setting, and in the larger society.	
16. Educators are familiar with legal, ethical, and policy issues, and take a leadership role in advocating for children, families, and themselves in a variety of professional, political, and policy-making contexts.	

CHAPTER 10

Equity in Teacher Education Standards and in Our Practice

Mieko Kamii, Amy Otis-Wilborn, Marleen C. Pugach, and Susan Redditt

The kids in my class are great. What makes it so challenging is that there's such a range of needs. You wouldn't believe the emotional and behavioral challenges some of the kids have. In my class, some kids are two or three years above grade level in reading, and some are two years below. We're a community, and we've worked really hard to make it a real community where everyone feels they belong. We believe in inclusion and reaching out to families and not leaving any child behind. Yeah, there's a lot of pressure for higher test scores, and obviously it's important. We work in teams and draw on all of our teaching talents but we need time, and we need focus. We want all of our students to learn. There's so much important work to do.

Achievement of high standards by all students is a criterion of equity in the current standards movement. But simply introducing standards into the educational change process will not result in equity in outcomes. This chapter describes how teacher education programs at two institutions, Wheelock College and the University of Wisconsin–Milwaukee (UWM), are developing program standards and assessments that make equity and diversity a central concern of teacher education. In this chapter we (a) describe the historical and political contexts of our institutions, (b) explain the need to be explicit in naming and defining equity in teaching standards, (c) examine the potential impact of

The dyad participants responsible for this chapter are Amy Otis-Wilborn and Marleen C. Pugach of the University of Wisconsin-Milwaukee and Mieko Kamii and Susan Redditt of Wheelock College.

teacher beliefs and behavior on students' achievement, and (d) provide examples of how we have moved toward more explicit standards and assessments of teacher candidates with respect to the issue of equity. Throughout this chapter we are reminded of the complexity of achieving equity in outcomes and the commitment we must all make to be persistent in our efforts to maintain equity as a focus of our work.

INSTITUTIONAL CONTEXTS: WHEELOCK AND UNIVERSITY OF WISCONSIN-MILWAUKEE

Wheelock College and UWM were paired in the Leading Edge Professional Development Schools (PDS) Network because both institutions prepare teachers to work in urban communities and schools, and because both are committed to altering beliefs and practices that contribute to unequal educational outcomes for children of color, children who are English language learners, and children from under-resourced families and communities. Additionally, both institutions focus on the inclusion of students with special needs. Although both colleges share common aims and concerns, we operate out of distinctly different historical and political contexts.

Wheelock College

Wheelock College is located in the heart of Boston and was founded in 1887 by Lucy Wheelock, whom many consider one of the pioneers of the kindergarten movement in this country. The college's mission—to improve the quality of life of children and families—organizes and informs the work of the entire college. This mission is pursued by offering multidisciplinary and multicultural liberal arts and sciences majors and professional education at the graduate and undergraduate levels for the fields of teaching, social work, and child life.

In 1987 the Wheelock College community began a college-wide conversation about what we would need to do to prepare teachers, social workers, and child life specialists to work effectively with all of the nation's children. Spurred on by the report of the Commonwealth's Joint Task Force on Teacher Preparation (1987),[1] work groups composed of faculty, administrators, and staff crafted proposals that resulted in significant changes at the college. In both the undergraduate and graduate divisions, the college (a) revised its curriculum and program offerings; (b) introduced multicultural perspectives into the curriculum; (c) altered the theoretical underpinnings of its teacher preparation programs; (d) shifted its understanding of field experiences and relationships with schools and communities; (e) created professional development school relationships in surrounding communities in which teacher preparation, professional development, and family and community engagement in children's learning were viewed as inextricably intertwined; and (f) made a conscious decision to diversify the faculty and student body. Since then, the college has taken on the challenge of integrating technology into teacher preparation to facilitate closing the digital divide.

Currently, faculty, administrators, and staff are looking through a critical lens at the college's academic, professional preparation, and student development programs. Work groups are proposing revisions to programs and devising new performance assessment systems that will provide information for ongoing program renewal.

Taken together, these changes have improved the college's ability to recruit, prepare, mentor, retain, and revitalize individuals at the college and in the schools who are committed to understanding and working with children, families, and communities in urban America.

The University of Wisconsin-Milwaukee

UWM is the single urban institution in the large, publicly funded University of Wisconsin system and has long defined itself in terms of its urban mission. With its roots as both a normal school and state teachers college, the institution continually regarded education as significant as it grew into a multipurpose university. Various partnerships among units at UWM and the community have existed for years and include the Schools of Architecture, Business, and Education.

Historically, the School of Education has always worked closely with the Milwaukee Public Schools (MPS). The majority of preservice field experiences for decades has taken place in MPS, and when the first professional development schools were established in the late 1980s, these partnerships were made deliberately with schools in MPS. Schools that were selected were not high-achieving schools, but instead, schools in which the capacity for connecting school reform and the reform of teacher education could be realized (Pugach & Pasch, 1994). In the late 1990s, a total redesign of teacher education began and was predicated on a continued commitment to preparing new teachers for urban schools (Hains, Maxwell, Tiezzi, Simpson, Ford, & Pugach, 1997), on creating a program and assessments that stressed this commitment, and on continuing and expanding our strong partnerships with MPS. This redesign was a grass roots faculty effort anchored in the belief that the reform of teacher education and the reform of urban schools are closely linked goals.

With the arrival of a new chancellor in 1998, UWM rededicated itself to serving the community in which it is situated. The current wide-ranging initiative to define the relationship between the university and the community, known as "The Milwaukee Idea," considers the borders of the university to be contiguous with the borders of the community. One of the major initiatives associated with The Milwaukee Idea focuses on ways in which the university can support the quality of teaching and learning for the children and youth of Milwaukee, in particular MPS, and builds on the existing partnerships between the university and the schools. This P–16 initiative is central to the current work of the university as a whole and the School of Education.

Contrasts Between Wheelock and UWM

UWM is a large, publicly funded, urban midwestern university offering a wide array of programs. Students attending UWM are mostly nontraditional; many support their own education through concurrent outside employment: the average age of the student body is 24 years; students bring to the university a variety of life and work experiences; and many are first-generation college students. At any given commencement one may find a mother and son or daughter graduating on the same day. In contrast, Wheelock is a small, northeastern private college with a focused mission on improving the lives of children and families. The vast majority of students in the undergraduate division are traditional students in terms of age and full-time status. Graduate programs reflect greater diversity in age, professional experience, and full- and part-time status.

UWM's and Wheelock's teaching programs operate in distinct political and policy environments. For example, the dominant issue in educational reform in Massachusetts at the moment is teacher and student testing. In contrast, vouchers for private and parochial schools headline public discourse about educational reform in Milwaukee, and MPS has just adopted a plan to curtail busing for the purpose of integration and is returning to neighborhood schools. Teacher certification requirements influence the way in which teacher preparation programs are structured, and Wisconsin *and* Massachusetts certification policies and procedures differ as well. Massachusetts has a two-tier system of licensure. Candidates for *Initial* Licensure must have completed a major in one of the liberal arts or sciences, passed the Massachusetts Tests for Educator Licensure (for example, elementary licensure requires passing three tests, Literacy and Communication, Subject Matter of Elementary Education, and Reading), and completed 300 hours in a classroom. *Professional* Licensure requires three years of teaching, and either the completion of a portfolio for professional licensure, or the acquisition of "an appropriate masters degree." To date, neither the standards for assessing professional portfolios, nor the content of "appropriate masters degrees" have been clearly specified.

Wisconsin, on the other hand, has only recently approved a standards-based certification and licensing plan that incorporates three "career stages." Beginning in 2004, Initial Educators receive a 5-year renewable license. To progress beyond Initial Educator, teachers must demonstrate growing competency based upon a professional development plan and earn a master's degree to advance to the highest level. Under this new certification and licensing structure, UWM will continue to prepare early childhood and primary/middle school educators both at the undergraduate and postbaccalaureate levels. Certification in special education is at the postbaccalaureate and graduate levels. However, a heavy, purposeful presence of special education is integrated into all regular teacher education programs.

Another aspect that Wheelock and UWM's programs share is strong relationships with local schools and districts through professional development schools and other school–university partnerships. Wheelock's partnerships began by working with teams of teachers in selected schools to support the development of new teachers. Out of these initial partnerships grew year-long internships, on-site seminars and courses team-taught by faculty members and teachers, and new professional development opportunities such as participating in teacher-as-researcher groups. At present, several whole-school professional development site partnerships flourish in Boston and Cambridge.

UWM maintains consistent connections with a number of schools in the MPS District. Currently, there are six PDSs in which a variety of collaborative projects and initiatives are ongoing. As part of the Collaborative Teacher Education Program for Urban Communities, preservice teachers complete all of their field experiences in MPS. The program has developed ongoing working relationships with key schools in MPS around these field experiences and the teacher preparation focus within each of the professional semesters.

The context for developing standards and assessments at the school, university, and state levels also is different for UWM and Wheelock. Each context, however, was a stimulus for pursuing our concerns about educational equity in urban schools. Joining Leading Edge provided both institutions an opportunity to address this concern together.

EQUITY AND THE LEADING EDGE PROJECT

As participants in Leading Edge, representatives of Wheelock College and UWM functioned as members of a cross-institutional network whose main purpose was to focus on standards and performance assessment for prospective teachers in the context of professional development schools. During the course of the 3-year project, we met at least three times a year as a full team from the six participating institutions; at each of these meetings we had several opportunities to talk with members from both of our institutions in addition to interactions that included all six institutions. Additionally, our conversations extended through visits to each other's institutions that helped us understand how our missions were aligned and how our programs differed.

In these discussions, we continually turned to issues of equity in teaching and learning and the enduring challenges we faced as teacher educators to build preservice programs that were serious about addressing the role that teachers'

perceptions of race, class, language, and culture play in thwarting or supporting achievement. We also searched for specific ways we might better help
teachers meet students' needs and close the achievement gap. Our local commitments to working in urban contexts meant that we had already placed the
issue of equity at the center of our respective institutional efforts. We came to
these discussions with concerns already in place about the lack of serious attention to equity in the 10 principles associated with the Interstate New Teacher
Assessment and Support Consortium (INTASC) model standards for beginning teachers, as well as in the five propositions of the National Board for Professional Teaching Standards (NBPTS). We recognized that in building
standards-based programs of teacher education, addressing the absence of explicit attention to equity in these standards for beginning and accomplished
teachers alike would be the focus of our joint work in Leading Edge.

As the six institutions in the network identified the focus of their work, we
became aware that each project had a strong connection with the issue of educational equity. Projects that addressed integrating technology, enhancing
teacher quality, and creating school-university partnerships, while not directly
related to the urban context, were directly concerned with fostering academic
achievement. In each project, at the most basic level, were questions not only of
access to educational opportunity but outcomes of those opportunities. Our
role in Leading Edge, as we saw it, was to keep issues of equity at the forefront
of all of our work and to connect dialogue about every issue we addressed as a
large group to considerations of equity.

Defining Equity: Confronting Our Failures

As the discussions progressed, we became aware of how commonly paired
words in our talk could become murky, indistinct, run-together ideas: "equity
and diversity," "multiculturalism and social justice," "high achievement and high
standards." As we read common texts, traded faculty meeting vignettes, and re-
told stories from the field, we found ourselves returning repeatedly to the single most troublesome and predictable outcome of standards-based educational
reform: the persistence of the achievement gap between students of color and
white students, between English language learners and native speakers of English, between students whose parents lack literacy skills and children of college
graduates, between the rich and the poor.

Our need to focus on equity is better understood in terms of our collective
failure to teach well large numbers of children whose race, class, language, or
cultural practices make them the targets of deficit explanations of educational
inequality. It is understood in our commitment to move beyond thinking of
children and families in terms of deficits from an arbitrary norm ("lack of . . . ,"
or the prefix "dis-" attached to words like "advantage" and "ability"), thus plac-

ing responsibility for educational failure on the backs of those we have failed. For us, equity was defined as "equitable educational outcomes for all students," and the refusal to relieve ourselves of assuming responsibility for all students' learning and achievement. We saw the challenge in our collaborative work, therefore, as assuming responsibility for actively working toward closing the achievement gap.

Based upon her research in urban schools and classrooms, Irvine (1991) writes,

> Teachers are significant others in their students' lives; as significant others, they affect the achievement and self-concept of their students, particularly black students. Because schools are loosely coupled systems and teachers frequently operate autonomously and independently, teachers' impact on the lives of students is perhaps greater than one might imagine. (p. 49)

As teacher educators, we believe in the efficacy of teachers not only to have a positive impact on students' learning and academic achievement, but to challenge and change current as well as future social contexts in which students will live and work.

These conceptions of equity framed our work with Leading Edge. Clarifying the meaning of equity for ourselves individually and for our teacher education programs was an important part of identifying expectations of our graduates and the role we hoped they would play in closing the achievement gap.

EXAMINING EQUITY IN POLICY AND PRACTICE

Having made the commitment to standards and performance assessment, it was important for us to examine how equity was addressed in national standards and educational reform recommendations. Exactly what standards were being set? Additionally, we needed to examine the relationship between standards and practice that may or may not support equity.

Equity as an Explicit Goal in National Standards

The National Commission on Teaching and America's Future (NCTAF, 1996) report makes it clear that attention to issues of equity and excellence are key to the success of the national educational reform agenda. The overall goal of educational reform, according to the report's authors, is that "by the year 2006, we will provide every student in America with what should be his or her educational birthright: access to competent, caring, qualified teaching in schools organized for success" (p. vi). However, translating this lofty goal into day-to-day programmatic preservice activities that result in teachers who are committed to providing this level of teaching to students in any school—but particularly in urban schools—requires an explicit level of commitment to educational equity on multiple fronts. At the level of policy, the NCTAF report goes on to state simply that "there are alternatives to perpetuating inequality" (p. 88). The policy action suggested is straightforward: "Increase the ability of low-wealth districts to pay for qualified teachers and insist that districts hire only qualified teachers" (p. 88).

But how will qualified teachers be defined in the context of closing the achievement gap between students of color and white students, between students in urban and poor rural schools and students in suburban schools? The NCTAF report suggests that "multicultural competence for working in a range of settings with diverse learners" (p. 76) will be required. Additionally, both INTASC and NBPTS are identified in the report as vehicles to achieve the kind of teaching that will result in more equitable achievement among white students and students of color.

However, the propositions and principles of these nationally recognized standards-based efforts to define what exemplary beginning and accomplished teaching look like are not particularly explicit about equity as it relates specifically to fostering equitable achievement. The report itself is focused on non-specific terms like *diversity*. For example, principle 3 in the INTASC model addresses the general issue from a diversity rather than an equity perspective. It states, "The teacher understands how students differ in their approaches to learning and creates instructional opportunities that are adapted to diverse learners" (INTASC, 1992). The explanations that follow suggest that teachers should address every possible kind of diversity: learning and performance, multiple intelligences, disabilities, cultural differences, English language learners, varied talents—and accommodate these differences.

While it is of course appropriate to expect good beginning teachers to be sensitive and responsive to difference, principle 3 is far less explicit about the reason for all of this awareness of diversity, namely, assuring improvements in achievement, particularly for students of color. If good beginning teachers are aware of the vast diversity of their students but are unprepared to foster a reduction in the achievement gap and open opportunities to their students as their foremost goal, how valuable is their awareness? New teachers may teach about various cultures but fail to monitor the expectations they themselves hold for their students. A diversity perspective as represented by these principles may or may not be paired with an explicit equity goal on the part of a particular teacher education program, a particular teacher education faculty, or a particular teacher education student. Only in the extended explanation of the INTASC standards do we even learn that a good beginning teacher "believes that all children can learn at high levels and persists in helping all children achieve success" (INTASC, 1992, p. 15), a statement that begins to broach the real issue underlying the commitment to diversity as espoused in the principle itself.

Similarly, the NBPTS documents do not address equity directly. The NBPTS standards for various content areas and age levels are all anchored in a set of five common propositions. Of these five, none is explicitly focused on issues of equity; rather, the assumption is that equity is best addressed if it is embedded in other core propositions. Two of these propositions specifically address the issues, but only in the accompanying explanations and not in the propositions themselves. The explanation of the first proposition, "Teachers are committed to students and their learning," states that accomplished teachers believe all of their students can learn and treat students equitably and also "are aware of the influence of context and culture on behavior" (NBPTS, 1996, p. 2). In the fourth proposition, which focuses on teachers thinking "systematically about their practice," accomplished teachers are to exemplify the following virtues: "curiosity, tolerance, honesty, fairness, respect for diversity and appreciation of cultural differences" (p. 3). However, nowhere do the propositions acknowledge that the achievement gap exists, that teachers and schools are implicated in its perpetuation, or that one of the great challenges is to prepare primarily white teachers to work in schools that serve predominantly students of color.

In other words, too much is left to chance in the standards in what is actually to be valued by good beginning teachers or accomplished teachers with respect to equity. If it is not spelled out deliberately, the goal of equity in achievement may be (and most often is) missed entirely, hidden among references to multiculturalism or diversity that provide a degree of comfort to those who may wish to avoid more direct confrontation with the more difficult question of equity in achievement, or among general references to good teaching for everyone, which are meant to subsume equity. Although we would agree that standards-based teacher education is a vast improvement over teacher education that is not tied to standards—making explicit the set of implicit expectations makes them accessible to learners and amenable to scrutiny and public debate—we would argue that it is critical for the standards themselves to be unequivocal regarding their stance on equity as it relates to achievement for all students, and not only on multiculturalism and diversity.

We focused our collaborative work on using standards and assessment as vehicles to assure that teachers who graduated from our programs reflected the knowledge, skills, and attitudes that would positively impact the achievement of children in urban schools. Additionally, we wanted our efforts to result in infusing issues of equity at all levels of the teacher education process (and of Leading Edge's work) so that we would deliberately revisit them on an ongoing basis.

Becoming more explicit about equity in our standards would help us directly address equity in our teacher education programs. However, we needed to be equally explicit about practices that create barriers for students in schools and classrooms which are the result of a teacher's attitudes and behavior if this standards-based process was to influence practice. In the next section, we characterize some of the major issues that were at the center of our dialogue and helped to clarify even further the barriers to learning for children of color and low economic status, barriers that we needed to address in setting standards and performance expectations for our teacher education students.

Equity: Explicit Issues and Practices to Address

One of the questions that emerged from dialogue among the six institutions in the Leading Edge project was, "How is teaching in urban schools different? Are there unique knowledge, skills, and attitudes in teachers who will teach successfully in urban schools?" The answer is both yes and no. King (1997) identifies many of the realities of urban schools: growing poverty of the families and communities they serve, limited educational resources (gaps in spending, inadequate facilities), inadequate teaching workforce (shortages and lack of qualifications), growing diversity in student body with concomitant decrease in diversity of teachers, demonstrated failure of schools to reach students as evidenced by academic achievement and dropout rates, and high student and teacher mobility (The Urban Challenge, 1998). King points out, however, that "Challenging experiences as well as the presence of viable communities are equally a part of the reality of the urban experience" (p. 183). Therefore, teachers in urban schools need to understand and work within the context of these realities. However, are these unique to urban schools? By neglecting these issues in any teacher preparation program, do we continue to marginalize their importance in the broader context of educational equity and reform? And while these realities are highly visible in urban settings, are they not present in suburban and rural contexts as well?

Batts (1998) developed a framework to describe what she calls "modern racism." She argues that while the behaviors may be different now, the basic assumptions are the same as they were 30 years ago. Although sometimes unconscious and well-intentioned, these behaviors have the same oppressive outcomes. Teacher beliefs and behaviors that obstruct student learning and achievement, particularly in urban schools, can be viewed using Batts's typology of five expressions of racism: dysfunctional rescuing, blaming the victim, denial of differences, avoidance of contact, and denial of the political significance of differences. The impact of these forms of racism on children in urban schools and classrooms includes assumptions about inferiority, viewing education as assimilation, and linking privilege with power.

Assumptions about inferiority. Batts describes the impact of two forms of racism, dysfunctional rescuing and blaming the victim, as lowered expectations and escape from responsibility. Teachers who operate out of a deficit perspective hold lower expectations for student learning. Their perspective may grow out of their own lack of knowledge or lack of commitment to all children. It may be based upon a belief that children in urban schools are disadvantaged because of the circumstances of their lives, because parents are not concerned about their children's education, or because others are responsible for the child's inability to develop academically. The teacher may choose to protect the child (dysfunctional rescuing), ignore the child (blaming the victim), or refer the child for special education services (escaping responsibility). As Irvine (1991) points out, "Much of the work on good urban teaching practice—indeed much of what we know about good teaching—rests upon teachers' convictions about the power of learning, the inherent capabilities of students, and the possibility of personal transformation" (p.184).

Education as assimilation. In a typical school district, over 80% of the teachers in urban schools are white and over 80% of the student body are students of color. Teachers in urban school, therefore, are teaching students with whom they do not share similar background experiences or cultures. Teachers may deny that there are differences among children and/or avoid contact with students out of discomfort. She or he may adopt a color blind stance, acting on the belief that all children are the same, regardless of skin color or cultural background, and should be treated the same in the classroom. This response essentially closes down other cultural world views or perspectives through which learning takes place and establishes a definable comfort zone for the classroom teacher. The goal is to assimilate students into the prevailing culture, the teacher's culture. To solidify the comfort zone, the classroom teacher has little contact with people of color, "making no effort to learn about life in communities of color" (Batts, 1998, p. 9). These types of racism create a conflict between the need for involvement of parents and the community in the education of children and the desire of the teacher to remain isolated and in control.

Linking privilege with power. Denial of the political significance of differences is practiced by individuals and institutions that minimize the impact of social, political, economic, historical, and psychological realities on the lives of people of color (Batts, 1998, p. 9). Tatum (as quoted in Scherer, 1998) describes this as " 'the fog around us'—the inequitable distribution of wealth, status, and influence that the advantaged groups take for granted" (p. 5). A white teacher, for example, may not recognize his or her position of privilege, which is the result of skin color and alignment of behaviors and beliefs with those of mainstream culture. Additionally, the teacher may not recognize or challenge normative institutional policies and practices constructed to retain control of various aspects of the educational process for students of color and policies and practices that minimize their access to, and opportunities for, meaningful and relevant educational experiences. These traditional practices include, but are not limited to, ability tracking, standardized testing, and the use of special education as an alternative. Within this form of racism, a teacher becomes a party to institutionalized racism rather than an advocate for students.

It is not just white teachers but all teachers who have the potential to engage in these forms of modern racism. Educators must learn to recognize privilege, racism, and the relative standing of our own positions within the sociocultural context. At the very least, we must learn how to prepare teachers who do not engage in teaching practices and support policies that inhibit children's learning, development, and academic achievement. Our task was to articulate what this looks like in teaching.

MAKING EQUITY MORE EXPLICIT IN STANDARDS-BASED TEACHER EDUCATION

The issues and examples raised in our cross-institutional discussion have strongly influenced the standards and assessment frameworks we have developed over the course of the Leading Edge work. In this section, we illustrate through three examples how our institutions have worked to build into program standards explicit issues that impact equity as we have come to understand and define it. Additionally, we have sought ways to use standards and assessments to keep these issues at the forefront of the teacher education process by continually making them a part of an ongoing dialogue.

Through the Lens of Core Values

At UWM, the reform of teacher education is anchored in a set of seven core values which are subsumed within the INTASC standards that are used for program approval. Recognizing that the INTASC standards lacked cogency with respect to equity, faculty developed core values that placed equity in the foreground and emphasized the central focus on equity in UWM's redesigned teacher education programs. For example, the first core value states, "Students who complete the Collaborative Program advocate for and provide equitable education to all children, but particularly for children in urban schools, and keep issues of race, class, culture, and language at the forefront of equity considerations," thus demonstrating that this is not merely a question of learning about cultures, but that inequities due to race, class and culture are prominent issues that UWM's preservice students and faculty are encouraged to grapple with throughout their preparation. However, even with the core values in place, we quickly recognized the need to go beyond our own rhetoric as represented by the core values (as well as the rhetoric of the INTASC standards themselves) to advance the goal of equity (see Chapter 8).

Our challenge continues to be how to keep the core value that focuses on equity (as well as the other six) prominent in the program. Although, as part of dedicated course work our students study issues of institutionalized racism and the schools' role in perpetuating it, our concern is how to foster a real commitment to equity in our students throughout the program. We do this in two ways. First, during each professional semester UWM teacher education students are enrolled in a Linking Seminar, the purpose of which is to revisit the core values in relation to the field experiences that occur during that semester. Students, therefore, regularly connect with what it means to enact a commitment to equity during their work with children and youth. Second, at the end of each semester, students engage in self-assessment around their growth in each of the core values. These activities are important for two reasons: (a) students know that they are going to be linking their field experiences to their own development in the context of the core values, and (b) faculty use reflective papers and other artifacts of students' work presented each semester as multiple sources of data that help determine not only students' knowledge and skills, but also dispositions around issues of equity in urban teaching. In addition, a group of experienced teachers from MPS are on special assignment to UWM to serve as clinical faculty and bring direct recent experience from urban schools into the teacher education programs.

Expanding and Deepening Program Standards

The need to be sensitive to the importance of the cultural context on teaching, learning, and children's development figured prominently in discussions of standards and assessments in Wheelock's teaching programs from the outset (see Chapter 9). Faculty members and cooperating practitioners shared examples of how good teaching in one context can look different in another. For instance, a teacher might use narratives or storytelling, in contrast to codes of conduct or rules, to teach students about moral and ethical behavior, civic virtue, strength of character, or human rights. Faculty and practitioners talked about how difficult it is for students to be engaged in learning when there is a mismatch between students' expectations of how a teacher is supposed to teach and their own teacher's style. For example, cultural beliefs differ about the kinds and amounts of authority teachers have in the classroom, and how learners should behave during lessons. Who should talk more, teachers or students? Are students encouraged to question or challenge what a teacher says, or is that a mark of insolence? Teachers respond more favorably to students whose behavior matches their own expectations which can result in differential treatment of students: engaging with or reprimanding talkers and ignoring or worrying about quiet children.

Building on these examples, supervisors spoke movingly of the complexity of understanding enough about differing teaching contexts to make valid inferences and fair judgments about the quality of teaching they see. One faculty member reminded us of the experiences of teachers of color in early trials of the NBPTS assessment process, and the parallel experiences of teacher-candidates of color in supervision conferences and courses at the college. She admonished the group to focus on the quality of teacher candidates' and children's learning experiences, not solely their behavior.

Everyone raised questions: What makes a classroom and school environment safe for learning for different groups of learners? What does hands-on learning look like in different classroom contexts? What is the relative importance of academic performance and care for others in the different cultures and therefore minds of children and adults in the classroom? What does the Wheelock way of teaching look like in urban settings for mainstream students and students of color? What about the experiences of students of color teaching in suburban contexts where they are in the minority?

Based upon these discussions, we agreed that our task was to develop broad, inclusive tools that would give students multiple opportunities to develop and then to document their achievement of critical knowledge, skills, and dispositions at the level of a novice practitioner. We further agreed that students must participate in their own assessment, that supervisors must understand the classroom and school context over time, that students need a safe environment in which to process teaching segments and hear concerns, and that assessors must be trained. With this, we launched into a review of our existing program documents and the INTASC model standards for beginning teachers. We decided to use the INTASC standards but to modify them to reflect our values, beliefs, and perspectives on the preparation of educators.

Wheelock's emphasis on equity and diversity is woven into the standards in several ways but is most apparent in three of the standards we added to the INTASC principles:

- Educators understand the social, economic, cultural, and linguistic contexts from which children come, and they communicate respectfully, from a strengths perspective, with children and families in the learning community.
- Educators build on the cognitive, linguistic, physical, and social abilities that children bring with them from their homes and communities.
- Educators employ multicultural, antiracist, antibias educational practices, and foster positive learning experiences and high achievement for all children.

As a faculty, we wanted to make visible and explicit in the standards our institutional and programmatic commitment to preparing educators who can teach all children. Our next task is to develop indicators or rubrics to help faculty, teacher candidates, cooperating practitioners, and outside assessors understand what these standards look like in everyday practice.

Performance Indicators as Evidence of Equitable Practice

The Post Baccalaureate Program in Special Education is a part of the Collaborative Teacher Education Program for Urban Communities at UWM. The core values, therefore, serve as the basis for the curriculum content and process in our teacher preparation program for special educators. However, we have worked to infuse these values into program standards, and further to incorporate them into performance indicators that clarify the knowledge, skills, and attitudes of special educators with an agenda for equity. This provides a way to consider evidence that would help assess the extent to which a preservice teacher might meet the standards.

There are five broad program standards that reflect five important areas: Child, Learner, Disability; Assessing, Interpreting Information; State-of-the-Art Curriculum; Collaboration and Leadership; and Ongoing Professional Development. Key concepts that focus on issues of equity are purposefully embedded in the language of the standards. For example, in the Child, Learner, Disability standard, although knowledge and understanding of the characteristics of learners with disabilities are important, the crux of the standard is focused on advocating for students and their families. The indicators help to point to the types of evidence we can use to assess teachers in this regard. We look for examples of how the teacher communicates and clarifies the rights of parents to information and participation in the educational process; and ways in which the teacher actively seeks and secures necessary resources and educational opportunities for students and their families (see Table 1).

The second standard, Assessing and Interpreting Information, focuses on what continues to be critical issues in special education in urban schools: tracking and overrepresentation of children of color. Important themes within the language of the standard emphasize the need for teachers to challenge directly inappropriate assessment practices that are often the basis for diverting students into special education, and the lack of accountability for student learning which keeps students in special education. Evidence for meeting the standard as defined by the indicators requires that the teacher: (a) develop a manageable system for ongoing accountability for student learning and communicating with parents about students' educational progress, and (b) protect students from misidentification by recognizing the potential for testing bias and using multiple kinds of information to evaluate students' achievement.

Table 1
Examples of Performance Standards and Sample Indicators

Performance standard	Sample indicators
Child, learner, disability Understands learners with disabilities in urban school, develops caring and supportive relationships, and actively advocates for equitable educational opportunities.	• Do I work toward educating others about the needs and rights of students and their families for equitable educational programs, services, and opportunities? • Do I actively advocate for equitable educational opportunities and just treatment for students with disabilities in urban schools by seeking equitable distribution of resources, access to learning experiences, and qualified teaching and support personnel?
Assessing and interpreting information Implements a student-centered approach to assessing and interpreting student performance that emphasizes students' strengths, challenges inappropriate and discriminatory assessment practices, and accounts for student learning and development.	• Do I have a manageable way to chart students' progress on meaningful learning targets? • Can I provide an up-to-date summary on at least a quarterly basis that provides an accurate and forward-looking account of students' performance and communicates clearly to parents? • Do I challenge assessment practices that are unfair and/or culturally biased?

The indicators are written in the form of questions that teachers, teacher educators, cooperating teachers, and others may ask in an effort to characterize performance in the field that is consistent with the goals and focus of the teacher education program. During the course of 3 years, the standards and performance indicators reflect greater clarity and definition. We have created specific field-based projects and observational tools that provide multiple sources of evidence of preservice teachers' performance and assess the impact of that performance on the achievement of students with disabilities.

MAKING THE COMMITMENT TO EDUCATIONAL EQUITY IN TEACHER EDUCATION

Once the commitment to equity is stated openly and accurately, how to achieve this goal within preservice programs becomes the primary consideration. Three aspects deserve attention: (1) how faculty address their own growth and development in relationship to equity, (2) what occurs across the teacher education curriculum, and (3) the extent to which, in our own pedagogy and practice, we reflect the same equity considerations we expect our graduates to practice.

Faculty Growth and Development

What happens when teacher education faculty are faced with what it means to confront their own beliefs and practices that may obstruct equitable education from occurring? Unfortunately, no assumptions can be made about the willingness or readiness of individual faculty members to be explicit about, or engage fully in, meaningful dialogue about equity or wish to confront their own knowledge and experience in this regard—or the lack thereof. Dialogue to promote faculty growth and development around equity cannot occur only at the early stages of program redesign or development, as an exercise in the development of standards or core values. It is simply too easy to rely on rhetoric about equity rather than engage in the personal growth that is necessary across faculty, students, or the society at large, for that matter. Our responsibilities as teacher educators require us to be constant participants in our own growth as a central means of fostering the development of prospective teachers— teachers who are willing to face the challenges inherent in helping students who have not achieved due to institutional barriers and modern racism.

At UWM, for example, inherent in the redesign of the teacher education program was the creation of a series of "dialogue spaces" that provide the ongoing structure within which considerations of equity are repeatedly raised as a function of program accountability, and actions to promote faculty development related to equity are planned and implemented (see Chapter 8). Dialogues may range in topic from how to structure faculty development to what readings are least likely to foster students' stereotypes about students in city schools to the relationships among diversity, equity and disability (see Pugach & Seidl, 1998). These spaces, which exist as part of a fluid organizational structure, permit and demand that faculty participate in equity-oriented activities as a form of personal as well as professional growth.

The underlying purpose, of course, is to engage in continuous improvement of the preservice program to assure that new teachers are ready to work actively to close the achievement gap. But program improvement cannot occur unless faculty recognize the interaction of their own actions and points of view about teaching and learning in urban schools with the beliefs and experiences preservice students bring to their professional programs. Typically, faculty assume that students need to do all the growing and do not look to themselves as part of the problem; this is an assumption we wish to debunk as part of the norm of doing the business of teacher education by continually revisiting our own biases, stereotypes, and actions in relationship to race, class, and culture. A school-wide annual Urban Education Forum contributes significantly to this effort.

At Wheelock, faculty growth and development has been, and continues to be, supported at every level and in a variety of ways. Recurring college-wide forums on racism, sometimes facilitated by outside consultants, at other times student-led, provide space and structure for community-wide dialogue on issues related to equity. Ongoing development takes place in undergraduate, graduate, and departmental meetings where faculty members periodically read and discuss common texts. It takes place in search committees charged with diversifying the faculty and staff; in curriculum committees where syllabi are reviewed for inclusion of multicultural content; and in student life committees where culturally sensitive cocurricular activities are planned. Speakers at opening convocations and honorees at commencement teach the entire community by story, admonition, and example about the many struggles, contributions, and achievements of diverse peoples.

Academia is a difficult setting in which to raise these contentious issues; criticism comes easily to academics and the risk of creating a platform for bullying rather than for scaffolding growth is a real danger. Like students, faculty are likely to be silenced in the face of colleagues who, with all good intentions, dismiss those who are not perceived as "getting it." An essential function of leadership in teacher education reform is relentlessly keeping issues of equity at the forefront through sustained local dialogue and action.

Infusing Equity-related Issues Across the Teacher
Education Curriculum

How might teacher educators move beyond a verbal commitment to preparing their graduates to work with multicultural populations toward a curriculum that fosters deeper understandings of the persistence of the achievement gap and how to close it? First, responsibility for achieving this goal must be shared across faculty members, which is why it is crucial for faculty to set explicit expectations for themselves to keep race, class, and culture at the forefront of their dialogue and their practice. In the curriculum itself, a structural means must be crafted to insure that students revisit their own growth and development with regard to how well they work with and teach students who have not been able to achieve in the past. At UWM, the core values are revisited each semester as students prepare end-of-semester presentations and portfolios. If the core value related to race, class, and culture has not been addressed throughout the courses in a particular semester of the program, the absence will show up in the students' self-assessments and ideally influence decisions about whether they move ahead in their programs. If an institution of higher education is serious about equity, students should be assessed on their growth in the realm of equity on a regular basis, and this requires faculty to consider how well they themselves are prepared to make such assessments.

This approach obviously argues against a model that relies on only one course in multicultural education or diversity. While fundamental knowledge and experience exists that might best be addressed in a dedicated course, typical courses may not address the achievement gap in a sustained manner. Instead, to address equity across the entire curriculum, a combination of dedicated courses and work in other courses must occur.

At Wheelock, students select from among designated multicultural courses in history, literature, human development, sociology, anthropology, the arts, and education, courses that enrich students' understanding of the histories, experiences, beliefs, practices, and contributions of non-European peoples and communities of color. All education courses in the teacher preparation core curriculum include multicultural content. As students acquire knowledge, they have multiple opportunities to examine their own assumptions about who the children and families they with work with are, how they think about varied sociocultural contexts for development and learning, and whether they can recognize strengths in every individual and every community. They are challenged to think about how these strengths can be harvested and transformed into activity and behavior that promotes academic achievement. Finally, they reflect repeatedly on the aspirations and expectations that they and the children and families they work with have for success.

Dedicated courses can provide an important framework for equity concerns, but this framework needs to be shared among faculty as an anchor to how they attend to equity within their own courses. For example, at UWM we created a new required course on language and urban teaching that focuses on second language learners, Ebonics, and teaching. These issues come up repeatedly across students' experiences as they participate in fieldwork in schools, not just during this course. Students also take designated courses in urban schooling and multiculturalism. Likewise, if the concept of white privilege is an important anchor, then all faculty need to be able to revisit this concept as problems or resistance arise among their students. So the structural decision to choose what is commonly called the "integration" model places high levels of responsibility on all faculty members. It can only be effective if all faculty members are dedicated to accepting their own need to address these issues on an ongoing basis.

In addition, the kinds of field experiences that are required also need to be carefully constructed. Because the stereotype that parents of students in urban schools do not care about their children's education is quite durable and persistent, experiences that bring prospective teachers into close contact with adults of color who live in urban communities are also crucial (Seidl & Friend, 1999). Field experiences in the community itself serve many purposes for those who wish to teach, but above all they have the potential to help build relationships between families and students. UWM is moving away from initial field experiences that are solely school-based toward community-centered experiences to enable preservice students opportunities to interact in authentic community-based activities with children and adults. Following this, their professional program is field-based within MPS every semester.

All freshmen at Wheelock complete 24 hours of field work in schools with extended day programs, Head Start programs, child care centers, Boys' and Girls' Clubs, YMCAs, and other community learning centers as part of a required course, Children and Their Environments. All sophomores enroll in a required year-long course in Human Growth and Development that includes two 30-hour prepracticum field experiences first with infants, toddlers, or preschoolers, and then with school-aged children, adolescents and adults in schools, afterschool programs, shelters, retirement homes, and community-based organizations. These courses and field experiences enable students to participate and observe in a variety of educational and human services settings, travel to different neighborhoods, familiarize themselves with community organizations, and interact with people from many backgrounds.

Holding up a Mirror to Our Own Pedagogy

As considerations of equity begin to permeate the teacher education curriculum, faculty members find themselves wondering whether their own pedagogy reflects the beliefs and practices they expect of their students. We use language differences to illustrate how an English-speaking faculty member might misunderstand writing errors made by English language learners whose primary language is Chinese. English and Chinese have similar sentence structure (subject–verb–object). However, in the Chinese language, verb tense is inferred from context; it is not marked grammatically. Not surprisingly, Chinese students for whom English is a second language frequently make errors with verbs. If one does not know this characteristic of Chinese grammar, one might wrongly assume that there is some blind spot or inexplicable error in Chinese students' processing of information.

Faculty must understand dynamics of race in how they interact with students. Steele's research demonstrates the vulnerability of minority students in the face of faculty who do what faculty members do all over the country—provide written feedback to students (Cohen, Steele, & Ross, 1999). Steele's work speaks to the need to create trusting relationships between faculty and students so that students do not misinterpret feedback as personal criticism; it speaks, too, to the great responsibility faculty have for understanding the implications of their actions. If teacher education faculty espouse a commitment to equity but are unable to practice it themselves, the depth of their commitment can validly be questioned.

FINAL THOUGHTS

Dialogue and conversation were the primary vehicles for our collaborative work throughout the Leading Edge project. Language was important—the words we used and how we defined concepts. Necessarily, this is where we began. We knew, however, that words were weak remedies in addressing persistent inequities in educational opportunity that children of color and children whose families struggle economically face daily in urban schools and classrooms. Although it is important to infuse language into standards that makes explicit the critical issue of equity in educational outcomes, we cannot relegate such important issues to standards alone. Within teacher education, we must be persistent in challenging ourselves, our students, and our institutions to follow through with actions and evidence that match the words we have so carefully crafted.

NOTES

1. Massachusetts Board of Regents of Higher Education and Massachusetts Board of Education, *Making Teaching a Major Profession, The Report of the Joint Task Force on Teacher Preparation* (JTTP), October, 1987. The JTTP was convened by former Commissioner of Education Harold Reynolds and former Chancellor of Higher Education Franklyn Jenifer. Its charge was to construct a blueprint for the improvement of teacher education in the Commonwealth of Massachusetts. The JTTP's recommendations to require an Arts and Sciences undergraduate major of prospective teachers and to create a two-stage teacher education and certification process were subsequently incorporated into Massachusetts teacher certification laws. They have been superceded by new laws.

REFERENCES

Batts, V. (1998). *Modern racism: New melody for the same old tunes.* Episcopal Divinity School Occasional Paper, #2. Cambridge, MA: Episcopal School of Divinity.

Cohn, G., Steele, C.M., & Ross, L. (1999). The mentor's dilemma: Providing feedback across the racial divide. *Personality and Social Psychology Bulletin, 25*(10), 1302–1329.

Hains, A. H., Maxwell, C. B., Tiezzi, L., Simpson, M. J., Ford, A., & Pugach, M. C. (1997). From individual and ambiguous to collaborative and explicit: Reform in urban teacher education at the University of Wisconsin–Milwaukee. In L. P. Blanton, C. C. Griffin, J. A. Winn, & M. C. Pugach (Eds.), *Teacher education in transition* (pp. 180–206). Denver: Love.

Interstate New Teacher Assessment and Support Consortium. (1992). *Model standards for beginning teacher licensing and development: A resource for state dialogue.* Retrieved 12/28/00, from http:www.ccssd.org/intascst.html

Irvine, J. (1991). *Black students and school failure: Policies, practices, and prescriptions.* New York: Praeger.

King, S. H. (1997). Toward the development of an improved urban teaching and evaluation process. In A. L. Goodwin (Ed.), *Assessment for equity and inclusion* (pp. 181–196). New York: Teachers College Press.

Massachusetts Board of Regents of Higher Education and Massachusetts Board of Education. (1987). *Making teaching a major profession.* The report of the Joint Task Force on Teacher Preparation. Boston, MA: Author.

National Board for Professional Teaching Standards. (1996, January). *Middle childhood/generalist standards.* Detroit, MI: Author.

National Board for Professional Teaching Standards. (1990). *Toward high and rigorous standards for the teaching profession.* Washington, DC: Author.

National Commission on Teaching and America's Future. (1996). *What matters most: Teaching for America's future.* New York: Author.

Pugach, M. C., & Pasch, S. H. (1994). The challenge of creating urban professional development schools. In R. Yinger & K. N. Borman (Eds.), *Restructuring education: Issues and strategies for communities, schools and universities* (pp. 129–156). Creskill, NJ: Hampton Press.

Pugach, M. C., & Seidl, B. L. (1998). Responsible linkages between diversity and disability: A challenge for special Education. *Teacher Education and Special Education, 21*(4), 319–333.

Scherer, M. (1998). Reading for equity. Perspectives: The fog around us. *Educational Leadership, 55*(4), 5.

Seidl, B., & Friend, G. (1999). *Community based teacher education: Learning from and with community organizations in the preparation of teachers.* Paper presented at the Annual Meeting of the American Educational Research Association, Montreal.

The urban challenge: Public education in the 50 states. (1988, January 8). *Education Week, 17..*

CONTRIBUTORS

Martha Erickson was an instructor in the Preservice Program in Childhood Education at Teachers College and is a doctoral student in the Department of Curriculum and Teaching.

Letitia Hochstrasser Fickel is Assistant Professor of Education at the University of Alaska Anchorage, where she is actively involved in school–university collaboration, serving as a Faculty-in-Residence at a local Professional Development School (PDS) . Dr. Fickel currently serves as Principal Investigator for the Alaska Partnership for Teacher Enhancement, a federally funded Title II grant project, and is continuing her research on teacher professional development and learning. She is the author of, "Teacher Community and Commitment: A Case Study of a High School Social Studies Department," in B. L. Whitford & K. Jones (Eds.), *Assessment, accountability and teacher commitment: Lessons from Kentucky*, as well as other publications. She completed her doctorate at the University of Louisville in 1998 with a specialty in teaching and learning.

A. Lin Goodwin is Associate Professor of Education and Director of the Preservice Program in Elementary/Childhood Education in the Department of Curriculum and Teaching, Teachers College, Columbia University. Her research and writing focus on multicultural teacher education, assessment, teacher beliefs, and the education experiences of Asian Americans. She is the editor of *Assessment for equity and inclusion: Embracing all our children*, and the author or coauthor of numerous articles and book chapters including, "Teacher preparation and the education of immigrant children," "Racial identity and education," "Multicultural stories: Preservice teachers' conceptions of and responses to issues of diversity" and "Voices from the margins: Asian American teachers' experiences in the profession." Dr. Goodwin also serves as a consultant and staff developer to a wide variety of organizations around issues of diversity, educational equity, professional teaching standards, teacher assessment, and curriculum development.

Gary A. Griffin retired in 1999 from Teachers College, Columbia University where he returned in 1996 after a 15-year absence. Between his two periods of service at Teachers College, he directed large-scale teacher education research at the National Research and Development Center for Teacher Education, served as Dean of the College of Education at the University of Illinois at Chicago, and was Professor and Department Head at the University of Arizona. Griffin began his professional career in education as a teacher in the Santa Monica, CA public schools, where he developed his lifelong concern with the relationships among teaching, the quality and character of schooling, and the preparation and continuing education of teachers. When he returned to TC, he served as Director of the National Center for Restructuring Education, Schools, and Teaching and worked with colleagues throughout the college on the critique, review, and revision of the TC teacher preparation programs. He served as Principal Investigator of the Leading Edge project described in this book. Griffin continued to be active in the American Educational Research Association, The Holmes Partnership, and a variety of national and regional educational organizations and agencies. He has written or edited 16 books and monographs, 34 book chapters, 30 journal articles, and numerous technical reports dealing with teaching, teacher education, staff development, school change, and curriculum development. His most recent book is *The Education of teachers: The ninety-eighth yearbook of the National Society for the Study of Education,* published by the University of Chicago Press (1999). Griffin earned his bachelor's, master's, and doctoral degrees from the University of California at Los Angeles. He currently lives in Rancho Mirage, California.

Susie Hanley has 19 years experience working in education. She has taught in public (K–12), government (Headstart), private, and alternative school settings. She taught primary age students for a dozen years and then transitioned into preservice and in-service teacher education. She has been the School-Based Site Coordinator for the Gorham Extended Teacher Education Program the last seven years with a university partner. She also earned a graduate degree from the University of Southern Maine in Educational Leadership. She is currently designing and implementing a set of structures and experiences for inducting new teaching professionals into her school district. Hanley also works as a NSRF Critical Friends Group Coach through the Southern Maine Partnership and the Gorham Schools.

Nancy Harriman is currently a principal at the Denmark and Brownfield Elementary Schools in the University of Southern Maine's rural partnership site, Western Maine. She previously served as a faculty member and Director of Teacher of Education for the University of Southern Maine. Her interests include assessment, collaboration, and inclusive teaching.

Ric Hovda is the E. Desmond Lee Professor of Urban Education at the University of Missouri-St. Louis and Assistant to the Superintendent of the St. Louis Public Schools. His interests are teacher education, urban education, school–university partnerships and PDSs, and professional development. He is co-editor of Professional Development Schools: Historical context, Changing practices, and Emerging issues (Parts I and II), *Peabody Journal of Education.* He earned his Ph.D. from The Ohio State University.

Sarah Jacobs coordinates the Elementary Teacher Education Program at UCSB. She is also Assistant Director of the Beginning Teacher Support and Assessment Project in Santa Barbara County.

Mieko Kamii is Associate Professor of Psychology, Director of College, School, and Community Partnerships, and Director of Assessment at Wheelock College in Boston, Massachusetts. Her current work focuses on assessment in relation to teaching and learning; on standards and assessments in teacher education; on equity and diversity in teacher education programs and in professional development schools; and on developing communities of practice that draw arts and sciences and education faculty members, school teachers and administrators, and family community and district stakeholders into dialogue and effective action to improve teaching, learning, and student achievement in urban schools. Dr. Kamii holds a BA in Political Science from Oberlin College and an Ed.D. in Human Development from Harvard University.

Walter H. Kimball is Professor in the Department of Teacher Education at the University of Southern Maine. He partners with school-based teacher educators in coordinating a postbaccalaureate yearlong preservice internship leading to initial teacher certification in both general education and special education. His scholarship interests are teacher assessment and designing Web-based courses and materials to support the internship.

Ann Larson is an Assistant Professor in the Department of Secondary Education, University of Louisville. She earned her Ph.D. in Curriculum and Instruction at the University of Illinois, Urbana. She is a former secondary and middle school English language arts teacher and currently teaches in a professional development schools model of a graduate teacher education program. Her work in collaboration with educators in schools is connected to Kentucky Education Reform Act initiatives. Larson also teaches graduate courses in curriculum for experienced teachers and works with teachers pursuing National Board Certification. Larson's research and teaching interests include teacher education, curriculum and assessment, curriculum theory, English education, and social foundations of education.

Alexandria T. Lawrence is an Assistant Professor and Coordinator of the Graduate Childhood Elementary Program at Lehman College, City University of New York where she is also involved in establishing a professional development network in high-need urban schools. She received her Master of Arts, Master of Education, and Doctor of Education from Teachers College, Columbia University.

Ann Lippincott is the Coordinator of Bilingual Teacher Education at the University of California, Santa Barbara. Her teaching focus is in the area of addressing the special needs of English Language Learners. She teaches language arts and English language development courses at UCSB. Her research interests include the manifestations of reflective thinking in practice, focusing especially on contexts in which teachers engage collegially in problem solving to understand their work in schools. In addition to her professional activities in the United States, Dr. Lippincott has earned an international reputation for her work with teachers in Micronesia, Argentina, Chile, Peru, and Uruguay. She has been a Fulbright scholar and an academic specialist for the United States Information Agency.

Patrice R. Litman is a research assistant at the National Center for Restructuring Education Schools and Teaching at Teachers College. She is interested in PDSs, and creating and sustaining school-based learning communities. She is the project coordinator for the Leading Edge PDS Network discussed in this publication.

Maritza Macdonald is Director of Professional Development at the American Museum of Natural History in New York City. Her professional experiences in research and evaluation, program design and administration, and graduate school teaching include positions as Senior Researcher and Evaluator for NCREST at Teachers College, Columbia University and as the Director, Advisor, and Instructor of the preservice teacher education program at Bank Street College of Education. She is committed to developing exciting and content-rich professional development opportunities for teachers at all levels. She also served as Project Director of the Leading Edge PDS Network project, the subject of this book, during its initial years. She holds a doctorate in education with specialization in teacher education and curriculum development from Teachers College, Columbia University.

Phyllis Metcalf-Turner is an Associate Professor in the Department of Teaching and Learning at the University of Louisville. She served also as a liaison to two urban Professional Development Schools and as Project Director of the Pathways to Teaching Careers Program.

Pat Morales has been a bilingual elementary school teacher in the Central Valley of California, an elementary school principal in that region, and for the past eight years has been principal of Peabody Charter School in Santa Barbara, CA.

Amy Otis-Wilborn is an Associate Professor at the University of Wisconsin-Milwaukee in the Department of Exceptional Education. She has been involved in teacher education and special education for over 15 years. Her work has centered on preparing teachers who work with children with disabilities, including deaf and hard-of-hearing. Along with this has been involvement in school–university partnerships as a part of teacher education and educational reform in general and special education. Dr. Otis-Wilborn directed the Four Cities Urban Professional Development School Network involving school–university partnerships in cities across the Midwest. Her research and writing have focused on issues of teacher education and teacher education reform (e.g., *When Best Doesn't Equal Good* [1994]). Developing standards-based teacher education and examining its impact on initial teachers within the University of Wisconsin-Milwaukee teacher education programs has been the focus of her most recent research and writing.

Marleen C. Pugach is Professor of Teacher Education at the University of Wisconsin-Milwaukee, where she directs the Collaborative Teacher Education Program for Urban Communities. Her interests include the relationship between preparing teachers for special education and general education, school–university partnerships, and preparing teachers for urban schools. She also co-directs UWM's *Preparing Tomorrow's Teachers to Use Technology* (PT3) grant. Dr. Pugach is author of several books, including *On the Border of Opportunity* (1998); *Curriculum, Special Education, and Reform* (1996) and *Collaborative Practitioners, Collaborative Schools* (2002, 1995), and co-editor of the book *Teacher Education in Transition* (1997). She was the 1998 recipient of the Margaret Lindsey Award from the American Association of Colleges for Teacher Education for her contributions to research in teacher education. Dr. Pugach earned her Ph.D. from the University of Illinois at Urbana-Champaign in 1983.

Susan Redditt is an instructor for Wheelock Graduate School's Off-Campus Programs. She is currently the co-designer and faculty tutor for the Online Writing Support Program, a content-specific, online writing assistance program for graduate students working on their Masters in Early Childhood Education. Her research and teaching has focused on multicultural curriculum development, multicultural issues in special education, and qualitative research in education with an emphasis on practitioner research. Working with the Leading Edge Network, she organized and facilitated a group of Wheelock Graduate School faculty who explored standards and assessment practices in teacher education with a focus on equity. Susan is also working with colleagues at the University of Massachusetts in Amherst and at Harvard University to develop coursework in the areas of inclusive schooling special education, and teacher research. Susan earned an Ed.D. in Special Education from Boston University in 1992.

Steve Ryan is Assistant Professor in the School of Education at the University of Louisville. His Ph.D. is from UCLA in Urban Schooling: Curriculum, Teaching, and Policy Studies. He is co-author of *Becoming good American schools: The struggle for civic virtue in education reform*, with Jeannie Oakes, Karen Hunter Quartz, and Martin Lipton (Jossey-Bass, 1999), and author of *Transitions and Partnerships: High Schools, Middle Schools, and Post-Secondary Institutions* with Anne-Marie Nuñez (Office of Vocational and Adult Education, 1999). His research and writing focus on teacher collaboration, teacher learning, and urban teaching and teacher education.

Anne Sabatini is an Assistant Professor of Practice in the Department of Curriculum and Teaching at Teachers College, Columbia University. She works primarily with preservice elementary education students.

Frances Schoonmaker is Professor of Education in the Department of Curriculum and Teaching at Teachers College, Columbia University where she teaches courses in curriculum, teaching, and supervision. She directed and served as codirector of the Preservice Program in Childhood Education from 1983–2001. Prior to this she was an elementary school teacher for twelve years.

Tanya Sheetz is a National Board Certified Teacher and teaches second grade at Isla Vista School, one of seven elementary schools that work in partnership with the Teacher Education Program at UCSB. As a school-based teacher educator, Tanya is a cooperating teacher and was active in developing UCSB's experimental program design.

Karen Siegel-Smith was a clinical faculty member with the Teachers College Preservice Program in Childhood Education and a classroom teacher at PS 87 in New York City. She is currently teaching in the Long Island public schools.

Jon Snyder is currently Dean of the Graduate School at Bank Street College of Education. He is also a Senior Researcher for the National Commission on Teaching and America's Future. His professional interests include teacher learning, the conditions that support teacher and student learning, and policy strategies that grow and sustain conditions that support student and teacher learning.

Robyn Ulzheimer is a teacher at PS 87 who has been involved with the Teachers College PDS partnership for many years. She has served as a clinical faculty member in the Preservice Program at Teachers College, Columbia University. She is featured in the NCREST video, "The Lightning Post Office." Ms. Ulzheimer is also an AACTE-MetLife Fellow. She has an MSEd from Bank Street College of Education and an M.Ed from Teachers College, Columbia University where she is a doctoral candidate in the Department of Curriculum and Teaching.

Betty Lou Whitford is Professor of Education and Co-Director of the National Center for Restructuring Education, Schools, and Teaching (NCREST) and Professor of Education at Teachers College, Columbia University in New York City. Her interests are school change, school–university partnerships, and qualitative research. Her most recent publication is *Accountability, assessment, and teacher commitment: Lessons from Kentucky's reform efforts* (2000) (with Ken Jones) from SUNY Press. She holds A.B., M.A.T., and Ph.D. degrees from the University of North Carolina at Chapel Hill.

INDEX

Education Program for Urban
Communities), 5, 141–164,
145
context, local, 143–144; 187–188
context, state, 188
core values, 151, 196–197, 202
coursework, 203–204; Linking
Seminar, 197
see also Dyads
faculty: leadership, 162, growth,
201–202
licensure, 188–189
Milwaukee Idea, 187
organizational structure, 147–148
Special Education Program, 156–161;
Post Baccalaureate Program in
Special Education for Urban
Communities, 199
standards, equity-based, 199–200
See also dialogue spaces, 141–163

values
equity, 196–197
faculty consensus, 14
dialogue, 144, 150; 157–161
match, 92, 112, 113, 120, 124
mismatch, 92–95, 125–126, 128,
129–130, 132, 137–139
programmatic, 88–91, 106–107, 151,
166

see also standards, program
student teacher, 112

Wheelock College, 5, 165–184
context, local, 186–187
context, state, 188
coursework: 176–178, multicultural
education, 176–178, 203–204
faculty: consensus, 14; growth,
201–202
history, 165
licensure, 188
standards, program, 172; equity,
198–199
standards and assessment, 165–179
influences: vision, 166, college
culture, 166, national standards
movement, 166, Leading Edge
PDS Network project
participation, 166, 167–168
lessons, 166–167
history, 167–173
Wheelock College and INTASC
standards, 169, 181–182
translating standards into
assessment, 171–173
NCATE review, 173–175
University of Wisconsin, Milwaukee,
178. *See also* dyad
vision, 166

Printed in the United States
1280500001B/417